The publisher and the University of California Press
Foundation gratefully acknowledge the generous support
of the Robert and Meryl Selig Endowment Fund in Film
Studies, established in memory of Robert W. Selig.

Violated Frames

FEMINIST MEDIA HISTORIES

Shelley Stamp, Series Editor

1. *Their Own Best Creations: Women Writers in Postwar Television,* by Annie Berke
2. *Violated Frames: Armando Bó and Isabel Sarli's Sexploits,* by Victoria Ruétalo

Violated Frames

Armando Bó and Isabel Sarli's Sexploits

Victoria Ruétalo

Foreword by Annie Sprinkle

UNIVERSITY OF CALIFORNIA PRESS

University of California Press
Oakland, California

© 2022 by Victoria Ruétalo

Library of Congress Cataloging-in-Publication Data

Names: Ruétalo, Victoria, 1971– author. | Sprinkle, Annie, 1954– writer of foreword.
Title: Violated frames : Armando Bó and Isabel Sarli's sexploits / Victoria Ruétalo ; foreword by Annie Sprinkle.
Other titles: Feminist media histories (Series) ; 2.
Description: Oakland, California : University of California Press, [2022] | Series: Feminist media histories ; 2 | Includes index.
Identifiers: LCCN 2021021919 (print) | LCCN 2021021920 (ebook) | ISBN 9780520380097 (cloth) | ISBN 9780520380080 (paperback) | ISBN 9780520977105 (epub)
Subjects: LCSH: Bó, Armando, 1915-1981—Criticism and interpretation. | Sarli, Isabel—Criticism and interpretation. | Pornographic films—Argentina—20th century. | BISAC: PERFORMING ARTS / Film / General | PERFORMING ARTS / Film / Genres / General
Classification: LCC PN1998.3.B62 R84 2022 (print) | LCC PN1998.3.B62 (ebook) | DDC 791.4302/330922—dc23
LC record available at https://lccn.loc.gov/2021021919
LC ebook record available at https://lccn.loc.gov/2021021920

30 29 28 27 26 25 24 23 22
10 9 8 7 6 5 4 3 2 1

*For Nicholas, Sofia, and Tony,
my sources of inspiration*

Contents

List of Illustrations   *ix*
Note on Translation   *xi*
Foreword by Annie Sprinkle   *xiii*
Acknowledgments   *xvii*

   Introduction   *1*
   The Signature of a "Bad Cinema"

PART I: BODIES AND ARCHIVES

1. Bodies through Time . . . Time through Bodies   *27*
2. Reading Bad Cinema through "Bad Archives"   *58*

PART II: CENSORING BODIES IN LABOR AND LEISURE

3. Disciplining Bodies through Censors' Shears   *83*
4. Collective Working-Class Male Bodies   *119*
5. Affective Intimate Interludes   *156*
   The Risky Female Body

Conclusion   *192*
 "You won with the censors. . . . They couldn't stop you!"

Notes   *197*
Selected Filmography   *231*
Index   *235*

Illustrations

1. Still from *Fuego* (1968) / 16
2. Ansisé and some Maká women in a still from *India* (1960) / 96
3. Ansisé in Iguazu Falls in *India* (1960) / 96
4. Advertisement for *Meat* (1968) upon its rerelease in 1979 / 102
5. Opening credits for *Intimacies of a Prostitute* (1974) / 111
6. A poster for *Insatiable* in 1984 / 115
7. Isabel Borja raising the Argentine flag at the end of *Last Love in Tierra del Fuego* (1979) / 117
8. Still from *Thunder among the Leaves* (1958) / 131
9. Stills from *The Shad Fishermen* (1959) and *Naked Temptation* (1966) / 133
10. Still from *Thunder among the Leaves* (1958) / 135
11. Spectators in *A Butterfly in the Night* (1977) and *A Madcap Widow* (1980) / 137
12. Still of Delicia in *Meat* (1968) / 146
13. Still of Siboney in *My Father's Wife* (1968) / 163
14. Two poses from the opening scenes in *Meat* (1968) / 165
15. Sandra from *Naked Temptation* (1966) / 166
16. Concepción's bad dancing in *Favela* (1961) / 169
17. Ansisé's ballet moves in *India* (1960) / 170

18. Still from the nude water scene in *Thunder among the Leaves* (1958) / *173*
19. Still from *Bewitched* (1976), which recreates *India* (1960) / *177*
20. The waterfall scene in *Bewitched* (1976) / *178*
21. Alicia in *Naked on the Sand* (1969) / *182*
22. Alicia's face in *Naked on the Sand* (1969) / *183*
23. Bárbara in *Ardent Summer* (1973) / *186*
24. Sandra on the grass in *Fever* (1972) / *187*
25. Close-up of Sandra with superimposed image in *Fever* (1972) / *188*

Note on Translation

The first time I mention a film title in the introduction I do so in the original language, followed by the closest English translation to the original and year of release. Thereafter I usually use the English name. Armando Bó's films had many titles as they played in different languages and to different audiences. In the case of *India*, *Favela*, and *Fuego*, I use the Spanish version as that was the title used abroad. If the film is not directed by Armando Bó, I include the director, country, and year of release. For more information about Armando Bó's films, please see the selected filmography. In the filmography I include all the English titles my research has uncovered.

For Armando Bó's films, there are discrepancies between when the films were completed and when they were released. All of his films were released first in Argentina, except for *Fuego* (1969), which premiered in New York before Buenos Aires.

Aside from film titles and unless otherwise noted, all translations are my own.

Foreword

*How Isabel Sarli and Armando Bó
Changed My Life*

ANNIE SPRINKLE

It was right after my lecture at the University of Alberta in Edmonton when Professor Victoria Ruétalo, PhD, approached me. I had been speaking about my work of forty-five years, researching and exploring sexuality in all its glorious and inglorious forms with a focus on my current interest, ecosexuality. She asked me if it was true that I had seen the movie *Naked on the Sand* when I was a teenager. She had read in an interview that I said the sexploitation film had a big influence on my life. It was the first film I had ever seen of a woman being free, being naked, having sex with multiple men, and even pleasuring herself (albeit in a soft-core way). Victoria told me the exciting news, that she was doing a book about the Argentinian director and star of the film!

The first time I saw *Naked on the Sand* was when I was fifteen years old, in 1970, just after it came out. It had been filmed in Panama where I was living with my family for four years. Back then the film was a huge sensation, absolutely scandalous, at least around my high school in the Canal Zone, Balboa High. The second time I saw the film was a week ago at sixty-six years old, when Victoria sent me a link to it on YouTube. What fun it was to watch this seminal film again after so many years.

The star of the film, Isabel Sarli, was as gorgeous and fabulous as I had remembered. She plays a young widow seeking to make a living to support herself and her son, but her bosses all fall in lust with her or want to marry her. About a third into the movie, Sarli's character goes on a romantic date with a potential new boyfriend (played by director

Armando Bó's son) around Panama City. The film captures the sensual delights I had enjoyed there so much; licking a *raspado* (snow cone) squirted with sweet condensed milk, the Chinese Garden fruit stand with its juicy mangos, guanabanas, and mamoncillos, the rush of jumping into the hotel swimming pool on a humid day, the colorful parrots at *el mercado*, the silky Chinese robes one could touch in the tourist shops, the dazzling sexy carnival costumes. . . .

In the next scene, the romantic couple takes a boat, escorted by playful dolphins, to Taboga Island, where I had spent adolescent family holidays along with my BFFs, Barbi and Maureen. The couple end up on a deserted, hidden beach where we too used to go. They get naked and make love for the first time, in a soft-core yet revealing way. I remember that to get to that same beach, we had to climb up and down a hill of jagged rocks. It wasn't an easy climb. I thought about the film crew having to carry their heavy equipment over those jagged rocks, and the actress Isabel Sarli's sumptuous, flawless body possibly getting scratched before her big skinny-dipping scene.

In Panama we teenagers were free to be relatively naughty, although none of us were sexually active yet. There were seemingly no age limits on vices. My friends and I could go into the Panama Hilton casino on the way home from high school. Sometimes men would give us a few quarters to play the slots. Apparently teen girls were good luck. I also remember the funky, smoky downtown theater where Maureen and I saw *Naked on the Sand*. No ID required. At the snack bar we could buy three cigarettes wrapped in banana paper for a nickel, and next door to the theater was a pharmacy where we could buy a few *bifetaminas veinte* (black beauties) for 25 cents each. No ID required. LSD, magic mushrooms, Panama Red, all easily available. In the movie theater, during *Naked on the Sand*, was the first time a man had exposed and rubbed his penis in front of me. It would be the first time of many more times to come.

My only other exposure to anything remotely like *Desnuda en la arena* was to the 1962 Hollywood film *Gypsy* and the hippie play *Hair*, both of which I had seen with my family in Los Angeles before we had moved to Panama. At the end of *Hair*, the cast was completely naked on stage. Yet *Naked on the Sand* was somehow not quite as family friendly.

The next time Barbi, Maureen, and I went to Taboga Island, we named our hidden beach cove "the Naked on the Sand beach," and we went skinny-dipping for the first time. Isabel Sarli had helped me overcome a little bit of my excruciatingly painful shyness. Suddenly my growing breasts felt less like fat and more like an asset. I wanted to be like Isabel Sarli, to wear those fabulous form-fitting dresses with bling, to have a big heart with big boobs, to wear heavy makeup, to pose perfectly provocatively in a bikini and high heels, to render men helpless when I danced the dance of seduction. . . . I wanted to get naked in the sand with the sun rays penetrating every pore.

At sixteen I had my first sexual experience—oral sex on the beach. Just two-and-a-half years later, I would become an adult film actress and centerfold model, as well as working in upscale Manhattan "massage parlors," having sex with all manner of men. A few years later, working my way through college, I would do the dance of seduction on the burlesque stage in costumes with bling and wear heavy eye makeup. Eventually, I would produce and direct my own films and become a successful artist with a lifetime of work about sex under my belt. Just as real-life lovers Armando Bó and Sarli made films together, I would eventually make films with my lover/wife, Beth Stephens. All my adult life I have lived by the sea. I'm an aquaphile and an out ecosexual. In retrospect, *Naked on the Sand* inspired me to become all that I desired to be. Va va voom!

Actress Isabel Sarli was controversial. I also became controversial and had to fight censorship and bad laws. Thankfully, I never had to do it in a military dictatorship like she did, although I did at times face arrest and jail. Today, remarkably, the same struggles continue between freedom and repression, pro-sex feminism and anti-porn feminism, sexual shame and sexual self-confidence, sin and virtue. In some ways, there is less freedom now. When I do college lectures these days, even with the now required multiple trigger warnings, I don't dare show some of my old sex film clips anymore, like I did twenty years ago. Post-AIDS attitudes toward sex and what's age appropriate have changed, a lot. Even with endless porn available in the privacy of one's own laptop, there are double standards. I can't show porn on campus without some kind of drama, even when everyone knows that college students are seeing it on the internet. In California where I live now, a person has to be twenty-one to buy cigarettes and to enter a casino where alcohol is served. It no longer feels relatively safe for fifteen-year-old girls to go skinny-dipping on an isolated beach.

The film didn't age well through my more politically correct senior citizen eyes. It makes fun of fat and elderly men. Isabel's prostitute character was sweet and loving, but she was stereotypically a cruel criminal who blackmailed men looking for love and sexy fun and ruined their lives. But still, it's a really fun, nostalgic movie to watch. Plus, it is a good thing to remind ourselves how influential Latin American films and Latina actresses have been on North American culture. I give *Naked on the Sand* my highest recommendation, two nipples way up.

As Professor Ruétalo will beautifully illustrate in this book, the films of Armando and Isabel featured sexuality, and sex is political. Pleasure activists Armando and Isabel fought the good fights for nudity without shame, with sex positivity, and for freedom of expression, all of which we benefit from today. Freedom isn't free.

Acknowledgments

Violated Frames began in the early stages of my PhD studies at Tulane University, when I took a class on the Poetics of Patagonia with Daniel Balderston. There I discovered the power of Isabel Sarli and Armando Bó's cinema. Unknowingly, I had signed up to comment on one of their last films, *Last Love in Tierra del Fuego* (1979), for an assignment. The version I saw had no nudity, was poorly made, and presented an incoherent story line with many unusual cuts; yet surprisingly its simplistic narrative and over-the-top melodrama intrigued me. I then discovered *Fuego* (1969) in Ana López's extensive library while working as her research assistant. Both instances sparked the fire of my curiosity, and for this I am truly grateful to Dan and Ana for introducing me to the Sarli-Bó duo many years ago in New Orleans and igniting the passion that underlies this project.

The research and dissemination of the ideas in this book were made possible by many small grants from the University of Alberta, namely the Endowment Fund for the Future Support for the Advancement of Scholarship and the Killam Research Fund. With these grants I traveled to Argentina and Paraguay to conduct the research for this book and presented at conferences throughout the United States and Canada. I was also fortunate to attend international conferences in Lima, Barcelona, and Vienna to introduce early findings of this research.

Extensive research would not have been possible without the gracious help of so many kind people working at the archives in Buenos Aires and

Asunción. I would like to especially thank Adrián Muoyo at the Escuela Nacional de Experimentación y Realización Cinematográfica library, who has truly been a wealth of information and provided important resources throughout the years. Thank you to the staff of the Museo del Cine Pablo Ducrós Hicken, where I found press clippings and books that have helped to nourish this project and give it depth. I am grateful to Roque González for making an extra trip to the archives to retrieve information for me, and for suggesting I travel to Paraguay, where he connected me to scholars and filmmakers. During my visit to Asunción, I was welcomed by Hugo Gamara, who runs the Fundación Cinemateca y Archivo Visual del Paraguay, and other film aficionados and journalists such as Manuel Cuenca and José Luis De Tone, who was gracious enough to give me a tour of the city and help fill in many of the gaps in this story. Special thanks to Juan Carlos Maneglia, who was extremely generous and shared with me the original scripts involving Paraguay, which he won in a contest after they were donated by Sarli. I am also grateful to Pablo Piedras for all his generous help and for introducing me to Nicolás Mazzeo, and to Nicolás for sharing with me his research into Octavio Getino's period as comptroller of the censor board.

I also want to thank the many colleagues and friends who throughout the years have fortified and fostered my work, granting me opportunities to share its development in discussions at the Latin American Studies Association and the Society of Cinema and Media Studies conferences, particularly through the Latino/a Caucus: Gabriela Aleman, Luisela Alvaray, Sarah Barrow, Catherine Benamou, Verena Berger, Nayibe Bermúdez Barrios, Gilberto Blasini, Christina Buckley, Olivia Consentino, Nilo Couret, Stephanie Dennison, Tamara Falicov, Paula Félix-Didier, Alison Fraunhar, Monica García Blizzard, Catherine Grant, Chris Holmlund, Matthew Karush, Dona Kercher, Susan Lord, Misha Maclaird, Leslie Marsh, Jeffrey Middents, Rielle Navitzki, Kathleen Newman, Roberto Carlos Ortiz, Tatjana Pavlovic, Pablo Piedras, Jonathan Risner, Yeidy Rivero, Carolina Rocha, Carolina Rueda, Ignacio Sánchez Prado, Paul Schroeder, Laura Isabel Serna, Deborah Shaw, Salome Skvirsky, Juana Suárez, Monica Szurmuk, Tzvi Tal, Dolores Tierney, Cynthia Tompkins, Cristina Venegas, Amy Villarejo, and Fernanda Zullo-Ruiz.

Thanks to my past and present colleagues at the University of Alberta, who were there for me daily and who have always been encouraging: Jennifer Askey, Laura Beard, Janice Causgrove Dunn, Russell Cobb, Claudia Cost, Ann De Leon, Eva Glancy, Naomi Krogman, Anne Malena, Angie Medeville, Janice Miller-Young, Tanya Parks, Lynn Penrod, Simone Pfleger,

Claudine Potvin, Tracy Raivio, Elena Siemens, Carrie Smith, Micah True, Dolores Wohland, Richard Young, and Heather Young-Leslie.

I am thankful to Susanne Luhmann and the Women and Gender Studies Department for the invitation to present at the Valentine's Day with Feminism. I also want to thank Víctor Goldgel-Carballo and John Nimis for the invitation to be part of the "Global Grit" Symposium at the University of Wisconsin–Madison, where I had the opportunity to engage with "trash" from the Global South.

It is impossible to be a scholar without the help and support of graduate students. They are central to shaping the research. For this I am grateful for my past research assistants, each of whom has contributed to the work, particularly Argelia Gónzalez Hurtado and Sandra Navarro, both of whose assistance was fundamental in the early days of the project. I would also like to acknowledge the many conversations in classes that more current graduate students have been a part of. Your insight and challenges have kept me on my toes and helped me to work through the major issues of this book: Laura Velázquez Velázquez, Sofia Rodríguez Monzón, Stephen Cruikshank, Elli Dehnavi, Derya Cinar, Anna Antonova, Jennifer Quist, Wangtaolue Guo, and Ross Swanson. Thanks to Zaira Zarza Blanco for being the best postdoc ever: she has inspired me with her infectious energy, passion, hard work, and dedication.

I am so grateful for the extensive comments and thoughtful guidance that both Richard Young and Marvin D'Lugo provided as I was preparing my proposal for this project. Thanks to the many mentors I have had throughout the years, particularly Laura Podalsky, Kathleen Newman, Catherine Benamou, and Ana López, all of whom in many ways have consistently nurtured and promoted my *latsploitation* work.

A very special thanks to Dolores Tierney, who has read this manuscript scrupulously and provided many valuable comments that have enriched both its content and style. Dolores is a true friend with her engaging and meaningful criticism, accompanying me from the beginning of our journey together into Latin America's "bad" cinema. I am also thankful to Lisa Cartwright and the anonymous reviewer for their insightful comments that have only strengthened the book.

I am extremely grateful to Raina Polivka for her sagelike advice and constant encouragement and excitement throughout the publication process, and to Shelley Stamp, the Feminist Media Histories series editor, for her faith in the project. Thanks to Madison Wetzell for her patience and the rest of the University of California Press team for their work behind the scenes. I am enormously appreciative of Annie Sprinkle's big-heartedness in writing the foreword. Annie Sprinkle's sexuality activism is at the core of this project. I thank Routledge for permission to reprint the article that first appeared in *Porn Studies* and forms part of chapter 3.

To my good friends Elena Siemens, Carrie Smith, Janice Causgrove Dunn, Tracy Raivio, Naomi Krogman, and Heather Young-Leslie: you are all female role models to me as both scholars and leaders. I cherish the glasses of wine and conversations we shared throughout the years, where we all had the space to dream.

Thanks to my friends Sharon Williams and Sandra Paolucci. After so many decades of friendship, you two have been sources of constant support and motivation.

Thanks to my dear friends Violeta Buckley and Wendy Gosselin, who were there at the tango bar long ago and helped obtain Sarli's phone number. Wendy has hosted me many times on my trips to Buenos Aires and connected me to her elaborate network of people in the city.

And last but certainly not least, I am very grateful to my supportive and loving family. I deeply appreciate my parents Brenda and Alberto Ruétalo for teaching me to be an independent thinker and not be afraid to roll up my sleeves and work. My grandmother Olga Ruétalo has stimulated me with her poetic soul and curiosity. Thanks to my sister, Mariela Ruétalo, and her wonderful family James, Serafine, and Naomi Oldfield, whose many laughs and fun times came just at the right time. Thanks to Carolyn and Gordon King: your good nature, openness, and embraces are sorely missed. Thanks to Rachel King who has challenged me to be the best I can be. This project would never have been completed without the help and support of my partner, Tony King. I thank you for your unconditional love. You are my muse, and you challenge me to mirror your abundant creativity and thoughtfulness. Thanks for helping me bring the children to this world and for being there to raise them when I was locked up in my room writing. To my beautiful and sweet children, Nicholas and Sofia, for always being wise and guiding mama to the last page, thank you.

Introduction

The Signature of a "Bad Cinema"

In the first decade of the 2000s, during one of my research trips to Argentina, I was sitting with friends in a tango bar, listening to a nostalgic *milonga* being played by a local band. I was exhausted, trying to find the Museo del Cine, which had moved locations, and looking for a way to connect with Isabel Sarli, for an interview as a foundation for my first exploration into her stardom. Deflated, but enjoying the sounds of the melancholic *bandoneón*, I noticed that my friend turned to the person next to her and asked: how can we obtain Isabel Sarli's phone number? A seemingly naïve question in an unlikely place, but the words, like a game of telephone, made their way from person to person through the intimate neighborhood establishment. And by the end of the night, I had the number. At this point in time, Sarli did not really do many interviews and only indulged me by phone. She still lived in Martínez, a suburb of Buenos Aires, with her many pets and two adopted children. The conversation I managed to secure was enough to write the article first published in the *Journal of Latin American Cultural Studies* that deepened for me a passion that took over two decades to develop into *Violated Frames: Armando Bó and Isabel Sarli's Sexploits*.

The anecdote settles what I suspected when I first started this journey: the popular celebrity was not only still relevant in Argentina but had also reached another status. Everyone, young and old, in that tango bar in the barrio that night remembered her legacy. For Argentines, Isabel Sarli was a name synonymous with sex. But she also represented the popular culture of decades past, particularly one of the darkest periods in the nation's history. Ever since she became Miss Argentina in 1955, her image and success have resurfaced in a long list of recognitions. Internationally she was an inspiration: her poses circulated on stamps in Japan;[1] the Chinese poet Wu Jiang dedicated an eclogue to her;[2] she was recognized by the Association of Film Critics of Mexico for being the most brilliant and discussed actress;[3] and she was honored with *carioca* and *paulista* citizenship for films made in Rio and São Paulo.[4] She was invited to film festivals all over the world from Colombia to France, Paraguay to Spain. Even at an old age and well after her retirement, she became an esteemed guest at the Festival de Cine de Guadalajara in 2008, and a retrospective of her work was featured in 2010 at the Film Society of Lincoln Center in New York. In Argentina, there were and continue to be many more instances that memorialize her inspiration—a rock band Isabel Sarly founded in 1986, the 2002 summer clothing line by designer Ona Saez with the star's images on T-shirts titled "South American Woman"—all featured in my first article. I have since discovered more instances, such as fridge magnets from local artisan markets and her embellished poses on the Nac & Pop's storefronts, a fast-food vendor that opened its doors in 2010 throughout Buenos Aires. They handed out a five-peso coupon in the form of a bill with none other than Sarli's image from *Carne* (*Meat*, 1968). In the popular culture world of Nac & Pop, the diva was worthy of a medium-shot image on coupons. The same one is reproduced on the truck of Frigorífico Fura, a meatpacking company fully owned by Argentine capital, as its logo explains, 100 percent "Argentine meat." All the aforementioned examples celebrate Sarli as a truly authentic Argentine myth, revalorized as part of everyday reality of a national popular culture.

Ever since 1956, when actor-producer-director Armando Bó and actress-producer-star Isabel "Coca" Sarli began their film experiments together, they provoked audiences by featuring explicit nudity that with time increasingly became more audacious, constantly challenging contemporary norms.[5] Their Argentine films shaped a growing fan base with a popular following extending beyond national borders. Between 1956 and 1981, Bó made twenty-seven films with Sarli. They included her first nude scene in *El trueno entre las hojas* (*Thunder among the Leaves*, 1958), a film that launched Sarli's stardom, and ended with the release in 1984 of *Insaciable* (*Insatiable*), following the dictatorship that had prohibited its exhibition, which finally happened three years after Bó's death.[6] Bó and Sarli made fast, independent, and cheap films popular throughout Latin America, parts of Asia, in Hispanic theatres and sexploitation circuits in the United States and European markets, a circulation that continues today through online versions of their work. Throughout their almost three decades of collaborative work, the duo fought the censors and critics to make rather unique erotic movies that were unlike any other in the history of Argentina, as well as holding a special place in world cinema.

This volume gathers the scholarship on the pair and introduces new approaches to explore their overall works, within the explicit Argentine context where censorship and regulation played a crucial role. *Violated Frames* mourns the loss of an important Film Censorship Board archive, which would have shed insights on Argentina's onscreen sexuality norms. Instead, this book proposes to develop a new, roughly constructed, or "bad" archive by exploring remnants of relocated materials to debate questions of performance, authorship, stardom, sexuality, and circulation in the Sarli-Bó films. Through the case of Sarli and Bó, the film historian can assemble a new history that begins in the nation and extends beyond it. The first part of the book, "Bodies and Archives," merges the various contexts for how to amass a sexuality archive with different bodies in post-1955 Argentina. The second part, "Censoring Bodies in Labor and Leisure," begins with the context of the new laws that expanded strict regulation of what was permitted in public and onscreen, moving on to explore the duo's films through the lens of bodies engaged in labor and leisure.

BECOMING AN AUTEUR: RISKY STYLE, PROVOCATIVE MODE OF PRODUCTION

"In all of Armando Bó's work, when all is said and done, coherence makes him seem like the only true Argentine auteur."[7]

Armando Bó's onscreen career was launched during the classical Argentine film period of modern studios, film stars, and elaborate film shoots: what was known as the "golden age." As an actor, he appeared on the silver screen in national productions from the late 1930s on, in such movies as *Ambición* (*Ambition*, Adelqui Millar, 1938), *Y mañana serán hombres* (Carlos Borcosque, 1939), *Fragata Sarmiento* (Borcosque, 1940), *Melodías de América* (*Melodies of America*, Eduardo Morera, 1941), and *La cabalgata del circo* (*Circus Cavalcade*, Mario Soffici,

1944), films which won over national and regional markets. By 1944, however, the Argentine film industry was on the verge of collapse.[8] The studios' fates had changed with Mexico's replacement of Argentina as the film-producing nation in Spanish America. War politics influenced the availability of raw film stock from the United States. By the time General Juan Domingo Perón came into power in 1946, there were already strong protectionist policies to shield the national industry, mainly through investment on production and with guaranteed exhibition quotas.[9] The industry did not thrive under Perón and continued to decline; but the waning of the studios allowed for independents to grow.

In 1948, Bó founded the production company SIFA (Sociedad Independiente Filmadora Argentina), after acquiring the rights for *Pelota de trapo*, a story about a poor boy who becomes a soccer celebrity, based on the writings of sports journalist Ricardo Lorenzo. Bó starred in and produced *Pelota de trapo* (*Ragged Football*, 1948), which was directed by classical film pioneer Leopoldo Torres Ríos.[10] As an independent and small company, SIFA's films were shot on the streets, and represented the tastes and desires of the popular classes. Through SIFA, Bó launched the career of Torres Ríos's son Leopoldo Torre Nilsson by producing many of his early films, including *Días de odio* (*Days of Hate*, 1953), a tale based on a Jorge Luis Borges story. The arduous trajectory of *La tigra* (*The Tigress*), a 1953 example also directed by Torre Nilsson, foreshadowed the eventual censorship challenges that Bó faced throughout the rest of his career with Sarli. Due to its lesbian undertones, *The Tigress* was banned and never fully premiered. All of the other films produced by SIFA were popular, generally based on sports, featuring Bó's athletic talents or other topics relating to local experiences in the barrio. Bó's roles as producer and actor helped him transition to directing his first feature with his star and muse, Isabel Sarli.

Laura Podalsky calls Bó's contribution a "cottage industry," referring to the small and often informally organized business model he developed with the production of over two dozen films based on a formula that he refined with time, using a regular cast and crew. Sandwiched between the studio industrial model and the new auteur practices, Bó's mode of production was very different, an amalgamation of both, while also unique in other ways. The fall of Perón's government in 1955 brought a change to the already ailing industry. The new Instituto Nacional de Cine (National Film Institute) or INC began to play an ever-increasing role in the shifting reality.[11] More foreign films were imported, and the weakening of the studio system opened a new space for independent cinema.[12] When Arturo Frondizi came into power in 1958, the INC, headed by Narciso Machinandiarena, began to support the work of independents like Bó and SIFA. Consequently, a new generation of filmmakers emerged, known as the "Generation of 1960." The New Argentine Cinema developed by independent auteurs critiqued modernity through a focus on the city, as Laura Podalsky explains in her book *Specular City: Transforming Culture, Consumption, and Space in Buenos Aires, 1955–1973* (2004).[13] Bó took another route. He was an experimenter and risk taker with a different vision in mind. With the release of *Thunder among the Leaves* in 1958, he homed in on a new formula of independent films featuring nudity, produced completely outside any state funding model. His autonomy gave him more freedom to develop a set of films that would never have been possible within the state apparatus of the INC.

While Bó established SIFA early on in his production career, collaborations with Sarli were of an equal partnership after the huge success of *Thunder among the Leaves*. Sarli owned 50 percent of every film she ever made with Bó; she worked as a producer drawing on her accounting skills and taking advantage of her fluency in English.[14] What began as a socially inspired cinema with realism at its base grew into at times seemingly preposterous topics with only one function: to feature his muse and partner. Bó worked within the ideals of his own star system. Most features, except their first made together, revolved around his starlet, whom he and the public "discovered" after her debut.[15]

Unlike the examples taken from classical cinema, where stars were empowered through their appeal within a studio system that bought and sold their features, the Sarli-Bó case highlighted the muse excessively, and it was almost parodic of the whole system itself. In some ways, the official acknowledgment of the true partnership of their work reflects the ideals of a star system that empowered Sarli to cultivate her own career within the partnership. Incongruous with other examples, Sarli's role in the film enterprise was unique in production history. Their partnership in business and their exceptional brand of films that revolved around star attraction led me to veer away from the study of the auteur. For clearly, Sarli, as a star, was very much a part of the brand. As their work grew together, she contributed her own dialogue and camera suggestions. She was a force and inspiration behind the camera as well as in front of it, keeping the company going. Since both Sarli and Bó were inextricably linked to the brand of films they made, throughout *Violated Frames*, I will refer to them as Sarli-Bó or Bó-Sarli to reflect the equally weighted role both auteur and star played in their common project. Their films, meanwhile, exhibit a unique film style that both of them had a hand in building, but more importantly while they each tried to make films outside their collaborative enterprise, they were unsuccessful and eventually returned to producing exclusively as a power couple.[16]

Regardless of their collective path, Armando Bó was a holistic auteur who fully contributed to the enterprise. He not only directed his own films but starred in them, produced them, eventually wrote the scripts or developed the story ideas, and composed the melodramatic and romantic music under the pseudonym of Eligio Ayala Morín. The arguments for the films were at first based on literary scripts that eventually developed a freer form. His first two productions were written by the famous Paraguayan Boom author Augusto Roa Bastos.[17] *India* (1960) was cowritten by José Martínez; and he adapted three other works: *Y el demonio creó a los hombres* (*Heat*, 1960), *Favela* (1961), and *Intimidades de una cualquiera* (*Intimacies of a Prostitute*, 1974). The rest were all penned by Bó.[18] The early productions used scripts; however, the written form eventually disappeared, evolving into a filmmaking process that just began with an idea and allowed actors to improvise the dialogue with some direction from Bó, adding to their spontaneity and confirming his trademark.

The new approach of foregoing written directions, developed after *La tentación desnuda* (*Naked Temptation*, 1966), required the cooperation of a cast that was comfortable with the unconventional method.[19] The cast always starred Isabel Sarli, playing characters each with different simple names and similar, usually humble traits. The director incorporated the medium shot as the most commonly used for capturing his starlet's most important feature: her breasts.[20] Armando Bó or his son Victor Bó costarred with Sarli as her onscreen lover. They relied on the same actors (Ernesto Baéz, Mario Casado, Santiago Gómez Cou, Miguel Ángel Olmos, Juan José Míguez, and Jorge Barreiro), who generally played modest working-class men. Occasionally, they featured notable local stars such as Alba Mujica, Jorge Porcel, Pepe Arias, Fanny Navarro, or José Marrone.

Similarly, they counted on a consistent crew; cinematographers trained in the studio system, like Julio Lavera, Américo Hoss, and Ricardo Younis all brought a practice of studio photography with a balance of frontal and back lighting to produce the shot.[21] Francisco Mirada was the main cameraman. When Bó bought a modern Cameflex camera, Mirada and he were able to experiment more.[22] For instance, they created in-camera superimpositions by returning the shot and continuing to film on top of the previous images. The infamous masturbation scene in *Fiebre* (*Fever*, 1972), discussed in detail in chapter 5, is accomplished using this method. Rosalino Caterbetti, the editor, helped Bó create a look that was fragmented and defied the rules of continuity. Orlando Viloni and Jorge Bruno provided the melodramatic makeup for Sarli's excessive appearance; Paco Jamandreu was her preferred costume designer, enhancing her extravagant star persona even when she played humble characters.[23] As music had a central role, generally alleviating the chaotic images, many popular and folk singers made appearances, such as Luis Alberto del Paraná y los Paraguayos and Los Iracundos. Bó was mainly an experimenter and risk taker from early on.

There are certain stylistic elements that make his films easily recognizable and signpost his own authorial signature. Bó's style entailed fast productions made cheaply with a crew and cast accustomed to his mode. The low cost meant that scenes were shot in one take. Inexpensive budgets and tight shooting schedules made elaborate transitions and multiple takes impractical. Bó tells an anecdote about shooting in South Africa. *The Virgin Goddess* (1975), a movie that was not directed or produced by him, stars both him and Sarli.[24] The director, Dirk de Villiers, relied on conventional methods. Bó recalls feeling anxious about the South African director's work ethic. De Villiers looked through his visor for a long time as he set up each shot.[25] What bothered Bó and contrasted with his own mode were the long shoots that repeated different takes until they were perfect.

In his own filmmaking process, Bó only had money for one take and would risk all by hoping that the shot would turn out just right. On the other hand, there were other reasons for not overstaging the shot. Bó was practicing a type of realism that could only be fostered with spontaneity. He was a believer in producing rather simple stories that spoke about everyday circumstances in the most impromptu and natural way. To achieve realism, he overextended himself to get the right shot, making people engage in actions as they would in real life, meaning he preferred setting up realistic situations rather than faking them. In part this drive explains why he eventually gave up writing scripts. He aimed to set up events so that they unfolded in front of the camera without interfering. For instance, he arranged the fight scene between Sarli and Alba Mujica in *Sabaleros* (*The Shad Fishermen*, 1959) by building up each side with comments about the other. Once the shooting of the scene began, Mujica was very agitated, and upon staging it, kept shoving Sarli's face into the water. Bó encouraged the scene to play out. They were performing it in a river that collected untreated sewage. Bó became obsessed with the realism of the shot and did not realize that Sarli was almost unconscious. She contracted hepatitis from the scene. The drive for a documentary feel in the early films continued and even took on a more familiar aspect with the inclusion of Super 8 footage from their international travels to reinforce its homemade impression.[26]

The cheap and fast modes of production resulted in the lack of continuity in the visual look of the films but also allowed for spontaneity in new ways. As Rodrigo Fernández and Denise Nagy argue:

> for Armando, the means and ends of the tools were dissociated; specificity did not exist; the limits produced distance. The shot is not cut, but overlaps. The editing does not omit but is redundant. The image in movement does not proportion continuity but exposes the fragment.[27]

What the authors mean here is that Bó's excessive style is both overabundant and fragmented. His ability to bring together seeming contradictions and yet produce a somewhat coherent film is a remarkable talent. It was a product of the blending of two systems, an old one with a set of norms and a new one that challenged norms at the level of style, mode of production, and content. Discontinuity in regard to editing and cinematography is the product of his quick filming techniques. The editing and montage sequences, clean cuts, and smooth transitions implicit in classical style are generally absent in Bó's version, an effect created by their devoted editor Caterbetti.

The awkward and clumsy montage in some ways is more akin to the auteur aesthetic of European cinema of the 1960s, a style that resisted coherent structure and perfection. Bó, like the French New Wave directors, mocked the elemental rules of continuity. But unlike the French auteurs, he made it look coherent even when it wasn't. From early on, since Sarli's first nude reveal, the fragmentation and visual discordance shows the true nature of the scene, a style particularly visible in the moments of sex onscreen, elaborated more fully in chapter 5. What makes scenes such as this first one seamless is the music that glosses over the fragmentation. Rodolfo Kuhn, a fellow director who belonged to the Generation of 1960, argues that despite all the many contradictions, Bó is rather coherent as a director. Kuhn believes Bó's fragmented effect is as impactful as Jean Luc Godard's *Breathless* (France, 1960).[28] One reason why Bó ignores the rules can be attributed to censorship.

Censorship made Bó's films easy targets, with the elimination of offensive shots and entire scenes. However, from *Thunder among the Leaves* onward, he established a way of allowing censorship-mandated cuts to happen, while at the same time still creating the anticipation of seeing more of Sarli's body, a strategy unique in his mode of sexploitation.

The films' content had two distinctive features: first, a social cinema that exposed exploitation, corruption, and injustice, and second, an element of sexuality, through Sarli's body, that grew to become the main attraction. From the beginning, innocent themes about unrequited love in *The Shad Fishermen* were paired with more substantial social topics exposing the exploitation of workers. Sarli's nude reveal in their first feature is seemingly dissociated from the story about human exploitation in a sawmill in the hidden jungles of Paraguay. Following *Thunder among the Leaves*, the films began to feature Sarli in more prominent roles, while still not promoting her to be an active agent in the story but rather a victim of circumstance. For instance, in *Heat* she moves from lover to lover in search of real connection but as a victim who is not empowered in her own future. Slowly, she begins to embrace her onscreen presence and adopt more powerful roles. In *Favela* she becomes a film star and works her way out of the Rio shantytowns. Her characters grew stronger in films like *Los días calientes* (*The Hot Days*, 1965) and *Naked Temptation*, where revenge for the death of her brother in the former and lover in the latter take place. In *The Hot Days*, she returns to El Tigre, a gateway town to the rivers and wetlands of the Paraná Delta with a fruit harbor, to find out what happened to her brother. She uses her sexuality to discover the true identity of her brother's killer and then manages to enact her revenge. Similarly, in *Naked Temptation* she avenges the men who have hunted her for half of the story and killed her lover. In later films, sexual norms become the focus of the story, beginning with *Meat*, *El sexo y el amor* (*Sex and Love*, 1974), and *La mujer de mi padre* (*My Father's Wife*, 1968), where father and son struggle for the prostitute's love. Notable in this period are *Fever*, about the love for a horse, and stories about prostitution, nymphomaniacs, homosexuality, and sexual dysfunction. In *Furia infernal* (*Ardent Summer*, 1973) Bárbara avenges the murder of her husband and her kidnapping, weaving a plan that eventually kills her captor and frees his victims.

Sergio Wolf provides a convincing analysis of the trajectory of their films, defining their work within three distinct phases. The first, encompassing their early four movies, is about setting limits and establishing the basic themes of exaggeration, crudeness, and exoticism, with a strong link to classical filmmaking through the convention of melodrama.[29] The second, what he calls the transition, begins with *Favela*, filmed in the shantytowns of Rio, and ends with *My Father's Wife*, about the struggle between father and son for the same woman, ironically starring Bó and his son Victor. The productions from this period are made quickly and cheaply, eventually discarding the script and giving music a more prominent role.[30] Morality ensures a contradictory position. As Kuhn has explained, the Sarli-Bó works were abundant with clear moral ideals.[31] And yet morality, as it makes its appearance through the dialogue and references to God, is continually being contradicted. The final phase comes after the release of *Meat*, and is defined by excess, new topics relating to sexuality, constant flashbacks, and indulgent music.[32]

Wolf's definitions can also be couched within the development of the sexploitation genre in the United States, which fits perfectly in the three phases described and adds another context that informed Sarli-Bó's path. The early films fit within the "nudie cutie" era, which featured nudity for its own sake. The subgenres of roughies, kinkies, and ghoulies dominated from 1964 to 1968, adding more violent and nonnormative sexuality to the offerings, like those found in Wolf's transition.[33] For example, *La leona* (*The Lioness*, 1964) is about the kidnapping of Susana by exploited workers at her husband's company. The film shows an interracial kissing scene between Sarli and Monsueto. By the late 1960s, classic soft-core movies included more sexuality and nudity, and daring proposals.[34] To map the development of sexploitation onto the description provided by Wolf makes sense: Bó-Sarli were responding to the demands of the world market. Also important to take into consideration are the laws that were developing in Argentina to control the amount of sex onscreen seen in theaters. In 1957, law 62/57 helped to centralize the film industry and allow for independent producers to grow. By the middle of the sixties (1963–66), new laws began to limit the possibilities of exhibiting sex onscreen, while already by the end of the decade (1968–69) law 18.019 brought the harshest regulation, permitting the prohibition of films. All three contexts disclose the competing pressures on the duo to adapt to national and international expectations.

The use of location shooting, mainly in marginal areas, identifies one of the main features of the Bó-Sarli productions. The shift from simulated spaces inside studios to the outdoors was common in the postwar years, particularly the 1950s, with the arrival of Italian neorealism that brought shooting into the streets. By the mid-1950s, the technological advances (lighter-weight cameras and more sensitive film stock) made the shift an inevitable and cheaper option for independent newcomers like Bó, since on-location shooting required no rental fees of studio space or highly lit elaborate and modern interiors. From the first films, the shooting locations were intimately connected to the funding of the projects and their status as coproductions. In this way, the duo traveled throughout the region, making movies in specific locations, some of which were in marginal filmmaking countries with underdeveloped film industries, such as Paraguay (*Thunder among the Leaves* and *La burrerita de Ypacaraí* [*The Girl Ass-Keeper of Ypacaraí*, 1962]), Uruguay (*Heat*), Venezuela (*Lujuria tropical* [*Tropical Lust*, 1964]), and Panama (*Desnuda en la arena* [*Naked on the Sand*, 1968]). Others were in more established filmmaking nations, like Mexico (*La diosa impura* [*The Impure Goddess*, 1964]) and Brazil (*Favela*, *The Lioness*, *Extasis tropical* [*Tropical Ecstasy*, 1978], and *Embrujada* [*Bewitched*, 1976]). In Argentina, location shooting took place in the provinces of Buenos Aires, the Alto Paraná, El Tigre, Tierra del Fuego, and other remote areas. Even the productions that didn't have funding from an international partner were filmed in some of their favorite exotic places, such as the border between Argentina, Brazil, and Paraguay at Iguazu Falls (*India*, *My Father's Wife*, and *Bewitched*). Marginal locations became a trademark of their cinema, easily integrated into the social dimension of the context but also, in its commercial aspect, appealing to the people in the whole country. By exploring settings in rural or natural landscapes, they were able to exploit the connection of the star to nature, as bodies and sexuality found their home in awe-inspiring surroundings.

From the very first collaboration, the Sarli-Bó productions were made with international private funding, facilitating their early entry into foreign markets, filming in exotic locations, and building a fan base abroad. On the other hand, the connections they established with key players both in the region and the United States helped open their work to new audiences.[35] In 1961, after the filming of *The Girl Ass-Keeper of Ypacaraí*, a representative from Columbia Pictures Argentina came to see Bó and bought the rights to distribute *Thunder among the Leaves* to all of Latin America. Around the same time, while on a trip to Central America and the United States, the pair met Orestes Trucco, who purchased the rights to distribute *The Shad Fishermen*, *India*, *Heat*, and later *The Girl Ass-Keeper of Ypacaraí*, the last of which premiered in New York on 4 July 1962.[36] The screenings in New York were all a success. When Columbia Pictures International, interested in their success abroad, then requested another film, they promised them *Tropical Lust*, which they had already agreed to produce in Venezuela after signing a contract with Lorenzo González Izquierdo, a local businessman. Sarli and Bó had toured all of Venezuela with *The Girl Ass-Keeper of Ypacaraí*, creating momentum for the star before releasing the Venezuelan coproduction.[37] The contract for *Tropical Lust* began their relationship with Columbia Pictures International, which was maintained on a film-by-film basis until the end, although it was never guaranteed Columbia would distribute all of their films. That would change with the release of *Fuego*, which consolidated their relationship with Columbia Pictures, especially in the late 1960s, at the height of their careers. When Bó realized that *Fuego* would not be released in Argentina, he decided to take it to New York, where it premiered and played for fourteen weeks on Broadway and Forty-Second Street at the Rialto Theatre. It took fourteen days to make, cost US $15,000, and made over $1 million in New York alone, according to the anecdotes.[38] The international focus meant that certain standards had to be maintained. For instance, their films used *tú* for the Spanish "you" instead of the usual Argentine *vos*, common in the vernacular.[39] Furthermore, different contexts required special concessions. In Japan during the 1970s, all the Sarli-Bó films screened, but the nudes were covered with spots in the pubic areas. Certain films entered different parts of Europe. One can still find French and Italian versions of *Fever*, *Fuego*, and *Intimacies of a Prostitute*. As Adrian Smith notes, there were plans to export four productions (*Naked Temptation*, *The Hot Days*, *Tropical Lust*, and *La mujer del zapatero* [*The Shoemaker's Wife*, 1968]) to the United Kingdom in the mid-1960s through Crompton Films.[40] However, as his research has uncovered, Crompton submitted the first one to the British Board of Film censors in 1966. *Naked Temptation* was refused the certificate and thus never released.[41] Crompton's inability to exploit the film brought an end to the whole project in the UK. The different distribution paths and their failure abroad invite new possibilities for further research projects.

In Argentina the Bó-Sarli films are generally disregarded as international and commercial, having little to do with the national reality. While there is truth that the duo played an important role in the regional circulation of Hispanic cinema and later entered the sexploitation markets transnationally, most of the films actually refer to the context of Argentina. They were originally made for a national market with an eye to attracting a more regional one. Therefore, *Violated Frames* begins in that nation: first due to the strong ties to the national and regional contexts that their cinema makes, but second because the Sarli-Bó work is a treasure trove for understanding sexuality, state censorship, populism, and popular culture in Argentina in the context of a history of regulation that spans three decades. The national lens will help unpack how the female body was censored from the time when the duo began making films until the end of the most vicious authoritarian dictatorship in Argentina's history. The Bó-Sarli films attracted a large popular audience. Sarli tells Néstor Romano about its changing face:

> First the men came to see me. The women came by the end of the 1960s. From the mid-1970s an intellectual and snob public, which wasn't mine, began to appreciate our cinema, relating it to a kitsch aesthetic.[42]

This shift from men, to women, and then to a more intellectual audience set the stage for a wide range of spectators and a popular all-inclusive culture.

In the first chapter, "Bodies through Time ... Time through Bodies," I use Diana Taylor's concept of "scenarios" to gather the many differing and at times contradictory narratives and affects surrounding the work and historical moment of the Bó-Sarli brand to understand the charged traumatic wounds of history left on the body and visible onscreen. Interweaving both narratives from the duo's work and scenarios from interrelated historical events (the threat of the return of Eva Perón's body, the founding supporters of Peronism and their ties to the worker's body, the emergence of the category of youth and its connection to the sexualized body), I attempt to encapsulate the changing dynamics of Argentina from 1955 to 1983. I argue that the Sarli-Bó movies entered into dialogue with the social volatility of the times, and I study how Peronism's populist affective mode delves into questions of taste. Analogously, the chapter looks at how, alongside Peronism, the Bó-Sarli films provided a place onscreen of national belonging for excessive bodies, which elsewhere faced looming threats that endangered their existence. The values that Bó exalted through his work with Sarli were somewhat old-fashioned, yet in true contradictory form they operated within an economy of risk, one where limits were certainly pushed by publicly displaying the private (bodies and sex) within a very traditional public space.

CRITICAL RECEPTION

Upon release of each film, the press was generally severe in its reviews. The excessive violence, bad acting, and simplistic plots were often criticized, while the cinematography and landscapes were lauded. Mostly, their work was seen as folkloric, melodramatic, humoristic, picaresque, and even ironic. The shock that it produced echoed in some of its criticism. Podalsky explains how the films "were ridiculed by contemporary intellectuals for *not* having any political or social bite."[43] Despite Bó's fight against censorship, no one defended the films publicly, and he was considered an outcast by his peers.[44]

It is not until the 1980s and 1990s that a brand-new appreciation took place. With the publication of Jorge Abel Martín's foundational *Los films de Armando Bó con Isabel Sarli* (1981), a new critical era was born. The book sets the scene for a newfound approval for Sarli-Bó. Full of anecdotes, interviews, images, and a thorough filmography, the compilation brings together a clear history of their work and grounds the many myths surrounding it. Kuhn's short thesis, *Armando Bó, el cine, la pornografía ingenua, y otras reflexiones*, followed suit.[45] In the introduction, Kuhn explains that in 1976 before leaving the country to go into exile, he signed a contract for a book on the Bó-Sarli films, using some of Bó's private archive. He sent the original to the publisher a year later, but because of the "difficult economic situation" they refused to publish it. He suspected, however, that they rejected his book due to his status in exile and because he was a "prohibited" author in the new regime. The graphic material that Bó had promised for his book went instead to Martín right before Bó died in 1981. After the return to democracy, Kuhn published an intellectual and more thoughtful criticism that reevaluated Sarli-Bó's work in spite of its ideology.[46] Kuhn's reflection appreciates the innovative unique style and authentic challenge to authority that they offered. In the 1990s two more books were released—*La gran aventura de Armando Bó, biografía total* and *Isabel Sarli al desnudo*—both of which reproduce much of Martín's work with additional anecdotes. The duo entered official national film history with their inclusion in the publication of *Cine argentino: Modernidad y vanuardias, 1957–1983*; a one-tome analysis of the film industry from after the 1957 cinema law and ending with the conclusion of the most brutal dictatorship in Argentina.

Internationally, when their most notable film, *Fuego*, which had a large following in New York during its initial run, was later released on VHS by the distribution company Something Weird Video in an English-language version, it in fact was responsible for stimulating and creating a second wave of global fandom. But even prior to that, critics like Roger Ebert were big fans, writing reviews for their films and appreciating their camp aesthetics.⁴⁷ It is no surprise that Ebert valued the Argentine duo; around the same time he then went on to cowrite the script for *Beyond the Valley of the Dolls*, a highly produced sexploitation film directed by Russ Meyer (USA, 1970). More recent works have been developed following the reappreciation of low popular cinema from the 1960s and 1970s in my 2009 book.⁴⁸ Due to *Fuego*'s success globally, many consider the Bó-Sarli work as internationally focused and distant from its Argentine context and reality. Conversely, to not consider the complications imposed by their mode of production, the Argentine social and political reality, censorship practices, the global framework of the sexploitation trends, and the affective register that exceeds the simplistic plots is to ignore the complex assemblage of circumstances that played into their work and established a rich popular audience.

HOW TO READ A SARLI-BÓ FILM: THE CASE OF *FUEGO*

The problem with using a simple plot-based and aesthetic analysis of one of their films, such as *Fuego*, is that any such reading will always be incomplete. *Fuego* is a film that can lend itself to many interpretations and contradictory analysis, yet none quite explain the actual slippery text.⁴⁹ What are the challenges of studying a film whose main attraction was the topic of sex? In many ways, *Fuego* is the epitome of the trope of an overly sexualized Sarli: a text meant for a mass male audience, an example of populism at the very least. Yet the images of crowds attest, and Sarli's anecdote cited earlier confirms, not only men attended the screenings. Moreover, *Fuego* reflects the tastes and pleasures of the "people" and the problematic way of defining such a group. It exposes the very worst aspects of popular culture that many critics despise.⁵⁰ Similarly, from a contemporary perspective *Fuego* can be seen as a retrograde and simplistic representation of sexuality, a misogynist statement on women's pleasure, and a very stereotypical representation of homosexuality (fig. 1).⁵¹ It is a simple exercise to watch the Sarli-Bó films today and deconstruct them as sexist, poorly made, and exuding all types of stereotypes. But the problem with those readings, not necessarily incorrect, is that they eliminate any further discussion on the value that popular cinema can provide. Furthermore, they assume a similarly progressive reading cannot be legitimately made. When I was visiting the University of Wisconsin–Madison to give a talk in a workshop about "Garbage Cinema in the Global South," a participant read the plot of the film as progressive from a third-world perspective. By

FIGURE 1. In *Fuego* (1968), Laura is devoured by Andrea in the opening scene.

juxtaposing progressive and regressive critical readings of *Fuego*, I will untangle some of the problems with staking positional interpretations of any of the Sarli-Bó productions. My intention is to not to belittle either point of view, as each presents equally convincing arguments that help to situate *Fuego*, but instead to show that in the end, to have a better grasp of the film's many layers and its complex context, one must change approaches. I will argue for an important shift in how to approach such examples, one that will guide the rest of the book.

Fuego is a "true story" about Laura, a nymphomaniac who cannot control her sexual urges. The name *Fuego*, which is never translated into English (only to French and Japanese), takes advantage of the Spanish and exotic original to describe Laura and her constant thirst for sexual pleasure. Laura meets an engineer, Carlos, who falls in love with her, and they finally marry. Despite her love of Carlos, Laura cannot be faithful to him because of her thirst for sex. Thus, Laura has escapades with her housekeeper, Andrea, and with other men she finds on her walks through the town. Carlos takes her to a doctor, who diagnoses her with a sexual neurosis and recommends that she see a specialist in New York City. They travel to New York to "fix" her ailments and restore her sense of monogamy. The cure is an utter failure, and she continues to find comfort in strangers' arms. Laura returns to Argentina, where she finally takes her own life. Carlos joins her in the afterlife when he realizes that he cannot live without her.

The film received some positive praise in its reviews, with comments such as: "there are no pretty heartthrobs here, everyone can identify with those who appear on the screen, to dream that they will be sought after by the exuberant Isabel Sarli."[52] However, it was heavily criticized in Argentina for its dialogue, cheap aesthetics, and excessive music.[53] In a more recent academic criticism of the film, Nayibe Bermúdez-Barrios reflects on its lesbian space. Referring to the character of Andrea, she argues: "the lesbian occupies a threefold space. In view of the situations in which she gets entangled, she becomes a tool for selling the film; due to her erotic and sexual interest in the protagonist, she is a threat to sexual "normalcy"; and through her role of working woman, she represents a menace to gender relations."[54] For Bermúdez-Barrios, the lesbian maid is "invisible through iconographic and cultural citations that reinforce the place of the lesbian within heterosexually regulated representations of space."[55] Her observations about the representation of Andrea provide an intersectional reading that includes the industrial and economic concerns that played a role in Bó and Sarli's success in profiting from a transnational market. She argues that the global reach of their films through the exploitation of Sarli's star persona motivates the content. Through the lens of the sexploitation genre, which functions as a socioeconomic and culturally conditioned aesthetic framework for the representation and consumption of images, Bermúdez-Barrios concludes that in the North-South trope, the South is easily consumable by the North.

While underestimating the pioneering effects of the duo and the difficult context within Argentina, Bermúdez-Barrios's analysis also falls short. Firstly, she is assuming that *Fuego* was made solely for the United States. The story is much more complex, because despite the seeming acceptance in the US market, *Fuego* was not easily adopted. Even with an already established relationship with Columbia Pictures International, Bó had to travel to the United States to seek distribution. He began by pitching *My Father's Wife* (1968) but was unsuccessful at securing the rights he sought. Only after introducing *Fuego* was he able to find a distributor for it and other films that followed.[56] Even though *Fuego*, like all the others, was originally meant for the huge fan base they had accrued in Argentina and Latin America, their consistent struggle with the ensuing censorship apparatus that was taking shape made it the only film that did not premiere first in Buenos Aires. As a matter of fact, when Bó was ready to process the film in Argentina, he was advised by a friend in the lab to take it to the United States, because the film would be outright prohibited in 1968, during Juan Carlos Onganía's military dictatorship and with the looming presence of law 18.019. To introduce the national context adds another layer of nuance in thinking about its North-South relationship.

Alternatively, the North-South paradigm could just as easily be read as a failure to find a real solution in the North. Carlos's attempt to seek a cure for Laura in New York is unsuccessful and they both return to the South. The North is not the haven that the South purports it to be. In many ways this was the resistant, less comforting path that Bó and Sarli personally chose. They could have easily gone to the United States to make their films. Sarli was offered work by director Robert Aldrich, which she refused.[57] Since she had a good command of the English language, the move to Hollywood would have been an easy one to make. Yet, English did not come easy for Bó, one of the reasons why he could not leave Argentina. Even when Columbia Pictures suggested making an English-language film, *The Virgin Goddess* had to be directed by another since Bó was not fluent in the language. When the duo finally resolved to move to the United States in 1980, SIFA was barely surviving and the INC had denied them funding for their last production, *Una viuda descocada* (*A Madcap Widow*, 1980). By that point, Bó had become sick and eventually died.[58]

Bermúdez-Barrios's observations about the problematic lesbian representation of the female worker forming part of a male fantasy is quite fitting. Notwithstanding, her analysis prevents further discussion. It fails to engage the role the films played in the development of onscreen sexuality that eventually continued in the 1980s, with identity movements erupting after the fall of the dictatorship.[59] It also imposes a more contemporary expectation of sexual norms onto a film that was made in 1968. While not an excuse for the stereotypes it presents, such an interpretation unfairly expects intellectual nuance at a popular level that was not a societal norm, even among intellectuals.[60] Is it that the film cannot contain the lesbian as she suggests, or is it that the film is about the freeing of sexual norms? Either reading could be made. Within the context of a restricted Catholic Argentina, the very existence of an onscreen lesbian may have had another effect. It also coincides with the 1960s' sexuality movements developing in the North that only arrived in full force in Argentina post 1983.

Similar to the lesbian issue, the representation of gay people offers a simple cliché. For instance, Adelco Lanza, who collaborated on films from the early days, performs on many occasions as a gay male character.[61] While the stereotypes of an overly mannered male reappear through Lanza's roles, the fact that he was included was a quite contentious choice that offended the censors. The same can be said for the lesbian representations found in various films, which I will take up more clearly in chapter 3 through the analysis of *Intimacies of a Prostitute*. The scenes involving lesbian references were censored or eliminated, even during the most open period with Octavio Getino as the director of the censor board in 1973. It is also reminiscent of the difficult time that *The Tigress* had in 1953, Bó's first confrontation with state interference. In the case of *Fuego*, the fact that the film premiered in New York first meant that Bó was able to include more risqué scenes, some of which were cut for the Argentine premiere in 1971. But perhaps the question of nonnormativity can be approached from a different angle. If the films were so regressive in their portrayal, why were they so influential for well-known sexuality champions such as John Waters and Annie Sprinkle? As John Waters has stated in his television introduction to *Fuego*, Sarli's character was an inspiration for Divine.[62] Facundo Nazareno Saxe and Atilo Raúl Rubino have jointly argued that the kitsch aesthetic developed through Sarli's costumes and makeup allowed for a camp reading that inspired Waters to create Divine.[63] They highlight the parody found in Divine as a drag queen version of Sarli and an insight for Judith Butler's iconic study in *Gender Trouble* (1990). Butler's drag queen performs femininity to excess, much as Sarli does throughout her films but particularly after 1968. It is the excess in Sarli, gay and lesbian characters, and the male lovers that make the Bó-Sarli films camp and set up nonnormative possibilities.

However, content-based analyses will always be insufficient, as they are not necessarily informed by the negotiations with the censors that took place and the specific context of each film. In the case of *Fuego*, it needs to be appreciated with its mirror *Insatiable*, filmed in 1978 but only released posthumously after the end of the dictatorship.[64] The two films are very similar to each other but happen in two different time periods. A span of ten years separates the two with two different contexts and within a history of censorship that will allow one to flourish abroad and the other to all but disappear. The questions of women's sexuality and the expression of sexual freedom of the body are central to both.[65] Nonetheless, there exists a sense of continuity between the two films due to their interrelated subjects. The differences that ten years make, and the release of the porno chic *Deep Throat* (Gerard Damiano, USA, 1972), opens up for the possibility of riskier scenes, such as a full-frontal nude shot of Bó himself. As permissibility was changing, there was a gap in the process that allowed for differences between films and how these were interpreted in the tighter Argentine context. The duo was seen as immoral, pushing the boundaries of acceptability, and in line with politically subversive actors. For this reason, it is more useful to think of the trajectory of the films and their place within a progression toward a more libertarian sexuality rather than being caught up in the specifics of one film. Individual texts were altered by censorial demands. Reading across films rather than only in one instance permits a more comprehensive look at the way that sexuality norms were transforming and how the Sarli-Bó brand was adjusting to these norms while also pushing their boundaries.

Currently there is increasing attention given to the preservation of explicit or adult films, such as the daring oeuvre made by the pioneering pair. Eric Schaefer's call to action on preservation has inspired a noticeable growth in the area of explicit film research, which became more official with the creation of the Adult Film Scholarly Interest Group at the Society for Cinema and Media Studies in 2014, the same year that *Porn Studies* launched as a journal.[66] Latin American film historians must enter the adult film debates and embark on the objective of filling gaps in the microhistories of explicit film trajectories. *Latsploitation, Exploitation Cinemas, and Latin America*, the essay collection I coedited with Dolores Tierney, which includes a section entitled "Sex, Sex, and More Sex," is a precursor to subsequent discussions taking place in the study of adult films. Tierney and I argue in the introduction that Latin American auteurs, stars, and places formed a large part of the earlier sex onscreen productions that circulated globally.

Yet much of the story of Latin American contributions in this field remains untold. *Violated Frames* fills this chasm and expands beyond sexploitation films themselves to incorporate practices of censorship and national policies on archives, as well as to more generally contribute to the emerging historicizing of gender and sexuality. In chapter 2, "Reading Bad Cinema through 'Bad Archives,'" I begin with the story of the disappeared Classification Board archive, which dates from 1963, the year of its creation, and ends in 1984, with the fall of Argentina's military dictatorship. The chapter explores the loss of the archive and its implications for film scholarship on the period, reflecting on ways of dealing with this loss by weaving in remnants that I have uncovered through relentless archival work underlining how these help in the process of reconstructing a new, albeit unstable, archive that continues to evolve.

Censorship and even self-censorship were undoubtedly contexts that must be taken into consideration when discussing the Bó-Sarli films.[67] As independent producers who did not rely on funding or credits, their productions continued to finance their upcoming work. Yet, despite their independence, they still had to abide by the rules of the state apparatus to release their films at home and internationally. Even from early in their career they found their films in court, as any individual could denounce one for offending acceptable morals. What is interesting is how Sarli's nudes were deemed more offensive than the northern examples of art films.[68] Chapter 3, "Disciplining Bodies through Censors' Shears," gives a history of various periods of film censorship in Argentina. It explores Argentina's film classification from as early as 1957, even prior to the formation of classification boards, up to 1984. Using the remnants of the file for *Intimacies of a Prostitute*, the only remaining but unfortunately incomplete Bó file from the film Classification Board archive, along with other archival materials (press clippings, surviving film versions, press releases, official laws, what little secondary work about the history exists), I help to reveal and suggest possible reasons behind the censorship of the Bó-Sarli films. In 1979, a retrospective of ten of their films played in the five-screen Multicine, perhaps suggesting the easing of censorship of their work. However, upon closer examination, the retrospective marked the end of Miguel Tato's reign, the official who was the most severe censor during their trajectory.[69] Even Tato's retirement did not ease the state persecution of the films, which were either prohibited or allowed to be released in heavily censored versions.[70] However, despite the many intellectual gatherings to protest any new measures, these excluded Bó and Sarli, the most persistently censored of the bunch.[71] Unlike their peers who either left the country in exile, died, or stopped making movies, Sarli-Bó persisted throughout the volatile period despite the many frustrations and threats they faced.[72]

Regardless of its sexual theme, on another level *Fuego* lends itself to other social readings. It is about a wealthy man who, despite his wealth, cannot buy what he wants. He desires a woman who cannot be contained. He tries to mold her into the "perfect wife" but does not accomplish it. Instead, everyday working men in the small town are able to enjoy her favors. The social implications of class go beyond Bermúdez-Barrios's intersectional reading of the maid. Chapter 4, "Collective Working-Class Male Bodies," begins with *Thunder among the Leaves* and references the whole oeuvre to analyze the gendered male body in its moment of manual labor. As an abstract concept, manual labor produced a specific type of affect that connected the body to Peronism, silenced in 1955. In the film, Bó makes work itself an explicit topic that later implicitly permeates all of his productions and thus defines the social aspect of his cinema. Politically tied to the workers' movement and a new niche audience, beginning with the male spectator, the films were not only limited to him, as Sarli's important role sets her always within a working-class position. Andrea, in this case, becomes a replacement for the new female spectator that enjoyed the films in the late 1960s.

Additionally, debates that centered around bad cinema need to include the role that Sarli-Bó had in provoking boundaries and questioning what was permissible and what was not.[73] By adapting and carefully weighing through different methods such as affect theory, historiography, feminist criticism, and intersectional analysis, *Violated Frames* thinks about how intersectionality through class and gender are used to either push those boundaries or create static provisions for women. The Sarli-Bó example provides the opportunity to explore questions relating to the history of sex onscreen, popular culture, and bad cinema. To counter Kuhn's characterization about naïve and moralistic pornography, one can look to Francis Ferguson to understand what is really at stake. Ferguson defines the archive not by its content but by its social use.[74] To participate in the production of knowledge about sex, one needs to think about the bodily anomaly and excess of the pornographic and its "capacity to crystallize the anxieties and desires of the society in which it circulates."[75] The pornographic, according to Ferguson, is about context not content—one can be pornographic without being sexually explicit. Studying Sarli-Bó results in more insight into the power structures in place during a period of the institutional building of strong apparatuses to control instances of sexuality and other "immoral" behavior on the screen. By doing so, I am proactively building the possibility of an archive that accesses sexuality in a period of sexual silences, to show who is excluded from the archive and who has access to it and why. To generate this sense of knowing by thinking of the archive of sex helps us move the debate from intention (criminal law) to effects of action (tort law) and decriminalize thought. Therefore, according to Ferguson, pornography, no matter how naïve, can become a part of the historical transformation in the mechanism of power relationships.[76] What then becomes powerful in its wake is its proximity to bodies—Peronist, youth, working-class, and gendered bodies. These bodies carry through them certain burdens that are expressed beyond just mere representation but through their intersections, identified by an affective turn.

In chapter 5, "Affective Intimate Interludes: The Risky Female Body," I discuss the "excesses" of leisure, specifically in exhibition, enjoyment, and the ecstasy of the everyday body. Focusing on moments of both contradiction and explosion of sex onscreen, the affective events provide potentialities that interrupt the already fragmented film narratives. Through posing, performance of "bad" dancing, the connections with nature, and the unleashing of female pleasure, I explore the possibilities of onscreen sex.

Sarli-Bó worked endlessly to produce a trademark that in the end, despite the state apparatus that was systemically developing to silence the clear body politics in their films, can be more readily tracked when we focus on patterns that permeate the whole of their work. Through assemblage, I find the repetition of the intersectional classed, gendered, and raced bodies, and how they meet at different historical junctures. Those events provide jolts for bodies that are marked but also allow for risk, discomfort, comedy, and pleasurable enjoyment. I argue that using affect to think through the onscreen body as a site of alternative epistemologies helps to rehistoricize and reorganize a group of popular bad films that have been highly dismissed for their purported lack of political or aesthetic content. I study the affective moments whose aesthetics and politics provide a potentiality for onscreen bodies; in performance and highly sexualized ones, those resurfacing throughout the films and thus connecting to a variety of audiences to belong in a complex matrix of national and transnational flows, ones that are always already social and political, and yet none of these at the same time. The excessive interludes of onscreen bodies allow for inscribing a new sense of time, one that ironically breaks from the simple narratives and quick dramatic action of each individual film. Instead of relying solely on representation as a methodology, which may provide some simple formulas encapsulating particular images' meanings, the body in the affectively charged moments becomes a thorny burst that can lead to more interesting and unstable connections. By isolating what the body can do but also what the body can be made to do, I find a way through seemingly trite and valueless productions to understand their continued appeal and lasting popularity, and perhaps take a more interesting and libertarian position on sexuality, work, and bodies that helps determine the specific audience the duo aimed to and did engage. Furthermore, my rough or "bad" analysis exposes the incompleteness, the gaps, the impossible drive for visibility of the sex act itself, and an anxiety about the unwieldy, disordered, approximate, uneven, and unfinished project of the bad that never seems to only signify.

PART I

Bodies and Archives

CHAPTER 1

Bodies through Time . . . Time through Bodies

I consider myself a fighter, a woman of the people.
—Isabel Sarli, 1999[1]

On 12 October 2012, President Cristina Fernández de Kirchner proclaimed Isabel Sarli an ambassador of Argentine popular culture. The decree declares:

> Ms. Isabel Sarli is considered a true representative of national culture, as much due to her talents as film actress as for being deemed a popular icon of her time and an emblematic celebrity of Argentine cinema.[2]

It authenticates a new perspective on the sensual star as one who "links the ethic and cultural values, in representing the synthesis of the image that the Argentine Republic wishes to project to the world."[3] Sadly, the words of validation arrived fifty-four years after the release of Sarli-Bó's debut film, a shocking launch that founded a body of work that was never officially sanctioned by the many governments in power during the development of their careers. They experienced censorship from their first public experiment.

This more recent gesture to recognize the star, under one of the latest iterations of General Juan Domingo Perón's original party, recalls a similar directive bestowed upon the naïve young woman who had won the title of Miss Argentina in 1955. Before heading to California for the Miss Universe pageant, Sarli met then President Perón, who distinguished her value by her beauty.[4] He said the following words to her:

You are worth more than 20 Ambassador Paz [the Argentine ambassador to the United States] because you represent the beauty of the Argentine woman, and you bring with you a message of good will to the people of the universe.[5]

The connection founded early on between the up-and-coming starlet and Peronism was only reaffirmed more recently in Sarli's old age, after the once scandalous films had become nostalgic relics of a distant era. Time left a mark on her onscreen body, but her latest recrowning as national ambassador formally acknowledges the central role the duo had on popular culture and sexual norms, and the enduring affect they still hold for Argentine audiences. Their role explains the ever-changing nature of narrations and mythology based on taste, stories that have a way of soothing past wounds. The official celebration that came years later did not remove the scars left on the sexual body but only helped to highlight the ironies found in Sarli's aging figure and promote the watered-down body of films widely available today on YouTube. This chapter returns to the historical context of 1960s' and 1970s' Argentina to gather the many differing and at times contradictory scenarios that surround the work and moment of the Bó-Sarli brand, in order to understand the traumatic wounds of history left on the body of the star and the oeuvre Sarli-Bó produced.

Diana Taylor explains that both narratives and scenarios help understand and better analyze histories. By using the term *scenario* to approach social structures and behaviors, Taylor draws from both the repertoire and the archive.[6] Simply put, the archive holds the enduring materials that are passed on from generation to generation, and the repertoire enacts embodied practice, memory, and knowledge.[7] For Taylor, scenarios carry localized meaning that pass as universally valid. As in Michel de Certeau's sense, they are practiced places, actions, and performances embodied by social actors. They are Pierre Bourdieu's habitus: structures that allow for reversal, parody, and change but remain generally fixed, imploring us to situate ourselves in relation to the scenario. And it is through scenarios that the archive and repertoire work together to constitute and transmit social knowledge.[8] The repertoire of the body operates in conjunction with the archive of history to create references that are by no means complete, a context that is always in the process of becoming because it is beyond total capture. As snippets in time that help fill in the picture of the past, scenarios also remind us that the portrait is permanently unfinished. They are mediated like the repertoire and the archive, a product of relationships, exchanges, and fluctuations rather than stability. By interweaving both narratives from the Bó-Sarli films as archives and histories from distinct and handpicked but interrelated events surrounding the merging of an assemblage of histories and contexts, I articulate how the Bó-Sarli films relate, react, and absorb such forces. The historical events and topics include Eva Perón's body, the founding supporters of Peronism, classed taste, the emergence of the category of youth, and the context of onscreen sexuality—all of which effected the changing dynamics of Argentina from 1955 to 1983. I also highlight the conflating scenes that gave meaning and produced affect to eventually allow the belonging of the duo's work in Argentine society, one that has more recently come with official acknowledgement in the law.

While Armando Bó was not a Peronist (he instead was affiliated with the Radical Party) there were elements in his work that could certainly align with the Justicialista movement, another name given to General Perón's party. Isabel Sarli, on the other hand, was an ardent Peronist at the time, a commitment sealed with her meeting the general as the representative for Argentina in the Miss Universe pageant. In this chapter I will begin with the premise that to explore the Sarli-Bó films one must understand the specific political and social scenarios from which their work draws inspiration, a time that coincides with the exile and return of Perón and the 1976 dictatorship that followed.

The period between 1955 and 1973 was an important and volatile time in the history of Argentina. It is also a period in which twenty-three of the twenty-seven Sarli-Bó films were produced. In the span of eighteen years there were nine different governments, only three of which were elected democratically (Arturo Frondizi, Arturo Umberto Ilia, and Héctor Campora). The rest gained power through military coups and in some cases from internal coups within the military, like those orchestrated by Roberto M. Levingston (in June 1970) and Alejandro Agustín Lanusse (in March 1971). Remarkably, until the Campora government in 1973, the constant absence from the political scene was Juan Perón and the Justicialista party, which was proscribed from its ouster until 11 March 1973, when Lanusse announced presidential elections and allowed a candidate to run for the first time since the leader's exile. For another three years the instability continued under a Peronist government, until the 1976 coup that brought in the most brutal dictatorship in Argentina's recent history.

Evident during the unstable stretch is the constant disavowal of Peronism and its meaning from public spaces. The movement and its leader were repeatedly erased from the public sphere in a way that ironically created an aura surrounding Perón's role in the nation's past. By discussing *Peronismo* and how its aura evolved, beginning with the body of Perón's second wife, I contextualize the work of Sarli-Bó. As Peronismo was the absent present during the era in question, I argue that the pair borrowed from the movement's tradition and melodrama, and appealed to its base (so-called *cabecitas negras* and working-class men), becoming most popular in marginalized areas around Buenos Aires and the rest of the country, much like the political faction itself.[9] Furthermore, their films (excessively affective melodramas with themes of social justice showing the plight of the marginalized), which featured a public anti-intellectual stance, were very much in line with its populist politics. Could the difficulty Bó-Sarli had with the censors be in part due to this seeming alignment?

To grasp the social, economic, and political factors surrounding the films, I delve into the support base of Peronism as it evolved from its foundation in different forces—working-class men, women, and youth—developments determining their spectators. The arguments that follow go beyond looking at the concrete base of their audience; I can only speculate retrospectively on this question by inductively coming to such a conclusion.[10] Instead, I connect Peronism's affective mode, which I argue can be found within Eva's body, to questions of taste linked to the group, trying to develop the historical base for the chapters that follow. As the lowly body of Peronism threatened to return, so did the possibility of sex that was imminent both in society and onscreen, a menace found in the material female body. In part, the complicated story for both the movement and the filmmaking practice relates to belonging and excess. Analogously, Peronism and the Sarli-Bó films provided a place for excessive bodies to belong in the nation and on the movie screen, despite the many risks that impended and endangered their existence, showing a fissure in that very system. I begin by explaining what I mean when I refer to Peronism's affective mode, which surfaces with Eva's body and consummates in the appearance and complete uncovering of Isabel's *cuerpo*.

SCENARIO 1: EVA PERÓN AND THE POLITICS OF AFFECT

In *La pasión y la excepción*, Argentine cultural critic Beatriz Sarlo brings together three narratives—the disappearance of Eva Perón's corpse after it was embalmed, the assassination of Pedro Eugenio Aramburu, president from 1955 to 1958 and leader of the conservative "liberating revolution," and two fictional short stories by Argentina's most prominent author Jorge Luis Borges—to discuss the role of affect in Argentina in the early 1970s and create one scenario. Playing off of Copi's interpretation of Eva in the theatrical piece *Eva Perón,* which debuted in Paris in 1970, Sarlo turns to her exceptionality as the founding element of the book that binds all three references. Because the ultimate and defining incident for her study is the disappearance of Eva's deceased body, Sarlo focuses on the construction of her figure while she was alive to show the journey it takes to become "sublime" after her death, a quality that refers to the work of Emmanuel Kant in describing unquantifiable greatness.[11]

Sarlo argues that Eva was exceptional among her peers and that her body personified a melodrama and camp aura during her lifetime. When compared to other colonel or political wives, Eva was not representative of the normative; conversely, she was thin, young, and blonde, more akin to a model than the mother or typical housewife body of other spouses.[12] Eva had a past: as a rising radio and film star, her overall image was defined by the extravagant fashion she flaunted. In one of her roles in *La cabalgata del circo* (*Circus Cavalcade*, Mario Soffici, 1944), she acted alongside Bó. Early on in her career, Paco Jamandreu designed her wardrobe and helped to conceptualize Eva's aura, an ultramodern look that could be described as fitting somewhere between Greta Garbo and Audrey Hepburn.[13] Her business suits hid the fact that she had no curves. The androgynous guise, at a time when women's fashions were homogenous, contributed to Eva's extraordinariness. Androgyny exceeded her style and seeped into her gestures, mannerisms, and actions.[14] For instance, Eva was comfortable with men. She addressed the opposite sex informally, a behavior that pushed the limits for women in the 1940s. Later Eva wore the most fashionable designer brands from Paris, an excess of elaborate dresses and jewelry helping to reaffirm her rags-to-riches story.

"Performatic" moments helped to define Eva's body, moving from melodramatic and camp to the religious realm in the end.[15] When she became sick, her celebrity deviated toward the tragic and "sublime," a quality reached through her passionate excess of hyperbolic cliché and redundancy. Her sublimity created a type of "auratic" in the Benjaminian sense, a presence that lives beyond the material now. As Taylor asserts, Eva's body ensures her reality and thus provides the authenticating materiality that sustains the performance of resuscitation.[16] After her death in 1952, her beauty and wealth were preserved as if at their peak by the latest embalming techniques. An expensive proposition to produce the most elaborate corpse at US $200,000, but Eva's body became the trace that threatened to reappear.[17] Ironically, the body gives authenticity to both ideological sides, the pro- and anti-Perón movements, as it takes on the authority of the regime and both sides work hard to capture and fix it: "to make and unmake" her myth, to borrow a 1987 phrase from Elaine Scarry. Eva Perón's body lies in the realm of the symbolic, as Sarlo states, but Sarlo's analysis of the archive (body as archive) alone only goes thus far, for she remains at the level of representation. Sarlo acknowledges that Eva's body produces a type of affect that justifies love/admiration on the one hand and hate/disgust on the other but does not emphasize enough its lingering power into the present. Sarlo's study is a first attempt to analyze how Peronism's affect through its excess created a sense of (not) belonging, a strategy that impacted the post-Peronist moment that followed, thereby leaving a trace or a wound that was never really reconciled and always threatens to return.

The affect found in the living and dead body of Eva can help reflect on the power of the movement's attraction. Affect, more than emotions, describes the body's capacity to move and be moved physically. From a Spinozian perspective, the body's perpetual becoming never reaches a final state but is in constant transformation.[18] Affect itself describes excess that cannot be fully represented, articulated, or defined. A surplus gap between what is meaningful and knowable and what is livable can never be erased, is beyond representation, and thus instead stands in for the remainder of the representable. The shift from thinking about bodies as material entities with defining qualities to one of belonging or not reflects the shift from identity politics to a politics of belonging not based on the concept of essence. While Sarlo's example of Perón isolates her, it also muffles the history and becomings of bodies that surrounded her and mutes those stories by emphasizing only the exceptionality of Eva, the commodity or star. What about the faceless bodies of the masses that surrounded her? How did their bodies belong to the project that became known as Peronism? Or how did bodies reject her aura through the anti-Peronist movement? How does the body of the exceptional relinquish political, economic, and symbolic capital to the have-nots? What emotional ties are provoked by such invocations of the past? If Eva's body was an archive of memory, then how is her body threatening to return? And what traces in popular culture reenact that potentiality? If Peronism featured the people as actors rather than spectators, than what role did they share in its return?

SCENARIO 2: PERONISMO RECONSIDERED
AND A NATION DIVIDED

> I ask myself, and if Juan returns where do we go? Ay, I have a doubt, I don't know what to do—well, in politics there is always doubt. If one only knew? I am sorry, sorry Chinese man, I put you back in my drawer, but times change, sorry. Ay, Juan how we wait for you, we are many who wait for you. You look good in shiny clothes, Juan! I say, are we as many as we want? The opposition says no that we are not many. However, . . . however, how nice it would be if everything could suddenly change. If this guy could, why couldn't I? What attraction does politics have? The balcony, a balcony, there isn't anything lovelier than a balcony. To be able to tell the people nonsense, the people fall for it. Yes, but of course, it couldn't be any other way. . . . but the town hall is yours. Yes, I know what I am saying, it's clear, the people already speak about you as Mayor Gambetta—phenomenon—Mayor Dr. Gambetta, the town of Long Lice is too small for you, you need a big city, perhaps New York first, Gambetta, Gambetta for the whole world.

This long monologue taken from *The Mayor's Wife* takes place after a friend comes to visit Dr. Gambetta, a medical doctor. Before his acquaintance arrives, Gambetta switches the picture hanging on the wall from Radical leader Arturo Frondizi (president 1958–62) to Communist icon Mao Zedong. His friend asks the doctor to support his candidacy for mayor. Dr. Gambetta says that he cannot do so because he will be running for the office of the mayor with another party. After the friend leaves, Gambetta begins the monologue as he replaces the picture of Mao with one of Juan Perón and then another of the same general, each image marking the two election periods won by the ex-president.[19]

The movie was shot in 1966 and released in 1967, during the Juan Carlos Onganía regime (1966–70), when leftist miniskirts and long hair on males became outlawed. *The Mayor's Wife* was the only film Sarli-Bó made with clear political references.[20] The irony and humor in the scene, showing the volatility of the candidate regarding ideological loyalty, would have been considered a critique of politics in general. That, in combination with the power-hungry actions of Gambetta as witnessed near the end of the monologue, when he openly desires to conquer the world, can also be read as a satire of politicians, Perón more specifically. Yet the underlying threat of Perón's return to power and the possible allegiance to his politics were a challenge to Onganía's regime. Despite the film's seemingly ambiguous political positioning, on the one hand critiquing Perón but through humor disavowing such critique, and because *The Mayor's Wife* is the only one of the duo's films that specifically relates to politics in Argentina, it serves as a key example to think about the relationship between their work and the outlawed political movement. In particular, one might consider that the *we* in the monologue clearly ties Gambetta, ultimately a sympathetic protagonist, to the controversial character of Perón and his party, one that did not officially exist publicly in 1967. For this reason, an outline of the historical complexities of Peronism and its challengers helps to better grasp the divisions marking the nation.

In September 1955, a coup toppled Perón and brought in another general to the helm, Eduardo Lonardi. Lonardi did not last very long in power since he was considered too moderate. Thus, in November Pedro Eugenio Aramburu replaced him under the new banner of the "liberating revolution" that aimed to de-Peronize the nation. On March 9 of the following year, Perón and Peronism became illegal, and it was a crime to use the party's symbols or discourses.[21] The military erasure of the past officially marked an era of clear division—a nation unable to merge opposing players in the game of class-based politics. Peronism thus took a position on the margins that ironically most likely gave the party an edge and allowed it to develop in ways that may not have been possible had Perón not been exiled.[22] While public demonstrations of its ideology were not tolerated, a pro-Perón uprising in June 1956 set a new standard for dealing with opposition.[23] The government decided to execute rebels as an example, and thus a form of state violence was born, one that may have left a particular trace in the nation's memory.[24] Violence was met with violence as a fresh brand of Peronism was allowed to brew and was even encouraged by Perón from exile.[25] It is his messages that called for violence and dissent encouraging groups to form; such as the left-wing guerrillas, the Montonero Peronist Movement or Montoneros, and others with similar revolutionary strategies tied to the leader.

In the period leading up to the return of Perón in 1973, the movement was already very different. There were many people trying to build a Peronism without Perón, not ever expecting his return.[26] When Lanusse called the election of 1973, he strategically did not allow anyone who was not a resident of Argentina to stand, hoping to keep the leader away from the democratic process despite seeming to open up the process. The new law did not prevent Perón from attempting another tactic—Héctor

Campora ran in his place and won with 50 percent of the vote in the first balloting. The plan was that once Campora was in office he would change the law, resign, and call new elections, giving the patriarch a new opportunity to win back his position cut short almost twenty years earlier. Perón returned on 20 June 1973 to a very different movement and a more clearly fraught Argentina. While troubled from its beginnings, at this point Peronism was ideologically more unstable. Neither left- nor right-wing, it was both and none at the same time. It was a truly populist movement that was constantly shifting to accommodate the many ideologies that it housed. Some of its followers belonged to leftist guerrilla groups like the Montoneros and others developed out of the Peronist Youth movement. However, there were representatives from the right as well, such as the newly established Triple A and union leaders who had been strategically placed in positions of power because of their political loyalty to the army.

Perón's return at the Ezeiza airport provided a scenario for the reperformance of the internal conflict brewing in the nation and more specifically in the party. Three million people, the largest mass gathering ever held in the country, showed up to welcome Perón back home.[27] The celebratory congregation produced a confrontation of opposing ideological factions. The crowds were shot at, leaving thirteen dead and 365 wounded.[28] Opposing ideological sides blamed each other for the incident. Regardless of culpability, the event enacts the virulent split in the party and nation, one that could no longer be ignored. Perón knew that he needed both factions to win the elections that Campora would call on 23 September. Unfortunately, his populist approach could no longer maneuver the severely splintered party. He had to choose between sides. By picking his third wife Isabel as his running mate and vice-president, and José López Rega, the mastermind behind the Triple A, as his secretary, Perón had clearly made a choice steering to the right. His position and strategy during a key and decisive moment defined the three years leading to the most brutal dictatorship in Argentina's history.

In exposing the traps of popular political movements, Jon Beasley-Murray shows how populism of the left can easily turn into populism of the right. In the case of Argentina, it was Peronism's foundations, its antagonistic relationships, and the many factions that it juggled that were to blame for the end to the left-wing movements that followed with the incoming dictatorship.[29] With hindsight, the concepts of right and left are troubling because of their static political picture: Peronism's history itself confirmed the problems with this picture. The multiplicity that encompasses the movement both throughout time and across people means that there is more value in a flexible perception of history that takes into account the clear shifts that adapt to the ever-changing social climate as it develops. Providing a complex but comprehensive picture of the ideology and practices without writing solely on Peronism is impossible and beyond the scope of this book. Nevertheless, the nuances and intricacies of Peronism cannot be ignored; one must be careful not to fall into the many traps that both cultural studies and history have laid out for us.[30] Without equating the work of Sarli and Bó to Peronism, there developed a strong connection to the political movement, one that in many ways took advantage of the marginal position Peronism had legally but also its commercial power. But instead of clear links between the movement and the pair, the relationship is more nebulous and connected to a commonality between what was happening in society as a whole and the duo's production history, both of which were born in specific political and social scenarios. The work of Sarli-Bó was neither subversive nor conformist, but its balance between both positions helped to affirm itself in the marketplace to a population that easily saw themselves belonging and relating to or reminding them of their political circumstances. In some ways, the Sarli-Bó films mirrored the balancing act that Peronism was playing with both ideological sides to ensure that it came to power. The end goal of the cinema was to guarantee exhibition of their films, at least locally, in order to make money at the box office for survival and continued filmmaking. But to do so they had to draw from a consumer base who bought into their films and what they sold. In many ways the original consumer is the same one that founded Peronism: working-class males subscribed to the Sarli-Bó brand.

SCENARIO 3: IT WAS THE PEOPLE WHO GAVE HIM HIS POWER . . . AND FLOCKED TO THE CINEMA

Perón adapted to societal changes to attract new voters to his party; first by tempting working-class men, then women, and finally children and youth.[31] History may have played out this way if one can account for the fact that in his first election (1946) only men could vote, and by his second term (1951) women had won the right to do so. On his return to Argentina, the youth movement that the general had launched during his tenure grew up to be an important sector in the 1973 elections. Moreover, the continuing and newly reconfigured youth movements were gaining much traction during the 1960s and 1970s and also helped

Perón achieve his comeback. All these circumstances reveal the different gender and generational groups that helped Perón to power throughout his political career. The changing landscape does not account for other defining characteristics of Perón supporters. Which men, women, and youth found his politics, affect, and project appealing? It was mainly the men and youth that gave Perón his support base, due to the highly patriarchal structures of society. While the youth grappled with issues of gender, in many ways they could not escape its limitations.

To return to *The Mayor's Wife*, the mayoral candidate, Dr. Gambetta, finds the balcony to be an important place where his power rests, as stated in the monologue cited at the start of scenario 2. Humorously, the architectural platforms become the main attraction for the candidate to enter politics. There is one scene when Gambetta practices his speech on a balcony on the ground floor. Its humor lies in the performatic nature as he speaks out to the supposed crowd with none present. The scene inscribes the body of the speaker, Gambetta, into the political, but the obvious absence of the spectator makes the effect flop. What the images clearly highlight is that for the balcony to be effective and affective, one needs corresponding bodies to feel its power, message, and passion. The use of the balcony and its role in the performatics of politics is emblematic of the style invented and perfected by both Eva and Juan Perón, who were known for their endless speeches on the balcony that consolidated their ultimate appeal to the masses. The scene in the film highlights, through omission, the importance of the observers or spectators and the role they play in its politics. The balcony is only as powerful as the connection to the masses allows. And the speeches work to create affect and establish a strong association between orator and receiver. The balcony produces an affective relationship with the masses, and ironically the division or barrier between the politician and the crowd almost disappears. Featuring Eva and Juan high above emphasizes the exceptionality of both in comparison to the faceless masses below. They loom over the people, whereas Gambetta has no spectators to oversee nor is he high above—the balcony he chooses is on the ground level.

Many attribute 17 October 1945 as the foundational moment of the Peronist movement because, despite the myths surrounding its history, neither union leaders nor Eva organized the mass demonstration that secured Juan Perón's candidacy in the upcoming elections and his immediate release from prison. On that historic day, a flood of workers walked from the suburbs of Buenos Aires to its center to demand their leader's release, which marked the rise of labor and the decline of other supporters. The crowd became the key component to Perón's success. The appearance of the multitude as one of the main protagonists of the erupting political drama ensured changes and the most profound effect on the working-class position in society, especially during his first term as president.[32] For instance, real wages for industrial workers, Perón's main base, increased by 53 percent between 1946 and 1949.[33] His government empowered the working class in a way the marginalized group had never experienced before. The state was the purveyor of new rights and a newfound prosperity for workers. As one of Peronism's most important historians, Daniel James, has argued, the caudillo recast the issue of citizenship in a new social context whereby workers, *pueblo* (people), and nation became one.[34] Perón's insistence on equating workers with *pueblo* and nation reproduced mass culture's depiction of hard-working, long-suffering poor as authentically Argentine.[35]

By making the correlation, Perón institutionalized class consciousness and worked toward class harmony rather than conflict. But his efforts to bring together the classes backfired, eventually causing him to lose power and incite hatred among many other groups such as the army, the church, and the oligarchy. While many contradictions characterized the movement, perhaps its most important is that it toppled class hierarchies by institutionalizing the working class and its struggle but simultaneously reproduced a false sense of class harmony. To better understand Peronism and its vitriolic counterpart, anti-Peronism, one can study the stereotypes developed by both groups to define their supporters, ones guided by social anxieties growing at a time of great change. To see the Peronist movement limited to a single group is always inexact as it also had many sympathizers from different backgrounds and for different reasons. For example, middle-class nationalists and manufacturers, who out of self-interest endorsed industrialization projects such as the nationally focused Import Substitution Industrialization and also evidently benefited from the increasing consumption of local products by raising the workers' wages, were both generally supportive of Perón. The simplicity of the conflict between groups allows for better fleshing out the presumptions at the base of the movement and its counterpart to understand precisely how Bó and Sarli's films fit into a socially and economically divided nation.

Los descamisados (the shirtless ones) was the name disparagingly given by the press to the workers who attended the first rally in support of the general on 17 October 1945, an ideological reference to

Mussolini's Blackshirts. In keeping with the unstable ideological position of the movement, Natalia Milanieso argues that inadvertently the term also evoked the "sans-culottes of the French Revolution, the most powerful icon of republicanism, egalitarianism, and popular political extremism."[36] *Los descamisados* referred to the Peronist multitude of men crowding the Plaza de Mayo, Buenos Aires's financial, political, and economic center, in that foundational moment. However, they were not as shirtless as the term suggests as many historic images, such as the infamous picture of three workers bathing their feet in the city fountain, prove.[37] The gathering in the plaza created the initial congregation, marking the rise of labor's importance and developing the image of Peronism as a working-class movement, one that solidified a connection between its leader-patron and the crowd. On December 15 of that same year Perón embraced the term given to his supporters and inverted its significance in a speech by saying: "While they may insultingly refer to us as shirtless riffraff, we believe it is an honor to have our hearts in the right place beneath a simple shirt instead of a fancy jacket."[38] The empathetic conception of the multitude as industrious that the leader promoted clearly ties it to material hard work. The *descamisados* presented a sympathetic image of the industrious working class that received benefits from Perón's programs and continued to help the leader in their undying support for his return to power.

The appropriation of *descamisados* and the reinscription of its meaning into the narrative did not happen with all stereotypes given by the anti-Peronists. The group created similarly affective stereotypes, specifically ones based on disgust, in an attempt to distance themselves from Perón's supporters. The negative view connects his followers with words like *chabacano* (gaudy) and *burdo* (crude),[39] both referring to vulgarity and associated with *lunfardo* and tango, a slang and musical genre originally banned on radios during the 1943 coup, which Perón reinstated in 1949 after a meeting with tango authors and composers.[40] Another term given to the masses was *cabecitas negras*, translated literally as "blackheads," originally an Argentine bird but also referring to different parameters such as filth, the dirty clothes worn by workers, their ignorance, and their instinctual nature.[41] The term makes reference to nineteenth-century and 1930s' racial distinctions such as the barbaric invasions of the mestizos, an allusion to Juan Manuel de Rosas and his plebe, and Hipólito Irigoyen and his *chusma* or rabble.[42] However, Perón avoided any discourse that hinted at ethnic or racial differences, erasing such markers to instead focus on economic ones. The anti-Peronist concept of the *cabecita negra* clearly racializes the masses and renews earlier ethnic traditions associated with other leaders.

Milanesio argues that stereotypes were grounded in anxieties over the invasion of people to the cities. By 1947, 17 percent of the population had migrated from the provinces, and 68 percent had settled in Buenos Aires.[43] Furthermore, interclass coexistence in public spaces, as well as safety for self and property, were points of contention.[44] The events in October characterized the shift that was taking place as the suburbs literally spilled into the city center. But at the heart of the matter is the idea that the taste of the uncivilized was a menace to the more European-centered culture of the city, especially Buenos Aires. It was the masses' inability to follow etiquette rules, adapt to urban space, and overcome "uncouth" taste that was the most threatening to the longer established Buenos Aires population.[45] In some ways the migrants embodied a process of transformation that "changed rhythms and appearance of principal cities, redefined social manners and codes of urban civility, broke with traditional standards of deference and respect, and liberalized norms of appropriateness and taste,"[46] unmasking apprehensions about processes of social, economic, and cultural change.

The divide came from both sides: Perón's sympathizers appropriated the slogan "Alpargatas sí, libros no" (espadrilles yes, books no), defining the priorities of the movement and distancing themselves from the elites.[47] The espadrilles, linked to the rural laborer, were a cheap shoe that was locally made and used by workers first in rural settings and later in the cities. It became the chosen symbol of the migration and material hard work of the poor. In contrast, books were linked to an old divide that was always at the foundation of the nation, the leisure class of the intellectuals and bourgeoisie, encompassed in the writings of classic authors such as Ernesto Echeverría and Domingo Faustino Sarmiento. While Perón's base transformed with time with the addition of different participants such as women and youth, who helped to redefine the movement in new ways, the main group of suburban working-class males formed its foundation. In many ways, Bó-Sarli tapped into a new, upward-rising, and exploitable consumer of cinema to expand and expose their unique product: the voluptuous star.

The class-based opposition between anti- and pro-Peronists clearly divides the national political landscape. On the cultural terrain, there was affinity between the Sarli-Bó products and the male worker of Peronism, one based in class with excesses whose specific tastes produced affective reactions from the opposing camp. In order to unpack the complexity of the ideas discussed here, it is worth isolating two different aspects to better bring together the context underlying the work of Bó and Sarli. The first is the use of affect: both Peronism and its opposition functioned to construct the question of class-based taste, one based on excess from the point of view of the upper class and on hard work from that of the "ill-mannered" lower class. The affect was used to determine what belonged and what didn't. As seen through the example of Eva and her corpse, the struggle to dominate her body thorough its description but also its possession was essential to both sides and differentiated one from the other. If this is the case, affect underlies most of the stereotypes discussed and constructs the mutual bitterness that drives class distinction at the base of Peronism. Through what Ben Highmore suggests is a "pedagogy of disgust," taste functioned to make clear those very same class distinctions.[48] The foundational work of Pierre Bourdieu, *Distinction: A Social Critique of the Judgment of Taste*, which has since been further expanded by social scientists, contributed to theorizing how taste remains socially loaded and bound up in struggles of power and inequity while not fixing it in any concrete way.[49] In the context of Argentina in the 1960s, the political dimension defines taste, the bad taste of a class that appreciates the excesses of the body by envisioning a different and distinct way of belonging, and thus helps to expose a new lens on the work of Sarli and Bó, as class-based taste becomes one of the defining characteristics of their "bad cinema."

SCENARIO 4: THE DISGUST OF POPULAR TASTE AND BAD CINEMA

In a central scene in *Heat*, after having been unfaithful to her husband Fernando, Marga is excited by the adventure she just had with another man, Marcos. Back in her bedroom, dressed in a negligée and half naked, Marga dances the cha-cha, a memory from the cabaret. Her attempt to seduce her husband fails as he ignores her sexual advances. Fernando is captivated more by his book than his hypersexualized wife, whom he barely sees. Entranced in his own world, Fernando continues reading Jean Paul Sartre's *Les jeux son faits – L'engrenage* (*The Chips Are Down*, 1948), in Spanish translation. Sartre's existential story is about two people from different worlds who meet in the afterlife and find another chance at life only to eventually repeat the same mistakes, securing their ultimate fate or death. The story reinforces Sartre's perspective that destiny always wins and references the social differences that keep husband and wife apart in the bedroom scene. The scene not only separates Marga and her lover from Fernando but also alludes to the cultural attitude of the advent of the Generation of 1960, a generation of intellectual filmmakers with antisensual characteristics, the antithesis of what the Bó-Sarli cinema was already becoming in 1960.[50] In essence, the bedroom scene exposes the choice between the espadrilles and the books, except that the shoes appear in the form of sexuality. Marga is enticed by the simple instinctual life of Marcos, a seductive criminal from the working class, rather than the boring existence of Fernando, the intellectual bourgeois who bears all the privilege of his class.[51]

Ironically, her husband in the end becomes consumed by his emotions, albeit the wrong ones, violence rather than sex, as he kills Marcos out of jealousy. The sexual disconnect represented in the scene substantiates many assumptions about the conception of taste and the differences that taste plays between the classes. Marga is instinctual and sensual just like Marcos. In the end she runs away and ends up on a rustic island, the Isla de los Lobos (Uruguay), where she meets the hard-working simple man who is able to succumb to his sexual instincts and give Marga what she truly needs: connection. *Heat* leans toward the instinctual rather than the intellectual. As their cinema was becoming more visceral in nature, utilizing sex and bodies as a product, their aesthetic and their repetitive plots embraced the concept of bad taste, the espadrille rather than the intellectual distant style of the bourgeoisie, the books. The underworld of sex, crime, and hard work are at the base of the Bó-Sarli films, an illicit world that features and centralizes the body.

Bourdieu's work on aesthetics introduced taste as historical cultural capital that gives value to specific objects and people. In his quantitative and qualitative study in 1960s' and 1970s' France, Bourdieu recognized that class as both a cultural and economic category was bound up in the conception of taste. He argued that the practices or cultural choices one makes are shaped by the combination of the social space in which one lives, the resources one has, and the inherited dispositions one is given, summarized in the following controversial formula developed by the sociologist: the habitus (inherited dispositions) + capital (resources) + field (social space) = practice (likes and dislikes).[52] By acknowledging that questions of class are detrimental in looking at how aesthetics are defined, Bourdieu produced a shift in how to think about such problems. The sociologist has inspired debates about distinction that take us through different film genres such as exploitation, the New Latin

American cinema, and pornography, ones contextualizing the Sarli and Bó body of work.

Taste is always relational and refers to a system of values that imposes certain distinctions. For instance, to speak of "bad" films one needs to be able to relate them to "good" ones, a comparison based on accepted norms in filmmaking. Any marginal cinema, therefore, is always having to justify its position and value in the industry and academy. Exploitation cinema struggles for distinction as "bad," "garbage," or "paracinema," through a relationship to the Hollywood mainstream or European art cinema. Eric Schaefer explains how exploitation films were at the margins of the Hollywood industry and thus emphasized difference rather than American ideals.[53] The work of Schaefer, Jeffrey Sconce, Joan Hawkins, and Mark Jancovich has helped to produce a shift in film scholarship from the canon or Hollywood to the so-called bad appearing on alternative screens.[54] Sconce argued that paracinema was not a category or genre but a reading protocol for a counteraesthetic devoted to all manner of cultural detritus.[55] Using Sconce's work, Hawkins further blurs the distinction and concludes that both high and low films have the same end goal: to challenge the mainstream status quo, while benefiting from the same reading strategy.[56] In her book, Hawkins valorizes all kinds of cinematic "garbage," meanwhile making distinctions between the art and garbage based solely in the intention behind the work. Both Sconce and Hawkins ground the assumption that everything that is garbage is thus subversive. The problem they encounter, according to Mark Jancovich, is that their position fails to acknowledge the struggles for distinction that exist and repeat the same errors they criticize.[57] Their theories are based on Bourdieu's concept of defamiliarization, which underpins bourgeois aesthetics, legitimating a concentration on form over function. The counterhegemonic tactic asserts the superiority of distanced aesthetic contemplation over naïve acceptance of illusionist mass culture.[58] Jancovich reveals that both are seduced by the lowly through adapting it to the bourgeois superiority of taste (the aesthetic). They elevate their audience over a duped mainstream one, privileging the middle-class white male spectator/fan and academic who can properly read garbage through an alternative reading strategy adopted from high art film.[59] By doing so they keep the hierarchy in place, only inverting it, superficially challenging the status quo without eliminating distinction based on class—instead, reinforcing it.

In the Latin American case, debates about poorly made films happened during the politicized movements of the 1960s and 1970s known as the New Latin American cinema. The umbrella term connects different projects with distinctive aesthetic aspirations through shared political goals of decolonization and resistance to the commercial Hollywood industry and European art cinema.[60] The filmmakers spearheading each movement wrote their own manifestos to clearly outline controversial positions reinforced by their films. See, for example, "For an Imperfect Cinema" (Julio García Espinosa, 1969), " Towards a Third Cinema" (Fernando Solanas and Octavio Getino, 1968), and "An Esthetic of Hunger" (Glauber Rocha, 1965).[61] The film *La hora de los hornos* (*The Hour of the Furnaces,* Argentina, 1968), which puts in practice the Third Cinema manifesto of Argentine directors/authors Getino and Solanas, rejected the aesthetic and politics of sleek and commercial First Cinema (Hollywood industry), and elite auteur European art cinema (Second Cinema). Instead, the filmmakers proposed practicing a Third Cinema politicized in its decolonial and revolutionary message, with an aesthetic practice that complements its material "underdevelopment."[62]

In reading the three manifestos by practicing filmmakers, critic Robert Stam sees a commonality through their "hybrid . . . chronotopic . . . common motif of the redemption of detritus."[63] While still pitting mainstream Hollywood against Latin American film movements, Stam finds comfort in the debates of the 1960s that saw third-world cinema expressions as valuable because despite their poor and unglamorous aesthetic, the new movements confronted Hollywood with an opposition worthy of study. Stam calls for the strategic redemption of the low, the despised, the imperfect, and the trashy as part of a social overturning where garbage recycles, revalorizes, and reaffirms what dominant culture throws away. For Stam, the power-laden "garbage" can be a social leveler: "Garbage signals the return of the repressed; it is the place where used condoms, bloody tampons, infected needles and unwanted babies are left, the ultimate resting place of all that society both produces and represses, secretes, and makes secret."[64] Yet his model, like that of Sconce and Hawkins, is still based on a value judgement that privileges one form over the other due to its laudable political message.

In *Trash: African Cinema from Below*, Kenneth Harrow criticizes Stam because "Trash can serve to soil their glitter, but if that is the only function to which it is put, all that will be needed to deal with it is a better cleaning service."[65] Perhaps Harrow's lesson teaches that rather than focusing on garbage, what becomes more important is the struggle for distinction itself. In an analysis of the work of Brazilian exploitation auteur Jose Mojica Marins, known internationally as Coffin Joe, Dolores

Tierney reasons there is a "cultural capital not in marginality itself, but in a certain kind of marginality."[66] She reveals the paradox at the center of the New Latin American Cinema through the films' circulation in US and European markets, and the European-educated position of their practitioners as that cinema "belongs to whilst nominally rejecting 'elite' culture, that is their explicit anti-neocolonialist and antibourgeois position."[67] The criticisms by Jancovich, Harrow, and Tierney show that discussions at the time about taste, class, and hierarchies in exploitation and the New Latin American Cinema criticism were all circular and based on definitions of being. Whether a film can be called good, artistic, bad, garbage, or paracinematic depends on the spectator/critic and carries with it a specific politics. By unraveling the politics of distinction and circumventing its circular nature, I find an awkward place in the politics of inclusion/exclusion and (not)belonging, as well as acknowledging that this book too circulates in the Global North. The bad cinema practiced by Bó and Sarli allows for exploring a specific audience and the relationships at the center of taste formation in 1960s' and 1970s' Argentina.

The work of Sarli-Bó intersects the political, historical, and social, where excessive bodies rely on both work and leisure, unsightly yet alluring sexualized and laboring bodies exposing what cannot belong. In that volatile place and time, such overabundant bodies carried with them many meanings and affects, at the precise intersections of a post-Perón era. In particular, the duo's films, accused of pornographic atrocity, find in the body a clear class- and gender-based politics that can easily be dismissed without its contextual grounding. Relying on affect both through the allure and disgust of popular taste and the unconventional stories of the films helps provide a path to approaching their work. The fact that the censors came to find the duo's work pornographic and contentious, and that it became more popular in Argentina despite its ongoing suppression battles, allows one to think about possible readings that were happening and perhaps being inspired on the ground instead of in the privileged space of higher learning. My approach aims to shift the discourse away from simple readings of the films' plots and bad form, while also acknowledging these, to encompass the complex interrelationship and interaction between the aesthetic, the content, the sociopolitical context, and the affect, that is, the senses that were being jolted and stimulated by the films' controversies, where belonging had clear political implications.

In a more recent study about the development of taste, David Wright links Bourdieu's ideas to Kant's work with the beautiful based on the sensory experience of the aesthetic.[68] In doing so, he justifiably points out that the beautiful is always already inextricably tied to its opposite, disgust.[69] Defined by the excesses of the oral and sensual pleasures of the flesh, disgust contrasts with good taste, which is usually assigned to restraint and management of behavior bound up in the rules of conduct, the changes according to context. For Highmore, taste is cultural power played out violently on the affective plane.[70] "The orchestration of perception, sensorial culture, affective intensities and so on . . . [produce] . . . resonances of other sensual worlds and on to the social ontology of bodies."[71] Through Highmore's assertion one can understand how anti-Peronists linked disgust to the bodies of the early Peronists or *cabecitas negras*. By taking the affective turn, which incorporates the way the body experiences class-based assumptions, this book thinks about the specific class divisions in place during the birth of the Peronist *cabecita negra* and beyond. The class struggles in Argentina from 1955 to 1983 create two very distinguishable groups and thus produce a type of exclusionary politics. Therefore, many of the concerns relating to bad taste correlate to gender and class, but beyond class also refer back to questions of race and ethnicity, which Perón himself tried to erase and ignore.

A parallel can be drawn between the so-called bad taste of the *cabecitas negras* and Bó's sexualized films, accused of being pornographic, offending the "good" taste of the bourgeoisie's art cinema.[72] In his article "Naked Ambitions," film critic Mark Jancovich rightly affirms that sexual behavior is overtly politicized and as such not only gendered but also classed, at the intersection of both. He argues: "Debates over pornography therefore need to be understood not simply as political struggles over gender relations, but also as political struggles between these different taste formations. Critiques of pornography are often the product of one class's visceral intolerance to the sexual taste of another class."[73] Jancovich suggests that instead one must look at the sexual tastes of class and the power relations in which different factors operate. He questions the trend in academic work that he terms "progressive pornographies," which reproduce cultural distinctions through an othering of lower middle-class taste. In so doing he concludes that struggles over sexual taste are more complex than either feminists or the "petite bourgeoisie" posit. The liberation of the body comes with a rediscovery of the self, and Sarli-Bó's films fit precisely at this intersection.

If indeed we turn to how affect plays out as a struggle for distinction in the Bó-Sarli oeuvre, then why not begin in the site of bodies? In the materiality of bodies, one can find that which defines the most marginal of taste and where the garbage or remnants lie. How were the bodies the center of Sarli and Bó's bad cinema? How did these bodies hold traces of class and memories of generations of oppression of all sorts (class, gender, race, etc.) at their intersection? How were the excesses and their connections to sex related to the popular audience, which flocked to consume onscreen bodies and the values the bodies represented? Bodies were material and sexualized and linked to instinctual practices relating to sex.

SCENARIO 5: BECOMING SEXUALIZED YOUTH

The 1960s brought a paradigm shift that featured at its center the role of youth worldwide. Movements like May 1968 in France featured the activism of students challenging authority on important political issues. Simultaneously, the youth sexual revolution in the United States and other parts of the world defied sexual norms and their patriarchal values. More politicized and sexualized, youth worldwide were unsettling established notions of what it meant to interact politically and sexually in the society. In Argentina, the category of youth developed from the 1950s to the 1970s and represented a wide range of political interests. The research on the category of youth by historians such as Isabella Cosse and Valeria Manzano shows the problematic relationship young people had with sexuality.

Youth needs to be seen not as a material category but as an abstract one that also enacts an affect and constructs a sense of (not) belonging. The Onganía coup that succeeded in 1966 and the repressive culture that his authoritative regime unleashed targeted both youth and ideological dissent. As a complex category, youth played an important role in the political and social movements of the 1960s and 1970s, and thus formed part of integrating sexuality into the changes that were taking place in society. In their idealistic attempts to change the future, however, they were still stifled by the past, for instance by patriarchy and the norms from which their struggles could not escape. In many ways the class distinctions that youth political movements struggled to change kept them in line when it came to gender and sexuality issues.

According to Manzano, youth is a sociocultural category associated with an increase in education and the culture of consumption.[74] Directly related to the "democratization of well-being" that Peronism delivered for a broad sector of the country in his first term in office (1946–52), the shift made education for the masses more accessible, leading to a leisure lifestyle that redefined what it meant to be young.[75] When referring to the youth, Manzano is speaking about young men and women between the ages of eighteen and twenty-four, 80 percent of whom lived in urban cities.[76] The youth were never a homogenous group, but there were certain trends that defined different participants, some of which can be traced back to Perón's second term in office (1952–55). For instance, increases in youth going to university rose from 5 percent of the people ages twenty to twenty-four in 1950 to 11 percent in 1960 and 20 percent in 1972, showing the development of a more educated youth population.[77]

In Perón's second term, he mobilized secondary school students and situated youth at the center of discussion. In 1953 he created the High School Students Union (Unión de Estudiantes Secundarias or UES) in an increasingly expanding sector. Between 1946 and 1955 the total enrollment of secondary students grew from 217,000 to 467,000.[78] Traditional sectors saw the UES as both a challenge to authority and a threat. By placing the youth at the center of public attention, Perón established a link with the generation that later became the Peronist youth movements and their offshoots of the early 1970s. However, youth as a category was not restricted to the Peronist party. Radical leader Arturo Frondizi also reserved a paramount role for young people. They were part of Frondizi's project of modernization of Argentina with imports of foreign products to be locally consumed. Simply speaking, the 1950s brought about a new consumer who took on different roles in society regardless of political banner. It was a tension that played out among the young and divided them into different ideological camps. Even those who shared similar ideologies created derivatives that carried with them important distinctions. For instance, many movements grew out of the Peronist Youth, while the Cuban Revolution of 1959 inspired others. Two of the main guerrilla groups formed by youth were the Montoneros and the People's Revolutionary Party, the military wing of the Workers' Revolutionary Party, which was a Trotskyist group. The divisions that characterized the different youth movements were too numerous and too many to outline here.

With the political opportunism of using a whole generation to improve electoral success came other changes that also helped to define the youth sector and eventually produce an inextricable link between them and sexuality. For instance, the work of psychologists like Eva Giberti was instrumental in attempting to mediate intergenerational conflict. She established the School for Parents in 1956 in an effort to eradicate harsh forms of patriarchy within family units and advocate for more youth autonomy.[79] Others like sociologist Gino Germani also advocated for the "urban modern family" that undid the backward patriarchal and archaic forms of its unit.[80] Changes in psychology led to the emergence of the new field of psychoanalysis that was taking hold in the capital city. Psychoanalysis brought a different understanding of sexuality by way of new professionals and the work at the University of Buenos Aires that referenced the Kinsey Report. Studies were promoting more open sex education.[81] Popular magazines were even following the trend of liberating sexuality. One such weekly, *Claudia*, first published in 1957, affirmed the importance of sexual gratification by leading with topics such as masturbation and female pleasure as part of the sexual development of a woman.[82] Others like *Satiricon* (1972–2005), a graphic humor magazine, reflected similar ideas humorously.[83]

Likewise, the new liberation of the body continued even in fashion. The miniskirt underscored the sexuality of women's bodies by showing more skin and curves. The trends throughout the decade launched a more fluid definition of gender as males wore long hair and women jeans to confuse the more rigid stereotypes of the 1950s. The new relationship with the body was a point of contention and a threat to conservative values. However, young people had no private spaces or even cars to explore the new more open sexuality. Bordellos and *casas de citas* or dating houses remained open during the mid-1950s, and in 1960 the city council of Buenos Aires passed a new regulation allowing hotel owners to offer rooms per hour to couples. The room-by-hour hotels, called *albergues transitorios,* or *telos* in the local argot, were the only places available for such liaisons. That same year, 169 new hourly hotels opened their doors; by 1967, 769 were operating in the city alone.[84] Adults and young dating couples used the newly created spaces for sexual explorations.

The connection between activism, sexuality, and bodies became a staple for the youth in the 1960s, one taken up again much later in the memory movements that emanated after the dictatorship, such as the case of HIJOS (Children [of the Disappeared] for Identity and Justice, against Oblivion and Silence). In one example, in an interview journalist Marta Dillon remembers her mother, Marta Taboada, a militant for the Revolutionary Front "October 17," whose political awakening grew out of an interest in eroticism.[85] According to Dillon, the right to pleasure remains to be won, but the idea of discovering the capacity for pleasure was at the base of the era, especially for women.[86] While feminism and gay rights groups were active on the ground, both were seen as a distraction from the main struggle, which was class-based in nature.[87]

Nonetheless, the Feminist Argentine Union and Women's Freedom Movement (MLM) were both feminist organizations founded in the 1960s. Few took up the cause: only fifty members were registered in 1972.[88] MLM was attempting to establish an important precedent when it came to bodies. As a second wave iteration, they questioned maternity as the defining feature of women and gave the right to women to make decisions about their bodies.[89] When the Homosexual Freedom Front was founded in 1971, same-sex attraction was seen as a "deviation" and a "psychological perversion," and had not been able to distance itself from the nineteenth-century stereotypes, leading to increased surveillance and repression. It continued to be perceived as a danger for the health of the national body; sexual activities had to be regulated to ensure the continuity of the nuclear family, as Donna Guy so eloquently contended.[90] Both movements were relatively weak and part of the educated elite, essentially the oppressors in the class war. The left refused to incorporate these issues relating to gender and sexuality into their agendas due to their political alignment with the bourgeoisie. As a matter of fact, the only point of agreement between gay rights activists, feminists, and the left was the condemnation of the commercial aspects of eroticism. When the Campora government took over for forty-nine days, right before Perón's return in 1973, there was a reprieve that was referred to as a sexual *destape* or unleashing, with new discussions on divorce and greater visibility of feminist and homosexual organizations. The opening was only temporary; however, the new *destape* did not accomplish much to erase the macho stereotype that continued to dominate, even in the most radical or leftist of insurgents. It was not until the mid-1980s, with the flourishing of identity politics after the end of the dictatorship, that the new social identity movements began to reshape the public sphere with more visible results on gender and sexual equality.

As a matter of fact, the example of the Montoneros, the country's leading political force that was attracting many young people, demonstrates how regardless of their political position the young people were relatively conservative when it came to sex and sexuality. Isabella Cosse's brilliant article "Infidelities: Morality, Revolution and Sexuality in Left-Wing Guerrilla Organizations in 1960s and 1970s Argentina" precisely outlines the role played by sexuality in the construction of revolutionary morality as a key dimension for understanding left-wing guerrilla groups active in Argentina. She argues that revolutionaries still based their actions on fundamental principles surrounding the family, sexuality, and relationships. The ideals of the middle class had ironically infiltrated a group whose main goal was to abolish classes. In fact, they imposed an "exalting virility, . . . promoting an ideal image of the revolutionary couple, which was both heterosexual and monogamous."[91] In her analysis she speaks of the Christian foundation, particularly the theology of liberation of Carlos Mujica, as part of the underpinning philosophy of the Montoneros.[92] She traces its development historically to concentrate on specific moments that changed the way the group thought about sexuality, a concept that constantly shifted.

While at first there existed more sexual freedom practiced by its members, by 1975 Montoneros imposed strict rules of personal conduct and applied harsh penalties to anyone who deviated from these rules. Romantic fidelity and political loyalty intertwined, leading to the creation, in October of 1975, of the Code of Revolutionary Penal Justice. In Article 16 of the document, infidelity was defined as having sexual relations with someone other than one's partner and equated with a crime of disloyalty. The reason for the new policy, which was absent from the previous version in the 1972 Code, was that security concerns had become a great threat, and the group believed sexual behavior could compromise military strategy. Furthermore, as Cosse rightly points out, the new contract also relates to countering the opposition's accusations of immorality and sexual excess, and the guerrillas as "drug addicts, homosexuals, and home-grown and foreign mercenaries."[93] It also suggests that promiscuous sexuality was being practiced, or else why address it in the code? Sex was a double-edged sword: on the one hand sexual violence that was synonymous with torture and the possibility of eventual treason to the cause were confused with romantic infidelity. Paradoxically, on the other hand sex was the only weapon that its members had to experience freedom and pleasure.[94] Cosse's analysis does not see youth as completely resistant; instead, she concentrates on other issues to disclose the generation's compound relationship with both practices and attitudes toward sexuality. Within the heterogeneous group, the ideas surrounding sex were by no means straightforward, and they shifted with context. However, one thing is certain: ideology and subversion trumped the excesses of the body. In moments when the former were challenged, the latter were constrained. Cosse, therefore, calls the sexual revolution of the period "discreet." In many of the radical groups, the importance of belonging meant that bodies and the excesses of sex had to adhere to more normative trends.

In part, the voice that is missing is the female one. The youth movements were still mirroring societal norms with women excluded from its structures.

As a category, youth is not central to the Sarli-Bó filmography, although there are exceptions, especially if one reads across films at the height of youth activity in the late 1960s. For instance, in the three comedies that they made (*The Shoemaker's Wife*, *The Mayor's Wife*, and *A Madcap Widow*), Sarli's portrayal as a young vixen takes on an important role as it contrasts greatly with her love interests and husbands in each. Stuck in small towns, she marries much older men that can provide for her and give her the commodities she so desires. But the dynamic of youth versus the older generation is clearly laid out in the plot of *My Father's Wife*. As the title suggests, the struggles between son (Víctor Bó, Armando's actual son) and father (Armando) for a woman (Eva played by Sarli) drive the narrative and action of the film, an irony played out between real-life father and son. The final battle between both characters is emblematic of the rebellion ensuing in society between generations. In the film, the father is victorious when Eva chooses him over the younger son. Yet in the next film, *Meat*, Víctor Bó is triumphant as he is Delicia's boyfriend. The clearly identified young couple work at the meatpacking plant. Sarli, who is Víctor's senior by eight years, presents a simple but youthful role through her attire and highly sexualized body, identified as part of the youth at the height of 1968. In *The Mayor's Wife*, Rosendo (Víctor Bó) is a rebellious youth, a journalist in love with Flor (Sarli), who opposes her husband, Dr. Gambetta, because he disagrees with his politics. In the depiction Rosendo is bothered by Flor's role in politics because it is not appropriate for women to be so active. Again, Rosendo reproduces the left's paradoxical position as he rejects Flor as a political equal even though he is fighting for a more equal Argentina. As a good male spectator, he desires Flor and hallucinates about seeing her naked. Sexually, he appreciates her excesses but is unable to fully accept women as equals. Ironically, the smoke in the only sex scene in the film covers her body and sexuality but leaves bare the political allusions to a movement that was duplicitous—endorsing sexual liberation but at the same time stifling its full possibilities. In *The Mayor's Wife*, Sarli's character does play a key role in her husband's political career. Sexuality and gender issues were key and central to the films on different levels. In spite of youth's discreet revolution, a more indiscreet one was happening onscreen and in the films of the Bó-Sarli brand.

SCENARIO 6: SEX ONSCREEN

As a new consumer group, youth were the target of competing film movements vying for their ticket purchases. They were important for the Generation of 1960, depicting a middle-class group facing angst in the modern-day city. Buenos Aires becomes "a map of their psyche."[95] When it came to sex, filmmakers dabbled in it early on, following Sarli-Bó's lead, but disavowed it until the late 1960s. For instance, *Setenta veces siete* (*The Female: Seventy Times Seven*, Argentina, 1962) is a key example of the differences between the generation and the filmmaking pair. The film stars Sarli in her only debut outside the duo's brand during Bó's lifetime, and was directed by the most recognized Argentine auteur, Leopoldo Torre Nilsson. Sarli plays a prostitute who is overcome by the monotony of her daily routine to become obsessed with a hole in the ceiling, which consumes her thoughts and brings about flashbacks of her past life. Time is excruciatingly slow, and the tedious repetition of the same scenes isolates the mental state of the protagonist rather than emphasizing her scantily dressed body. While Torre Nilsson chose Sarli, a known sexual bombshell for Argentines since she had already starred in six films with Bó, the film avoids the Bó-Sarli formulas expected by popular audiences. Instead, *The Female* displaces the promise of sexuality, which is ever present as a danger but never delivered. In its place, the existential crisis of the working protagonist overwhelms the repetitive and slow-moving narrative, akin to the Sartre book that consumes Fernando's attention in *Heat*. The intellect in both cases prevails over the longings of the flesh. Ironically, in exploitation circles abroad, extra scenes were added to *The Female* to provide the missing sex onscreen, an act that debases Torre Nilsson's authorial intention.[96]

Furthermore, in varying degrees sex became central on the agenda of all youth representations. Even the benign *El club del clan* ("The Gang's Club," Guillermo Hinestroza), a popular TV show that aired on channel 13 on November 10, 1962, featured the modern bodies of young people, yet they were clean-cut. The sex in *El club del clan* was analogous to the Doris Day and Rock Hudson pictures, as Alina Mazzaferro suggests, limited to kissing, focused on the face rather than the dangerous body and flirting with a seeming revolution, but in the end matrimony always won and social, gendered positions were clearly maintained.[97] The youth on the show were inoffensive rebels not very threatening to the older generations and essentially conservative in nature, as the main objective of the women was to find a man to start a family. The show embodied "lo merso," the bad taste of the lower classes. In many ways they are Sarli-Bó films light, but unlike *El club del clan*, the duo's work had elements that made them difficult to categorize as purely conservative, especially when in comparison with such TV shows and the other sex comedies of the dictatorship era. In the realm of film, Laura Podalsky identifies two shifts during the late 1960s, "a shift toward light comedy or farce and a focus on aspects of contemporary culture that were mildly titillating."[98] In the first case, she is referring to the Italian light sex comedies from the mid-1960s and those imitated in Argentina, such as productions by Aries Cinematografía like *Hotel Alojamiento* (*Accommodation Hotel*, Fernando Ayala, 1965), *El professor hippie* (*The Hippie Professor*, Fernando Ayala, 1969), and the "cottage industry" developed by Bó.[99] Podalsky argues that the success of films produced by Aries Cinematografía and Bó "demonstrate the way that cultural producers were responding to and creating a more permissive attitude about the presence of sexuality in the public sphere."[100] A conscientious appearance was accompanied by more spaces where youth met and expressed themselves. Buenos Aires was the center for such a statement, the center for consumption, which of course included the consumption of bodies.

The city of Buenos Aires was starting to carve out a space for the new generation that demanded to be heard, a culture promoted, for instance, by the work of psychologists like Giberti and Germani. As Oscar Terán explains it: there was a network of bookstores such as Verbun, Galatea, bohemian intellectual bars, independent theatres, Lorraine Cinema, and other film clubs playing Bergman, Godard, Truffaut, or Antonioni films.[101] In the intellectual culture of the city, at its center was the Instituto Di Tella, an establishment that was founded in 1958 and supported by funds provided by Guido Di Tella and later the Ford Foundation. The Di Tella intended to promote, stimulate, collaborate, participate, and intervene in all types of initiatives, works, and businesses that were educational, intellectual, artistic, social, and philanthropic.[102] The institute wanted to produce art that exported easily to Europe. On the other hand, the Di Tella was symptomatic of the modernization project proposed a decade earlier by Frondizi, the liberal democratic ideal of the cosmopolitan generation, one that clashed with the politicizing projects of the youth that enveloped Buenos Aires, the outskirts, and spilled across the rest of the country. A key montage scene in the New Latin American film *The Hour of the Furnaces* by Argentines Getino and Solanas highlights the role that the Di Tella played through advertisements, English music and culture, and a partying clip. The scene concludes with an increasing bombardment of images of pure violence—Vietnam, severe hunger, and war called "monstrosity dressed up as beauty"—ending with machine-gun-like shots of intermixed images, a rich critique of the connection between art and violence. During the 1960s, when the youth were seen as agents of change, a new vitality brought to the university made it a hub for radical thinking that pushed innovation in new ways.[103] Youth were generally divided into two camps: the radical leftist guerrillas and the cosmopolitan worldly youth obsessed with fashion and trends.[104]

The seemingly conscious displacement of Buenos Aires in the Sarli-Bó films leaves a significant mark on their work that cannot be ignored. This authorial decision may have been guided by financial considerations (it was cheaper to film outside the city), which has interesting effects on their work. All of the duo's films are shot and set in either foreign countries, remote locations, or small towns. There is an obvious absence of the big city from their movies, which in some cases may appear only momentarily in an urban scene but is always already displaced and never named. Even when featuring locations abroad, including important fellow industrial film nations such as Brazil and Mexico, Sarli-Bó always show marginal locales in the favelas, Iguazu, and beach towns in Brazil, as well as the southern Mexican state of Yucatán. Other foreign locations represent the margins of the film industry: Paraguay, Panama, and Uruguay, where little to no film production occurred except for Bó-Sarli's films.[105] In Argentina, the three comedies *The Shoemaker's Wife*, *The Mayor's Wife*, and *A Madcap Widow* feature small towns. Other films (*The Hot Days*, *Naked Temptation*, *My Father's Wife*, *Fuego*, *Fever*, *Ardent Summer*, and *Last Love in Tierra del Fuego*) are all set in rural locales or in the far south. Still others, *Intimacies of a Prostitute* and *A Butterfly in the Night* are far less about place but do always seem to come back to the notion of the far south. The obvious absence of Buenos Aires, the capital city, which embodied youth and modernity simultaneously, coincides with the margins of the nation, ironically the areas where Peronism thrived.[106]

Fast-forwarding to the dictatorship, a different type of film featuring sex was being made. The most notorious examples were the films directed by the Sofovich brothers, such as *Los doctores las prefieren desnudas* (*Doctors Prefer them Nude*, Gerardo Sofovich, Argentina, 1973). The sex comedies featuring Jorge Porcel and Alberto Olmedo, similar to the Italian sex comedies of the mid-1960s, introduced up-and-coming *vedettes* such as Susana Giménez and Moria Casán, and included a mix of comedy of errors and erotic elements.[107] In his third volume about the history of sexuality in Argentina, Federico Andahazi mentions the genre as examples of dictatorial sex.[108] He accuses the males of portraying dumb lads with the only objective being to spy on naked women and eventually touch them. Women, on the other hand, were the victims and were depicted through two extremes as either naïve and dumb or as conniving and calculating by taking advantage of the men. Milanesio calls these films "conservative" because they, like *El club del clan*, "exalted marriage, traditional gender roles, and respectability, while punishing any sexually liberated characters."[109]

Andahazi argues that such products functioned to create a sense that the screening of sexual material was open and free, while nonetheless hiding the actual censorship that was behind the Process of Reorganization, which was the nonthreatening description of the political violence of disappearance, torture, and murder of dissident groups. He goes on to say that the *destape* or unleashing that took place after the end of the dictatorship in 1983 was very different from the one blossoming in Spain after Franco's death in 1975.[110] In Argentina, the films that were produced in the aftermath of the dictatorship were committed to uncovering the political and social reality of the nation. Meanwhile, Spain's own *destape* led to the *movida*, and with it a set of new sexual norms that were clearly seen onscreen, the most famous example of which is Pedro Almodóvar's first feature film, *Pepi, Luci y Bóm y otras chicas del montón* (*Pepi, Luci, and Bom and Other Girls like Mom*, Spain, 1980). The difference Andahazi highlights lies in the fact that Spain, under dictatorial rule since 1939, never had an opportunity to develop the same permissive attitudes that blossomed in Argentina between 1955 and 1976. Albeit sporadic, the discreet revolution mentioned earlier remarkably allowed certain versions of the exhibition of sex onscreen.

Despite producing a three-volume look at the history of sex in Argentina, Andahazi never once mentions the work of Bó and Sarli. This is surprising, given the role the duo had in pushing the limits of what was screened. When compared to the sex comedies of the dictatorship era, the work of Bó and Sarli appears obviously different and cannot be simply categorized as complicit with the regime, especially since during the dictatorship only four films were made (*A Butterfly in the Night*, *Insatiable*, *Last Love in Tierra del Fuego*, and *A Madcap Widow*) and only three were ever released because *Insatiable* was banned altogether.[111] From their first exposure, Sarli's onscreen sexploits allured, intrigued, and disgusted her onlookers. By the time the dictatorship happened, she had already made the revelation of female bodies more than a mere possibility: it was a staple. However, policing and restraints kept films like *Insatiable* offscreen, being banned the same year that *Los hombres sólo piensan en eso* (*Men Only Think about That*, Enrique Cahen Salabery, 1976) played in theaters.

In compiling many disparate and fragmented narratives and scenarios as part of the context in the post-Perón period from 1955 to 1983, and dabbling in a more distant past, this chapter has constructed a heterogeneous, untidy picture of a volatile epoch in Argentine history. Yet the multiple scenes described interrelate and interconnect to develop a sense of attitudes, divisions, and associations that better contextualize the Bó-Sarli work, a body of work that archives sex, fantasy, desires, bodies, actions, and pleasures. At the intersection of many different influences, the duo's work made intimacy public and challenged the limits of what can be seen on the screen. The problematic site of such boundaries defied the power relations that were so deeply ingrained in society and those that existed beneath strict sterile Catholic norms. But most importantly, the Bó-Sarli oeuvre places the body as the central site of that change. This book builds a conflicting history surrounding attitudes, rejections, taste, and affect, in hopes of establishing a foundation to understand how knowledge about the body was produced and reconstructed through Argentine history, one that returns to the affective mode enacted by Eva Perón and her sublime female body to connect with the body of the star.

CHAPTER 2

Reading Bad Cinema through "Bad Archives"

Freud had little faith in archives: in his psychoanalytic theory they are frequently described as sites of censorship since acts of remembering are closely related to forms of forgetting.

(Sigmund Freud Museum, Vienna, Austria)

The provocative words in this epigraph appear on the wall of the Freud Museum in Vienna, built in the home and practice of Sigmund Freud, where he lived for forty-seven years and produced most of his major contributions to the developing field of psychoanalysis. Coupled with documenting the life and works of the science's founding father, the museum details the history of the discipline, which he built alongside other practitioners living and working in the same Viennese community. The museum's walls, furthermore, collect and narrate a veiled account of the political oppression experienced by Jewish people that eventually led to Freud's flight to London in 1938 after the integration of Austria into the Third Reich. The epigraph that begins my reflection underscores the role psychoanalysis plays in the construction of both memory and forgetting, announcing the fractious nature of archives while warning of their powerful position in erecting certain interpretations of that past.

The social turmoil of the past establishes an uncanny parallel between the context of oppression experienced by Freud in 1930s' Austria because he was Jewish and that of Argentina in the 1960s and 1970s due to political or social reasons, a setting that implicates a more recent state-sponsored program to forget, or a remembering of a different kind. This chapter tells the story of the loss of a significant archive of Argentina's Classification Board that awaits a hopeful development. Despite the catastrophic gap the absent archive signifies for historians, I consider new ways of approaching the study of popular film in Argentina. I also contemplate how challenges to film research continue to haunt contemporary scholars who have accepted the task of constructing histories about traumatic and turbulent pasts, a perpetual flirtation between knowing and oversight, two sides of the same coin, and thus an act of censorship itself, as this chapter's epigraph recaps.

THE CASE OF THE DISAPPEARED FILM CENSORSHIP ARCHIVE

The tale begins in the Ente de Calificación Cinematográfica (Film Classification Board, herein shortened to Classification Board), an official body created in 1963 and responsible for overseeing all films screened in Argentina until 1984. The work of the Classification Board gained moral and legal ground once the state passed law 18.019 in 1969, giving it the official authority to make material cuts to the films it received for review.[1] To be screened in the country all films required authorization through a certificate of classification, and thus the institution kept a file for each of the films that were vying for access to national screens. The files contained details about offensive scenes, dialogues, actions, and plots compromising national security and morality, according to law 18.019.[2] Furthermore, there were files kept with the film clippings of the scenes and shots that were cut by the classification body or by the directors themselves, who were asked to deposit clippings with the office. Once the Classification Board was disbanded in 1984, both types of files were moved to the then Instituto Nacional de Cine, the precursor of the contemporary Instituto Nacional de Cine y Artes Audiovisuales (INCAA, National Film and Audiovisual Arts Institute). Researchers accessed the written files in the early 1990s and began to publish preliminary secondary documentation about the process the Classification Board followed from its creation to its end and the types of films that were censored throughout the era.[3] Mostly providing a general overview of censorship and how it functioned ideologically, the aforementioned studies do not delve into the particulars of censorship with close readings of films, directors, or specific subjects to understand what was found offensive during the different periods of the Classification Board's history. While the work that has already been done is foundational, its generalizations, common to new inquiries on any given topic, make it difficult for current scholars to explore directions in censorship studies that may require important details hidden in the many files lost in the archives.

Sometime between the mid to late 1990s, the scholarship and thus access to the files ended abruptly. After many years of unsuccessfully searching for the mythical room full of files and their potential answers to budding research inquiries, I decided to write the current chapter, which reflects on the circumstances and consequences of the archive's disappearance. The many dead ends I encountered have led me to one conceivable explanation for the archive's vanishing. It appears that between 1995 and 1999, during the Carlos Menem neoliberal years, the director of the INC, Julio Máharbiz, wanted to microfilm all the paper files and then destroy them, as they were taking up too much physical space.[4] Apparently, the microfilming process was flawed because the transfer was not clear, thereby producing an unreadable product. Although Máharbiz was aware of the technological failure, he continued with the project until its completion. Once the microfilming was done, the paper files were destroyed, bringing a sudden end to what could have been a treasure trove of endless future research projects.[5]

My research and quest throughout the years to try to access both paper and filmic files have come up empty-handed, and I am now left with this lackluster explanation. While the account may have some basis in truth regarding the paper documentation, it still does not explain the whereabouts of the film clips, which offers hope for their making an appearance at some point in the future. Nonetheless, as far as I can tell, the story about loss has meant the end of an archive and implies the destruction of probably one of the most valuable deposits of the dictatorial period in Argentine film history.[6] I can say for certain that the ultimate fate of such material cannot be known until someone finds it or officially verifies the narrative of its whereabouts. Until that time, it will be a difficult path to the construction of knowledge with the current tools at our disposal. In this chapter I grapple with the role that archives play in knowledge formation, principally in the knowledge of nonsanctioned popular culture featuring sex, and how to construct that history despite loss—in a sense how to make the lost repository of information *be-come*. The chapter is interspersed with references to alternative resources that I have collected to help in reconstructing the history of onscreen sex in light of the disappeared archive.

Questions of state power are central to the issues discussed herein. According to historian Peter Fritzche, in different contexts wars trigger archive construction, because the archive functions as a mechanism for memorializing logics of military and political power.[7] During wars, archives assert the centralized power of authoritarian regimes. Similar cases in Nazi Germany, Nazi Austria, and colonial Latin American centers of power (Mexico and Peru), to name a few examples, have proven that archives were vital to the formation of the state and its overall authority. A similar argument can be made for Argentina in 1968 as militarization developed a central role as a state apparatus, which eventually led, eight years later, to the most brutal dictatorship in the nation's history (1976–83). Ironically, that period of dictatorial rule is known for its purposeful lack of documentation, particularly not documenting the many who disappeared before and during military rule. If no archives of *los desaparecidos* exist, then their disappearance cannot be proven. This makes the archive of the film Classification Board all the more critical because it is the only official record kept by the state to document its power. However, later, once the past problematic power structures become exposed, the archive was eliminated. Generally, during the war, censorship forms the public record, while once the war ends any proof of the repression is erased in its aftermath. Could the example of the postwar cleansing of the Argentine film archive have been a method to undo, erase, or ignore the military and political power that prevailed during the government's most openly repressive period? And if this was the case, does it show a sense of societal guilt felt by bureaucrats or politicians in regard to the nation's past? While the answers to these questions may never be known, the issues they raise are worthwhile pondering, even if only to engage with future reconstructions of an absent record. Furthermore, the destruction of the archive establishes an intent, on the part of state and institutional leaders, to obstruct future engagement with the materials, an intent that may never be proven but must always be suspected.

Confronting the possible loss of rich material resources forced me to write the most self-reflective chapter to guide my methodological approach throughout *Violated Frames*. In considering the archive, I ponder my own personal struggle with conducting historical film research in Argentina even given the help of many wonderful people who have contributed to my work in endless ways. On the other hand, I also contemplate the challenge of exploring a topic that has very little *value* or meaning to most people in the fields of film and Latin American Studies, because of its commercial appeal and perceptions of its being below standard.

It is no coincidence that I started the chapter with an epigraph taken from the Freud Museum in Vienna. For me, the work of Sarli and Bó is central to understanding the history of sexuality in Argentina and throughout Latin America at a time when sexuality was becoming more public and is the object of repression. Freud is key in the discussion of sexuality and was an important thinker about questions relating to memory, providing a basis for the current scholarship on mourning. While scholars have moved on from psychoanalysis in sexuality studies,[8] Freud is still relevant in thinking about memory as a way of encountering the past. Cultural critic Andreas Huyssen makes a strong connection to him and history as he reflects on memory.[9] Huyssen's theories provide a basis needed to understand the value of the work in *Violated Frames*. For Huyssen it is the "tenuous fissure between past and present that constitutes memory, making it powerfully alive."[10] He argues that the "struggle for memory is the struggle for history and against high tech amnesia,"[11] a forgetting associated with the same "neoliberal techniques of forgetting" that Nelly Richard describes in the Latin America of the 1990s.[12] The case about the lost archives clearly fits with other arguments made in the aftermath of the dictatorship about President Menem's terms (1989–99) of neoliberal policies and a state-sponsored drive to forget and erase the recent violent past.[13] Confronted with the accelerated pace of temporality that the future has brought, memory and history are the contested forms for Huyssen, a way for the present to hold onto or control time. Memory for Huyssen is not frozen, as it is something alive and growing while different from the static archive.[14] On the other hand, there is always the danger of commodifying the memory of the past through "museification" or trying to keep it static, as cultural critic Susana Draper explains.[15]

Violated Frames consciously works against the commodification of memory, time, or history toward showing how the past continues to live in and through the present. In thinking about the past, I return to the present and explore the interconnection between the two by deliberately constructing an alternative archive, actively engaging in a discussion about what that archive may look like and furthermore helping to build a version that acknowledges its roughness and incompleteness at the same time through its be-coming a "bad archive."

My purpose is twofold: firstly, to acknowledge the great loss—the gap in knowledge for film scholars interested in the role the state has played throughout the history of Argentine cinema—and secondly to openly confront the disappearance by thinking about ways of compensating for the buried archive as I approach the work produced by the Bó-Sarli duo. In an attempt to recreate the history of censorship and sexuality in spite of all of the stated obstacles, I argue that as an example from popular cinema their films helped to define sexuality by bringing a new type of pleasure to the screen that (dis)orders the middle class fantasy of sexuality and aligns itself with the politics of the period. Popular culture fills many voids during specific social, political, and historical moments, time that continues to reflect on the present and future in a nonlinear fashion. Furthermore, popular culture of the past can both hide and highlight important aspects of society and its surrounding attitudes in the past that persist into the future.

The present chapter serves as an introduction to the next, which further examines the particular details about censorship in Argentine cinema throughout the period of the Sarli-Bó productions, coinciding with the coming of age of erotic cinema in the nation. On the other hand, the ensuing discussion functions as a theoretical basis for a methodology of how to study the past when confronted with loss, a loss simultaneously mourned and surmounted by finding new ways of filling in the gaps or piecing the fragments together. Archives have an important role to play in the patchwork of history: they define the way scholars see and interpret the past. Taken further, film as an archive also offers another contested form, one that complicates archive's central role. Finally, I want to take a closer look at the state of archives in Argentina, to better explain some of the reasons for the loss. I conclude by using the buried archive to consider how its absence affects the work of film historians and scholars of the past. Under the circumstances, film historians need to better compensate for gaps to achieve the goals of understanding the past with the materials available and at their disposal, in a conscious effort to go about piecing together a version of the past without the official nucleus that could bind particular interpretations. Said in another way, the project is about erecting history *from the outside in* rather than from the inside out, in order to better grasp an important era in film production and its role in the history of sexuality throughout the region without forgetting the tension that exists between loss and reconstruction.

CURATING THE PAST

In thinking about archives, one imagines places that preserve memory. Memory itself evolves from its containment as an in-camera private thought to its liberation through worldwide public access. Archives are literal and concrete spaces where those scholars involved with historical inquiry engage with material objects, whether they are artifacts, documents, or films.[16] As living repositories of memories, they are never static, for they adopt a new life from the point of view of each critic who enters to interpret them. On the other hand, as historian Dominick LaCapra reminds us—there are dangers in fetishizing their sites, mistakenly allowing the belief that they are substitutes for some sort of "'reality' of the past, which is 'always already' lost for the historian."[17] LaCapra insists that any recreation of history will always be flawed because in the end it too proves to be a mere construction.[18] Archives were never really as "raw or primary" as one may have expected them to be, they were always assembled by someone to lead future researchers in certain directions.[19] Furthermore, as value given to the artifacts changes with time, what is saved can take on a less treasured role than what is discarded. To return to the epigraph found in Freud's Museum, the appreciation given by the curator of the materials paradoxically becomes both a site of memory and a form of forgetting.

Jacques Derrida probably best articulated the archive's contradictory essence in *Archive Fever*, one of the most thorough reflections on the topic. In his reading of Freud's act of archiving, Derrida identifies two opposing forces at work: the death drive and the pleasure principle. On the one hand, in every repository there is a destructive force that incites forgetfulness, amnesia, and the annihilation of memory, but also the eradication of the archive itself.[20] On the other hand, there is the accumulative undertaking of collecting, organizing, and conserving the human record. Derrida argues that the dual, yet antithetical function is intrinsic to all repositories. For instance, if one considers precisely what is included or excluded from the archive, it becomes evident that the act of registering already imposes a "poetics of exclusion," as David Greetham has called it in the title to his essay (1999), underlying a social need to "want to preserve the *best* of ourselves for those who follow."[21] Ironically, the "*best* of ourselves" may not necessarily be what future generations will want to know about our past. Herein lies the struggle between two drives, and the core problem in the case of the censorship archive in question. What is kept and what is discarded, because it bears no recognized value, does matter and is relevant to any discussion about the past and society's principles and beliefs at the time of its obliteration or protection. It is in this way that the historian understands archives as repositories of "good taste and bad faith."[22] Similarly, Frances Ferguson reminds us that the struggle in pornography happens through belonging to the archive: that which is excluded is precisely that which is considered invaluable in bad taste, or somehow deviant and not worthy of preserving or belonging to the archive.[23] Foucault was right to suggest that archives are precisely "monuments to particular configurations of power"; they represent the order of the day and hold within them the power that created them.[24]

While one cannot properly judge the question of values in an absent archive, its very nonexistence shows up the lack of meaning in the preservation of memory in film production in general. However, some saved files did survive as remnants in copies of the original data. The resource I refer to comes from Octavio Getino, filmmaker and previous comptroller of the Classification Board during the open period in 1973 and later director of the INC from 1989 to 1990. In the mid-1990s, while doing research for his book *Cine argentino entre lo posible y lo deseable*, Getino had access to the extensive paper archive that existed and was housed in the INC. He photocopied parts of the files that were relevant to his book. At the time of his death in 2012, his wife donated the copies as part of his personal archive to the library at the film school, Escuela Nacional de Experimentación y Realización Cinematográfica (ENERC), at the INCAA. Among the forty censorship files saved, many documented foreign films (e.g. *Mad Max* [George Miller, Australia/USA, 1979], *Pink Floyd "The Wall"* [Alan Parker, UK, 1982], *Xica da Silva* [Carlos Diegues, Brazil, 1986], *Carrie* [Brian De Palma, USA, 1976]) and others were political movies (*The Hour of the Furnaces* [Fernando Solanas and Octavio Getino, 1968], *State of Siege* [Costa-Gavras, France/Italy/West Germany, 1972]). Only one was from an erotic Argentine picture, a Sarli-Bó production: *Intimacies of a Prostitute*. The files copied by Getino are incomplete, but a look at all forty reveals the general anxieties of the censors and the challenges both national and international productions were experiencing. The files also serve as a sneak peek into the process developed by the Classification Board. Seen from such a perspective, Getino performs as an unintentional curator. Through his choice of examples to illustrate his arguments in the book, he isolates a variety of films that provide access to parts of the "raw" material. While certainly not representative of the whole archive, unknowingly Getino does offer a small window into the world of the lost original.

And yet a closer look at his finished product, the book about Argentine cinema, reveals a problem with Getino's curating, one endemic to all curatorial acts. In his work, Getino makes a well-defined connection between cinema and dependence, in a repetition of a dependency theory framework that was popular in the 1960s and 1970s, and which overwhelmingly influenced his own Third Cinema documentary directed with Fernando Solanas, *The Hour of the Furnaces*. The book offers a sweeping history of film production in Argentina and identifies two divergent paths for its practice. The first constitutes bourgeois inspiration for consumption by upper classes that includes an aesthetic cinema inspired by European standards, defined as Second Cinema in the manifesto that he cowrote with Solanas. The second, a popular cinema meant to attract working-class audiences, is a tradition that begins with early director José Ferreyra, originally inspired in popular culture, and continues through the work of Argentina Sono Film and filmmakers such as Mario Soffici, Leopoldo Torres Ríos, and Hugo del Carril. While Getino sees popular cinema practice as neither the ultimate expression of Argentine film nor aligned to his activist Third Cinema manifesto, he holds a nostalgic appreciation for such early proletariat depictions. However, his own biases become evident when he acknowledges and esteems the many forms of popular cinema that existed in classical film production, ones that were somehow allied to the working class. He expects early divergent paths to coalesce into the only option exemplified in his own ideological masterpiece, *The Hour of the Furnaces*. The approach taken by Getino simplifies the period with broad strokes and limits all other expressions of popular cinema that uneasily express working-class struggles. Getino conflates, for instance, the work of Bó and Sarli with the more international and commercial cinema that was made by Aries Cinematográfica; for example, that of comic duo Jorge Porcel and Alberto Olmedo, the sex films of Libertad Leblanc, and the cinema of Emilio Vieyra, who is justifiably accused of supporting the military regime.[25] Such vague categorization may arguably have merit, as Bó did share many similarities with an internationally accepted version of Argentine cinema. Bó and Sarli were responsible for pioneering international collaborations through coproductions and working with distributors like Pel-Mex and Columbia Pictures International that later adopted Vieyra's and other popular productions. However, Getino ignores the vein of Bó-Sarli work that continues earlier popular examples. For instance, he does not see that *Thunder among the Leaves*, Augusto Roa Basto's first film script (an author responsible for many films discussed by Getino as exemplary of an emerging type of proletariat cinema) also fits into the same debate.

Throughout Getino's book, the sharp demarcation of political cinema and its struggle with censorship as opposed to the other films produced became the only desired direction for Argentinean cinema in its resistance to dependence. Getino's values and tastes are clearly exposed in the archetype he offers. His political agenda mediates the eventual archive that he leaves behind. With his text he does provide images of many of the photocopied documents that he curates for the book, which are meant to make his overall point and only provide a glimpse into the vast raw archive that previously existed and that he consulted. Of course, at the time Getino was not aware of the crucial role he was playing for future historians, as his is one of the few remnants of the past archive still preserved. Nonetheless, to work with the fragments provides an obvious obstacle, because we are already working with the values and tastes of just one curator.

To build an archive of the past is to encourage critical thinking in the future, and thus ensure an ongoing engagement with history, giving it renewed life. In *Archive Fever*, Derrida makes clear that to build an archive is not only to preserve the past but also to further affirm the present and more importantly the future.[26] Destruction of the archive represents for Derrida a failure of the present in its responsibility to the future, a valid point that further connects to Huyssen's conceptualization of memory and its relationship to what will come. By recognizing the existence of the lost archive, I am engaging with discussions about how the state censored films and why certain decisions were made at different moments of the Classification Board's history, highlighting and even encouraging its future life, an acknowledgment that must be given to the intentional but also inadvertent function of Getino's work. I may be limited by Getino's own investigation because his curating restricted future research directions, but I am also enriched by the little curating he did do. To borrow Derrida's words, I am reminded of the reproduction of power found in archives: "There is no political power if not control of the archive, if not memory. Effective democratization can always be measured by this essential criterion: the participation in and access to the archive, its constitution, and its interpretation."[27] "Access," "constitution," and "interpretation" of archives are key stages crucial to producing an informed and democratic society.

Yet Derrida's words also inspire reflection about how archives are institutionalized. Who builds the archive? To what end? And conversely who destroys the archive and why? In the case before us, were the censorship files considered threatening? Or was it just a question of apathy on the part of some bureaucrat who could not be bothered to save them? We may never know the answers to those questions. What one can hope for and practice is advocating for the resurgence of archives for their added value: I think about the ways the past can relate, influence, and affect the future. Perhaps the files may turn up in some dumpster or buried in someone's closet. While I still hold onto hope, I also agree with Beatriz Sarlo, who believes that it may be worth reconstructing some ideas so that "all ideas don't disappear 'gnawed away at our habit of forgetting.'"[28] Even if the files are lost forever, I can take some comfort in what Anjali Arondekar reminds us: only with the production of more stories about the losses can a future be-coming take place.[29]

FILM CHALLENGES THE ARCHIVE

To consider film as an object to be documented further introduces new complications to the concept of collection, exposing many paradoxes. In her consideration of the construction of time, Mary Ann Doane explains that film confuses the notion of the archive with its function to preserve an object or artifact thought to have original value or meaning. In the case of film as artifact, the medium is constrained by its affinity with "contingent and always potentially meaningless detail."[30] Furthermore, Doane borrows Walter Benjamin's concept of the aura to describe film as "anti-auratic," due to the dissemination of multiple copies without an original.[31] While archival desire or "fever" is meant to stop the vertiginous movement of mechanical and electronic reproduction, the argument is hard to maintain in the case of film due to its characteristic as a consumable product and the need to make multiple copies for distribution, whether it is locally or worldwide. Therefore, to speak of an original is even more problematic in the case of Bó and Sarli's films, as censorship of their work globally ensured the existence of many different versions in circulation at any one time. What offended local institutions differed between cities, countries, and cultures. For instance, in Japan many parts of the body were blacked out or covered, while in other markets the versions screened were the uncut ones not acceptable in Argentina. They may even have had extra scenes filmed and assembled by producers abroad with different actors because they were not as steamy as they wanted. Furthermore, as their films were dubbed, not subtitled, the various language versions also produce meaningful differences.

Despite the circulation of multiple variations at the time, today not all films still exist. A "natural" censorship reduces many of the inconsistencies as films are still lost. Such elimination has meant that three of the films made by the duo are to date completely lost (*Tropical Lust*, *The Lioness*, and *Sex and Love*). The case of *The Lioness* is most interesting to any study of its censorship—it was not allowed to enter into the more "liberal" United States because in the film Sarli's character kisses a black man (Monsueto), an act considered illegal in a period when miscegenation according to the Production Code was not permitted onscreen.[32] More recently a copy of *India*, thought to also be lost, was rediscovered in the archives of the Museo del Cine Pablo Ducrós Hicken and restored. The new version was shown at the Buenos Aires International Festival of Independent Cinema (BAFICI) in 2012, offering a glimmer of hope for the recovery of other disappeared material.

Aside from the lost films, access to many of the duo's other films is now facilitated by their worldwide resurgence and a second wave of fandom, as most films are available in their entirety on YouTube.[33] After the end of the dictatorship and its censorship of many films, and with the growth of cable TV in the 1980s, many of the Bó-Sarli films were shown on late night TV, even the fully prohibited and never before screened *Insatiable*, a movie about a nymphomaniac who lives with a husband who accepts her sexploits with other men. Now fans have made the duo's films available on the web, making any claim to Benjamin's aura described by Doane not only highly questionable but also truly laughable.

Doane suggests that film should be seen as an archival process instead of just an expression of art, which especially reaffirms the shift toward film historiography that has been taking place in the field. For instance, film can be considered both a historical artifact and a document of a given moment. Similarly, the work of Philip Rosen agrees with Doane's proposal. He has led a film historiography movement with a complex and in-depth reading of André Bazin. Rosen advocates for a historical approach to film using Bazin's term "change mummified." In the oxymoron, Rosen endorses historical knowledge that has as its center the relation of change to stasis.[34] Here he speaks of "radical historicity" defined as "historiography that knowledgeably confronts the instabilities of the relationships that modern historicity establishes between past and present."[35] It acknowledges both the problems of constructing pastness in the present and the corrosive premises of modern temporality. Pastness cannot be excluded from the present, and thus Rosen speaks of a hybrid temporality conceived as being grounded in and embodying the "unavoidable interplay of present with pastness that modern historicity cannot overcome and that is basic to its rationale."[36]

The shift proposed by Rosen and taken up later by scholars of adult cinema makes a complex and self-conscious version of history more central to film studies, one that allows for inclusion of the past in the present and future, as well as aligning nicely with the parameters of

Violated Frames.[37] How will reading the work of the duo help us look at pastness in the present of their work? As their oeuvre becomes more relevant within the context of recent studies on sexuality and film, I begin to appreciate their production as both artifacts and documents of the past that can take on a new life with the engagement of more current trends in the interdisciplinary studies of Latin America, film, sexuality, feminism, and affect.

Another archive, which like the Classification Board has been lost, is the one containing the many film clips physically eliminated by the Classification Board during its tenure under official law until 1984. The clips were supposedly housed in the INCAA, and it equally proved as inaccessible as the Classification Board files, despite my attempts at access. I still hold onto hope for rediscovery of its material because the story that may explain the loss of the files does not describe the disappeared clippings. Given both missing archives, I turned to another possible source of information that may fill a missing void, but which carries its own problems: the documentary film directed by Diego Curubeto called *Carne sobre Carne: Intimidades de Isabel Sarli* (*Meat on Meat: Intimacies of Isabel Sarli*, Argentina, 2007), about the duo's censored material.[38] Sarli donated Bó's personal archive to filmmaker and film critic Curubeto. The archive contained the many cuts made throughout the years by Bó himself to his own films, those kept in excess of the ones made by the Classification Board. The documentary provides an inside look into the problem of censorship for the duo from a fan perspective, but it is full of rich, fascinating material such as split screens of the censored scenes with both before and after versions. Similar to Getino's curating, Curubeto serves the same function with a new censorship archive that his documentary becomes, judging and proctoring the most important aspects for him as an Isabel Sarli fan and aficionado of exploitation in Argentina.[39]

But the case of Curubeto's documentary raises another question about archival material being kept through private ownership and what that can potentially mean for access by scholars. The same struggle continues to be fought as the only cinematheque in Argentina is a private institution that has made it difficult for researchers to access its collection.[40] While the Museo del Cine Pablo Ducrós Hicken does hold collections, the Buenos Aires government owns and controls its collections locally not nationally. The national INCAA does not prioritize preservation as part of its mandate. For many years, a movement has been growing to develop a public cinematheque, in the same vein as

Mexico's Cinemateque, which would preserve collections in the appropriate conditions and give access to researchers to such collections. Its main function was to bring together different archives, such as the many paper and filmic ones referred to in this chapter, to one location and make preservation, storage, and restoration a priority, allowing access to future scholars. Perhaps had such a project been further along and in place at the time of Sarli's donation to Curubeto, she may have considered donating the material to the public institution in lieu of the private collector.[41]

Adult film scholar Eric Schaefer advocates for the preservation and archiving of material relevant for the study of adult movies (films targeting adult audiences including both hard- and soft-core).[42] He has made a convincing argument about the necessity to regulate the materials that exist, identify where they are located, and ensure that measures are being taken to safeguard their long-term availability. Schaefer backs the historical turn in film studies, for which Doane, Rosen, Paul Willemen, and Miriam Hansen have also advocated, to also encompass the study of adult movies.[43] In doing so, he urges that more academic rigor should be accorded to the adult movie genre by using archival documentation of the films, and he calls for the collective work of archivists and scholars to guarantee their "access, acquisition, and preservation."[44] Albeit American-centered, his call becomes highly relevant to our censorship study in Argentina, especially as I understand that Schaefer justifies his invitation by suggesting that scholars are drawn to the films because they "'engage a larger field of contextual issues' [citing Sconce]: religion and morality, social relations, law, biology, psychology, and issues of identity—not to mention 'the three Ps': politics, power, and pleasure," all central to our current study.[45] Schaefer's call fully accepts the archive as purveyor of truth, as an activist summoning the importance of the material and justifying the field of sex onscreen.

Additional work has been done in the essays that make up *Porn Archive*, a project to connect the very act of archiving with the establishment of the distinct category of pornography, making it a site for both the production of knowledge and pleasure. Some of the essays in the book further acknowledge and consciously pose the many problems inherent in the task of archiving, some of which will prove useful, while also advocating for the study of the "pornographic." For Tim Dean, one of the book's editors, pornography documents pleasure, and more specifically sex, fantasy, desire, bodies and their actions, enabling intimacy to enter the realm of the archive.[46] He argues that one cannot think of affect without including both pleasure and lust, important emotions used by sexual minorities as part of constructing cultural memory. Similarly, Linda Williams suggests that pornography constitutes a mode of thinking about bodily limits, intimacy, and power. She argues that pornography studies have challenged us to think differently about our bodies, representation of them, and sexuality. Pornography always already bears some limit, has a border that it challenges or pushes: "[it] . . . needs to remember that it must always exist at the problematic site of this limit."[47]

To advocate for the preservation of film and other archival documents, especially in Argentina, regardless of their content, I propose a more comprehensive and inclusive understanding of the past that embraces the many gaps and missing archives, in order to relate it to the present. What better way to crystallize the anxieties and desire of a society than with offensive sexual materials of the past? In the Sarli-Bó films alone, there are traces of the very same limits Williams exposes as they open the seams to show what is missing and what is promised, though most times never delivered.

FILM ARCHIVES IN ARGENTINA

Taking Schaefer's challenge seriously requires careful pondering about the condition of film archives in Argentina. This task is thoughtfully considered by a booklet edited by the Argentine Association for the Study of Film and Audiovisual Material, titled *What Have I Done to Deserve This? A Research Guide to Audiovisual Media in Argentina*, which laments the sorry state of archives relating to the audiovisual medium.[48] While the booklet does not even acknowledge the existence of a censorship archive, its focus on the main, more official repositories proves useful for consideration and makes its task more urgent. According to the editors, there are seven main reasons why the conditions of general archives in Argentina are poor:

1. The lack of public policy in the preservation of local heritage
2. The absence of a social consciousness about the importance of preserving national heritage
3. The weakness of an institutional framework that reveals itself as inefficient, inadequate, and incapable of adapting to the changes in the area of the preservation of archives
4. A lack of relevant and effective regulations for the protection of audiovisual heritage

5. A shortage of professionals educated in the areas of gathering, conservation, and preservation of audiovisual archives
6. An absence of instruments and support for professionals in the areas of collection, conservation, and dissemination of archives
7. No funding for research, recovery, preservation, and dissemination of audiovisual materials[49]

As the cited reasons suggest, the problem of archival memory can be summarized and directly linked to issues surrounding funding. However, questions of space and lack of information about the whereabouts of some of the collections due to the absence of a tradition of valuing historical documents and its study in the nation are also influential underlying reasons.[50] The regrettable state of actual collections means that only ten of the three hundred silent films made in Argentina still exist today, and as much as 50 percent of the sound films have been lost.[51] The sole state-supported entity, the INCAA, has never made preservation a priority, and although the privately owned Fundación Cinemateca Argentina has played an important and even pioneering role in the history of film preservation in Latin America, it has more recently made access to this material more difficult.[52] Thus, preservation comes through films kept under private ownership, such as Cinemateca, or the release by TV channels onto the small screen, as has been the case with some of the Bó-Sarli films.[53] Fernando Solanas, film director and senator, initiated a project called CINAIN (Cinematheque and Archive of National Images) through law number 25.119, which had as its sole objective to preserve film memory and to alert people to the dangers of the possible disappearance of film and paper archives.[54] The bill dates back to 1999, yet only passed into law in 2010.

The long journey of the bill into law shows the arduous struggle for change in the attitudes toward film preservation the government has through the INCAA itself. When the law was proposed in 1999, the director of the INCAA, Julio Máharbiz, did not support it.[55] This is no surprise, since Máharbiz was allegedly the one responsible for the destruction of the Classification Board archive in the first place. The bill, passed in 2010 under the leadership of Liliana Mazure, director of the INCAA at the time and the presidency of Cristina Fernández de Kirchner, only went into effect on 27 March 2017 with the official inauguration of CINAIN directed by Fernando Madedo under the government of Mauricio Macri. In its short lifespan, CINAIN's impact has already been felt in the community, making important inroads in the preservation and dissemination of archives.[56]

CONSTRUCTING MEMORY AROUND A LOSS

Given the current state of archives, in conjunction with the acknowledgment that archives in themselves are already fraught with many contradictory and competing dilemmas, What do the compound issues discussed mean for the work of this book in constructing memories in process of becoming, memories that may lead to new forms of knowledge about the past? How do film historians compensate for loss in order to approach the cinema of Sarli and Bó? To begin to answer some of the questions posed here, I return to the ideas guiding scholars of archival exclusion trying to look at different or subaltern voices within official archives that have clearly muted or purposefully erased all marginal presence. The researchers I engage with read history into the remnants, gaps, silences, and absences found in official documents and other sources, proposing different reading strategies as a theoretical framework that has helped me rethink the gap in information. These methods work with the somewhat unique situation of the censorship archive in Argentina. The methodologies I am proposing here help me enter the context in new ways and yet in the end they all have one common goal: to expose the fallibility of the archive, uncovering what is missing without fully eliminating it. The overview that follows is by no means exhaustive. Instead, it is meant to be a sweeping explanation to help expose the validity and utility of an assemblage of critical theoretical ideas for my own engagement in the debate.

A. *Reading against the Grain, along the Grain, and at the Limits of Visibility*

The work by postcolonial critics who have been confronted with the conundrum of colonial archives offers a good point of departure. Scholars show how official state documents erased many voices and perspectives from the past that are no longer directly accessible. In doing so, they have developed and proposed different strategies for accessing hidden, erased, or disappeared histories. For instance, postcolonialism's leading theorist, Gayatri Chakravorty Spivak, grapples with the past and argues that writing, including literature, is complicit in the imperial task of constructing while simultaneously destroying or disappearing.[57]

Taking a deconstructionist approach, Spivak identifies the paradox of the archive and implies that through the politics of inclusion, the erasure of memory takes place. She calls for its displacement by reading without a trace, finding the voice of the Rani of Sirmur, and making visible the "native informant" and the pressures on women in colonized societies: "a call to interrogate, without paralysis, to challenge, without ending the promise of a future."[58] Spivak finds ways to read against the grain of the archive by exposing the project of imperialism and uncovering voices that were abolished during that enterprise. Spivak's call helps to reveal and acknowledge the silenced voices in the lust-filled cinemas of the 1960s and 1970s. In doing so, film historians better understand the project(s) driving different authoritarian regimes, first within the imposed laws of censorship and its practice during a period of various dictatorships, and later during the cleansing neoliberal venture in the 1990s that worked hard to eliminate the possibility of mobilizing traces of their voice into the future.

In contradiction to Spivak, scholar Ann Laura Stoler does not want to read "against the grain" of imperial history, but instead "along the grain," thus giving the same title to her book, *Along the Archival Grain*. Stoler positions herself differently to Spivak in that she is more interested in the principles and practices lodged in particular archival forms and processes.[59] She believes that by using such a methodology the critic draws attention to the *roughness* of the archive and elucidates why empires strove to put unintelligible systems in place. Stoler emphasizes the importance of subtlety when it comes to the study of archives. For example, she discusses three possible reasons for exclusion: (1) there may not have been a need for writing down certain information because it may have been already common knowledge, (2) perhaps it could not yet be articulated by those doing the writing, or (3) it simply could not be said.[60] The important distinction and different explanations offered demonstrates that silences or gaps in archives may be as a result of multiple and oftentimes contradictory epistemological and political anxieties, which may be conflated to one reason. Stoler's concept of along the grain adds a level of sophistication that can be helpful when reading against the grain, especially in thinking about how the Sarli-Bó films may have been read through lower class and student or youth movements at the same time as patriarchal social structures. Working with the official laws and the file fragments from Getino's collections to reconstruct the important context helped me in the task of thinking about why, in particular, Sarli's body had been offensive to the censors during different periods of precarious social and political moments that constantly shifted.

Anjali Arondekar's *For the Record* adds yet another level to the reading of the archive. She tries to include contemporary conceptualizations of sexuality in the historical colonial archive. Arondekar asks: "Can an empty archive also be full?"[61] By looking at the space of absence, she is trying to show both how sexuality is made visible and the limits of that visibility. It is one thing to say that the archive can never be complete, but scholars always read as if it were full, exposing one of the many faults of the practice of history. Arondekar proposes a type of reading that *re-presents* absence and becomes the very condition of the possibility for the book's archival returns. Therefore, the archival object of sexuality emerges after it is gone, and a be-coming can conversely only take place once more stories of its loss are re-produced. *Violated Frames* is part of that account of absence, and with it I hope to inspire others to reconstruct narratives of further losses in the same project and to re-produce necessary stories to fill in other gaps in 1960s' and 1970s' Latin America.

B. *The Repertoire*

In her book *The Archive and the Repertoire*, Diana Taylor brings a layer of complexity to the question of the archive as she includes the repertoire as part of the archive's inherent other. For Taylor, the archive and the repertoire are two distinctive yet interrelated forms of knowledge. By acknowledging the role each plays, she values the importance of the repertoire, the embodied and live act, the live performance that always disappears. In making the shift from written to embodied culture and from discursive to *performatic*, she calls for a modification in methodology. Taylor gives the repertoire political, affective, and mnemonic power. The body is an intermediary, a receptor, a storehouse, and a transmitter of knowledge. Memories and survival strategies are transmitted from generation to generation through the *performatic* that includes ritualistic bodily and linguistic practices. Such practices have histories that threaten and promise to return what is erased. Performance, thus, becomes visible and meaningful within the context of the phantasmagoric repertoire of repeats.

Taylor refers to an example that is relevant to our context, the bodies of the Mothers of the Plaza de Mayo and HIJOS (Children for Identity and Justice against Forgetfulness and Silence) who turn their bodies into billboards, conduits of memory. Both groups wear photo IDs on their bodies, the same IDs that were erased by the archive, materialized into lived bodies with memory, displacing the official record produced by the military dictatorship. Taylor's contribution underscores that the archive cannot be limited to written form, as it can reside in the most material of places, such as the body. And although it inevitably will disappear, its traces do manage to return in a myriad of ways. Taylor's text takes us away from the classic notion of archive to think about other forms that produce the repetition of the past. By drawing our attention to the lived bodies, those appearing before Bó's camera lens and documented as still shots of the repertoire, the spectator and film historian can read what may have become offensive in the bodily gestures and beyond the representation. Why were certain bodies censored? What actions came across as distasteful? Taylor provides a material point from which to access some difficult social, political, and ethical questions. In the absence of official written answers, those kept in the archive, the bodies on the screen, and the bodies recorded in Curubeto's documentary begin to both fill the void and provide a memory of embodied performance, as examples of raw materials that precede the disappeared archive but also as archives in themselves or documents, since they are recorded and have passed on to researchers of today and tomorrow.

C. Constructing Roughness

Finally, another approach comes from a very different source, an article about rough sex films. Eugenie Brinkema suggests that any pornographic archive should be rough, not smooth, because it is only through roughness that one can grasp its incompleteness, the gaps, the impossible drive for visibility. She exposes the many anxieties about the unwieldy, disordered, approximate, uneven, and unfinished. By insisting on the elimination of loss, one is admitting a loss. Instead, Brinkema proposes a bad archive: a mortal, sketchy, all interruption and no privilege type of archive. By embracing destruction and loss, Brinkema encourages memory to remain rugged, thereby letting history become interrupted and uneven. To let bodies, their openings and entries, be difficult, and even fail. In her gesture of becoming: "The archive's entries remain in a state of being ever about to enter the repository, without being determined by it, without having been archived."[62] She teaches how to wrestle with the broken and conscientiously embrace it, affording a probability beyond nostalgia and frustration.

All three of these different but interrelated methodologies offer strategies that invite an overall concept of becoming—they rightly point to the incompleteness of the archive, the importance of embracing a given loss, and the implicit shortcomings of the truth in the record. "It makes sense, then, that any project involved in redefining how we construct history should seek out alternate forms and versions of historical documentation."[63] Confronted with the interrelated issues that comprise other forms of knowledge such as the repertoire, as well as the way that official archives can be read against the grain or along the grain by welcoming their roughness, I unravel a version of the past that is not necessarily comprehensive but ventures into new and valuable areas of research, such as the case for sexuality, the affective, and histories of pleasure and lust. Despite the fact that the official documents are at the moment almost all but absent, I use various methods as inspiration to approach the subject from different angles to reach a better understanding about the role of bad movies in bad archives.

I have not lost hope that official documents may one day come to light, but nonetheless I currently rely on the ruins and fragments that I have been able to piece together to follow the lead taken by capturing unorthodox and new knowledge, without losing sight of its inherent deficiency. The rest of *Violated Frames*, and the history of film censorship experienced by Bó and Sarli, relies on important documents I succeeded in uncovering through hard work that in many cases happened due to others' generous sharing. Traces have helped me to piece together a history and reconstruct some of that lost past, albeit a consciously incomplete and ever-becoming one.

To summarize, different sources have aided in the recreation of an unfinished yet increasingly flourishing history of sex onscreen. The sources in the book include Curubeto's documentary *Meat on Meat*, which includes Armando Bó's archival footage; the forty files photocopied by Getino and left to the ENERC, particularly the one on *Intimacies of a Prostitute*; the different filmic versions available, whether in other languages or showing extra or different scenes; the original documentation published about the Classification Board by scholars who were able do research in the archive; the secondary sources written about the work of the duo; the official laws of the period continually updated to tweak and reflect the latest administration's growing agenda on censorship; the guidelines that the military released expanding on such laws and explaining the proper ways to interpret earlier laws; the film scripts that were donated to Juan Carlos Maneglia relating to the work of Bó-Sarli in Paraguay; and the press clippings found in the archives at the Museo del Cine and the library of the ENERC.

In looking at the different sites of memories in Argentina that have popped up within the last fifteen years, there is a clear trend toward what Susana Draper calls "selective forgetfulness [that] has turned into a surplus in terms of controlled memory."[64] We have a seeming contradiction: on the one hand, the production of spaces where memory thrives but is still static and reproduced for consumption purposes (museums, torture centers, parks, shopping malls); on the other hand, the loss, deterioration, and disposal of artifacts and documents, such as the censorship archive that has been censored itself through an aggressive and violent act of destruction. The act produced the disappearance of a wealth of information during the neoliberal years of the Menem presidency when perhaps one repository was representing, to those who destroyed it, the worst of the past. This is a failure indeed, one that has limited our own ability to reconstruct not only the past but the future. And yet, despite the seemingly insurmountable obstacles I have outlined, I continue to push forward in my quest to interrogate that obsolete past and rebuild alongside it a rough, unsmooth version that reluctantly accepts its failure.

PART II

Censoring Bodies in Labor and Leisure

CHAPTER 3

Disciplining Bodies through Censors' Shears

> He restrains himself, he sweats, and then
> with his silver scissors
> he trims away her body
> he cuts her skin
> he deforms her face
> and that way, mutilated, he carries her loaded
> onto the screen ... which bleeds.
>
> —Sui Generis, 1974

The lyrics to rock band Sui Generis's 1974 hit "Las Increíbles Aventuras del Señor Tijeras" (The Incredible Adventures of Mr. Scissors), about the work of the infamous film censor Miguel Paulino Tato, also known as Néstor, details the mutilation of a female on the screen, a brutality that violently assaults the gendered body of the star and the public act of sex itself as the screen bleeds from its many attacks. Tato, known as the most severe censor in Argentine history, carries a legacy that only reveals part of the story of film censorship in the nation. Despite his anecdotal reputation, censorship neither began nor ended with him. By 1974, when Tato became the director of the Classification Board, censorship was already systematic and institutionalized. He carried it to its darkest hour—the beginning of the nation's worst dictatorship (1976–83)—a time when many liberties were abolished and state violence akin to the screen massacres of the censors was rampant. However, film censorship history begins earlier and covers many governments, both democratic and de facto, which passed laws ensuring its methodical implementation.[1] While military governments were responsible for instituting unconstitutional measures, legitimate ones did nothing to change them, and vice versa. Rather, the law only became stricter and state control of what was screened in public increased, until censorship was finally abolished in 1984, following the end of the dictatorship. The seemingly impenetrable apparatus produced some fissures or hiccups in the system when changes to the law were ostensibly within reach but never came to fruition.

The song lyrics cited suggestively disclose the private nature of the censoring task, an ironic intimate exercise in outlawing the display of public intimacy itself. The words tell the story of how the censor, away from the public eye, secludes himself in a dark room to conduct his work.[2] He engages in a close moment with the film star and thus completes his duty, which begins as a deceptively caring but nonetheless dominant sexual act ("the man lays her down on the rug / touches and kisses her") that transforms into an act of fanatical torture ('he restrains himself, he sweats / and then with his silver scissors . . . [begins his chore]"). In his darkened chamber he contains her body, denies her identity, and physically violates her ("trims away her body / cuts her hair / deforms her face / and that way, mutilated . . .") before releasing her back to the screen, "loaded" like a gun. The words candidly indicate that it is the film censor who absurdly and incongruously accesses a level of affective connection with the film/star/body in its whole original uncut version, while deciding which parts of the body and frames of the film need to be altered. The song, which was also victim to its own cuts, describes the moral hypocrisy implied in performing an act of prohibiting.[3] It also establishes a definitive correlation between censorship and torture, seeing both as sadistic violations of the female body, the sex act, the materiality of the film, and the artistic product.

My aim in this chapter is to reconceptualize the process of film censorship, not only by describing how it works and its evolution throughout a tumultuous period in Argentine history of constantly changing governments but also by exploring the kind of aggression films were subject to. The chapter deals only with film censorship, as it was the one clear apparatus the state had to control cultural production. Censorship was not consistent across media, but it had a clear institutional development in the realm of film. Despite the fact that some films were screened underground, what I am interested in is the commercial exhibition of films to mass audiences. The persecution of movies as objects that received censorship raises the question of why they were considered to be dangerous, which culminates in the seemingly final and clear-cut verdict given by the guidelines of film production released in 1976. First I will show the development of film censorship as a systemic apparatus that anticipated the oncoming dictatorship, where clear parameters for filmmaking became transparent. Then I will summarize the trajectory of the Sarli-Bó films within the national project of regulation, before focusing on the case of *Intimacies of a Prostitute*, the only surviving file of their joint work from the missing censorship archive, photocopied by Getino and available at the Escuela Nacional de Experimentación y Realización Cinematográfica (ENERC). *Intimacies of a Prostitute* is a film completed in 1972 and finally released in 1974 just before Tato's reign (1974–79) as director of the Classification Board. I argue that by the time he took over the Classification Board there was already an efficient yet labyrinthine apparatus in place, suggesting that the personal moment described in the song was in fact much more public, as many intruding hands and scissors were involved in the film's release. The study of film censorship cannot be linked to any one cause or individual; it is an ongoing process that expands a long history as old as the early experiments on celluloid. Manipulation was clearly taking place as films were stepping up to challenge existing notions of morality and politics. I will argue that the work of Sarli and Bó presents a fruitful example for the study of both industrial and moral censorship because their productions helped to define the limits of what was permissible, especially in the realm of sexuality.

Given the disappearance of the censorship archive, the sole survival of parts of the *Intimacies of a Prostitute* file also makes the film an urgent, unavoidable, and compulsory example. The documentation found in its file outlines how ideological positions were staked between the producer/director and the Classification Board, alluding to the issues that Bó's work presented. I also imply that ascribing any notion of intrinsic artistic value to the film (often through the perspective of a single auteur study) is complicated by the fact that there were many individuals involved in altering the final version eventually released.

To compile the convoluted and incoherent historical process of censorship, I divide the chapter into four parts. The first will detail three key laws in 1957, 1963, and 1968–69 to argue that as time progressed, legislation tightened and institutionalized a national policy to include the growing voice of church and interest groups along with more engagement of the state, while at the same time reducing the role of the industry. Newly published laws built tighter administrative structures meant to regulate the industry as three themes began to surface that were detrimental to the work of Bó-Sarli and impacted local film production, exhibition, and distribution: namely, funding opportunities, classification, and regulation of international collaboration. All three were used by the state to control what was screened nationally and abroad. Eventually, the Catholic Church as well as family-based interest groups took a more prominent role in defining criteria, particularly those surrounding film censorship.

In the second part, I focus on Bó and Sarli's trajectory as they challenged the legislation and thus experienced roadblocks at every turn, even when the laws were open and accepting of more experimentation meant to reinvigorate the industry. To view their career through the laws allows for a better appreciation of the work they were doing in challenging an apparatus that was ultimately limiting certain types of expression. Censorship was a constant for their first film produced together, but as the regulation tightened so their films adapted to find new ways and venture through the process of classification until the circumstances no longer allowed for adaptation.

Third, I will spotlight the case of *Intimacies of a Prostitute* to understand the intricacies of releasing a movie during a period of strict laws and another more open period, to ask the type of questions that the archive could have better helped understand: What was so offensive in the pair's films? Why were they targeted from early on? To look at the case of *Intimacies of a Prostitute* gives an opportunity to analyze the varied and contradictory issues at stake.

In the fourth part, I will discuss what the guidelines established by the dictatorship in 1976 meant for the film industry. If the act of censorship is a private examination, torture, and muzzling of a public display of the body, then to shift the cuts from frames to body may imply that more than just the print becomes the victim of censorship. The body and its affect are also victims. This chapter sets a foundation for the next two that follow, where onscreen bodies of working males and the sensual female star become the lens through which to analyze and appreciate the value of Sarli-Bó's onscreen sexuality.

CONTROLLING THE INDUSTRY AND LEGISLATING TASTE

Although this chapter focuses on regulation as it developed after 1955, the history of regulation begins as early as the 1930s and adapts to different political agendas. For instance, a first attempt in 1938 to pass a cinema law that promoted, controlled, and surveyed film production and exhibition activities failed because it was wholly rejected by the increasingly powerful and growing industry.[4] The first iteration of the INC was created in 1933 only to be dissolved in 1944, during the military government preceding the presidency of Perón. Then the state replaced the INC with the General Direction of Public Spectacles, which became a protectionist body for the industry, supported by Perón until he was ousted.[5] As film historian Clara Kriger explains, during Péron's government:

> Harsher censorship instruments were not necessary. Cinema did not give state functionaries the opportunity to interfere in the abstract art, neither modernists nor businessmen were willing to risk their businesses.[6]

In other words, the studios worked with General Perón's government to support a politics that was mutually beneficial for the industry and the state.

The implication was not that political or personal persecution did not exist. The documented cases of star Libertad Lamarque and auteur director Carlos Hugo Christensen, who both had to leave Argentina to develop their careers in Mexico and Brazil, show otherwise.[7] Nonetheless, as Kriger argues, censorship was informal and inconsistent. It was guided by personal relationships rather than political ones, as the examples of actor Fanny Navarro and actor-director Hugo del Carril confirm. Both were ardent Peronists but still fell victim to authorities because of conflictive associations with Raúl Alejandro Apold, the public servant who worked for the Secretariat of Information and the Press and who sanctioned, applied, and managed the regulation of Argentine cinema.[8] Yet censorship has a longer history when as early as 1910 one can find instances of its imposition on specific examples, albeit only at the municipal level on a film-by-film basis and through the process in the courts.[9] Distinct from what preceded it, the post-1955 period witnessed the federal institutionalization of film censorship, beginning in the late 1950s and officially ending in 1984.

The first step toward centralization came in 1957, when President Pedro Eugenio Aramburu (1955–58) enacted law decree 62/57, which changed the film industry for good, thus beginning what proved to be an increasingly constrictive period, leading to official prohibition of entire productions in 1969. Law 62/57 brought the INC back to oversee and save the dying film industry by providing funding, mainly through loans, to worthy projects. It coincides with a shift in the industry from an elaborate studio system to more independent producers. Law 62/57 expressly denounces censorship, imposing a six-month prison sentence on any individual intentionally obstructing the production and distribution of movies.[10] However, many see it as the beginning of a period of increasing governmental control over the industry.[11] Yet the new law established an ad hoc classification committee, headed by the INC with representatives from the industry, authorized to deem whether films were appropriate for an audience under eighteen years of age. The assembled group also included members from the wider arts community, such as the cultural industries, writers, and the Academy of Letters and Fine Arts. In this law there is a clear statement that films could not be cut or prohibited unless there was a judicial order to do so, maintaining previous practices that allowed only local courts to intervene in such matters. The beginning of a new process to centralize the industry gave the INC and the state more authority to determine what was being watched nationwide.

The decree consolidated the INC's role as arbiter of taste. The institution was responsible for classifying films into two categories, labeled A and B. Those with an "A" classification had access to funding, prizes, exhibition in better cinemas, and full exploitation abroad. Alternatively, the films with a "B" class were not eligible for funds nor guaranteed exhibition, although they were not denied exportation rights. The contradictions of the new state politics and the different interests at play were already becoming apparent. First, the knee-jerk reaction against Perón's economic nationalism fostered foreign influence and stimulated imports, bringing more foreign films into the country and benefiting the exhibition sector. The law explicitly stipulated that the INC stimulated coproductions with foreign nations. By 1966, the import quota was abolished.[12] Second, the moribund local industry, in which independent producers were replacing dying studios, needed state support to better compete with the recent injection of Hollywood product into Argentina. Nonetheless, new funding models were directly linked to quality and subject matter. Of particular interest is a paragraph in the law that states: "The loans will be given taking into account the moral and material responsibility of the producer, the quality of the script, the artistic and technical team."[13] By reinstating the INC and giving it a role of differentiating films and driving collaborations, the government thus privileged certain productions. In other words, the state was guaranteeing quality and formalizing a measurement of taste. Ironically, at a time when the nation was moving beyond government intervention toward market forces, the film industry was in the hands of the state, controlled by a few individuals in the INC who decided the fate of each product. Moreover, at the core of law 62/57 was the assumption that quality drove national film production.

The next important shift in legislation took place in 1963, under President José María Guido, fifteen days before Arturo Humberto Illia took over the government. Decree 8.205 created the more formal National Classification Honorary Council, a continuity of the Sub-commission from 62/57 with a notable change in the constitution of the overseeing body: the added involvement of direct government members (Ministry of Education and Justice, Ministry of Defense, and Ministry of the Interior) and civil leagues representing the interests of minors, the family, and the church. While others have claimed that censorship was not official until later on in the decade, this decree, like its precursor, explicitly speaks about freedom of expression except in the case of "educational reasons or protection of public morals, good customs, or national security," implying a protection of minors that began to encompass public screenings in general.[14] The move created an apparatus relying on taste, state, and moral interest rather than artistic merit or freedom of expression. The main explanation for the shift was framed as quelling the rising threat that could be seen onscreen:

> To protect public morals, especially in all of that which directly influences minors, affected more each day by different mass media, spectacles, and publications that risk and attack the social validity of values of the greatest hierarchical spirit . . .[15]

In general, the state, following the council of the church, was adopting a paternalistic role by deciding for the people what they needed to see and appreciate, a role that began with the youth but extended to encompass all of society.

At this point, the National Classification Honorary Council was established separately from the INC, under the Executive Power, giving more authority to the state and clearly steering control away from the industry to the government. This begins a new phase in classification, not only of films but also of culture in general into two camps: the true and the false in regard to sexuality, religion, and national security. The job of the government, with the help of the church, was to safeguard culture, and film in particular, and keep it from "ideological infiltration and softening of the internal front from the corruption of customs,"[16] a narrative in line with Cold War discourse that was driving political thought throughout the Americas at the time. It is important to note that the mentioned rhetoric was explicitly infiltrating the legal parameters surrounding cultural products. Meanwhile, terms such as *public morals*, *good customs*, and *national security* remained rather vague but were becoming the accepted norm. Nonetheless, both the church and the government became involved in the interpretation of the new legal restrictions for film production, whereby religion was clearly interfering in the state and its laws.

There were various indications that the role of the Catholic Church was growing in Argentine society and would thus influence the policies implemented in 1963 and throughout the period. Earlier, Perón's move to legalize divorce in 1954 sealed the conflict between his Justicialista party and the church. The general's downfall a year later was supported by the ecclesiastical hierarchy, a group that favored more participation of religion in civil matters during both the "liberating revolution" following Perón's fall and the ensuing even more conservative "Argentine revolution" of 1966. The local church's agenda became transparent with the publication of *Guía cinematográfica* in 1962 by Catholic Argentine Action, a nonprofit organization working since 1931 to promote Christian values in the nation. The purpose of the guide was: "to offer people interested in film culture some current necessary elements to facilitate and orient their work," as the inside cover to the fourth edition explains.[17] The reference guide contains an introduction by the Archbishop of Buenos Aires, Antonio Cardenal Caggiano; the Encyclical Letter written by Pope Pius XII on motion pictures, radio, and television; a decree approved by Second Vatican Council on the media; and finally a guide that categorizes all the films shown in Buenos Aires from 1954 to 1962, updated yearly.[18] The ratings in the guide were separate from the state's own classification. Meant for a Catholic viewer, it provides recommendations for each film rated from 1 (acceptable for all) to 6 (prohibited for all). The Bó-Sarli films were included, and movies such as *Favela* received a 4 (for Reserved: these films expect a spectator to differentiate between confusing values that are sometimes positive and negative).[19] *The Impure Goddess* and *The Lioness* were classified as 5 (Not recommended: the bad elements are dangerous even for people with good judgment).[20] And the rest received a 6 (*Thunder among the Leaves*, *The Shad Fishermen*, *Heat*, *India*, and *Tropical Lust*), where evil is posited as attractive and fundamental ideas and principles are distorted; thus ultimately, not considered appropriate for any Catholic audience.[21] While directed at practicing Catholics, the guide nonetheless demonstrates the moral stance that the church adopted regarding bodies and sexuality. In the case of Bó-Sarli, a simple film like *Thunder among the Leaves* received a 6 classification. The film's content, which features Sarli's first nude scene in a river and the revolt of the workers against their foreign oppressive boss, suggests that there were many elements that were considered provocative. Surprisingly, it is the nude scenes along with the film's political and social aspects (discussed in the next chapter), which may explain why the film came across as offensive to the church hierarchy. As Getino notes:

> Sex, morals, politics, ideology, freedom of expression, everything was under the microscope in moments when the church and governmental organisms of repression coincided in a common mission, which was "to survey and protect the national being and the morals of all Argentines."[22]

Getino is referring to the late 1960s. The guide set the stage and a standard by which state policies continued to adopt Catholic elements in its creation of an apparatus, thus influencing national values and societal moral beliefs.

Second, the fusion of state and church coincides with the appointment in 1963 of Dr. Ramiro de la Fuente, a lawyer and ardent Catholic, to head the newly legislated National Classification Honorary Council with greater powers and a much more prominent role in the period. An ultraconservative Catholic, known as the Argentine Torquemada (a reference to the Spanish Inquisitor imposing the rule of the church), de la Fuente reigned unchallenged for ten years across the presidencies of José María Guido, Arturo Humberto Illia, and Generals Onganía, Levingston, and Lanusse. Prior to his role dictating values of films, he was a representative in the International Catholic Office of Film in Argentina, a parallel organization to the one responsible for the *Guía cinematográfica*. The role of the church throughout the historical process discussed in this chapter was a contentious one that merits its own study, a task that is unfortunately well beyond the scope of my project.

After the coup d'état that brought Juan Carlos Onganía to power in 1966, a major piece of legislation in relation to culture in general and film in particular tightened the rules even further. The new government instituted the "Argentine revolution," modeled after General Francisco Franco in Spain, which promoted a national culture inspired by rural and local traditions but also open to universal Christian values. Immediately after coming to power, Onganía imposed law 16.955, which returned the general tenets of 62/57, instilling a two-tiered classification system that once more relied on the INC as arbitrator of taste in its awarding of funding and prizes. In 1968 the new minister of the interior, Guillermo Borda, together with the counsel of de la Fuente, began to implement a much stricter and clearer vision of the law that eventually led to law 18.019, which legalized well-defined direction on censorship.[23] From

1957 to 1968, the parameters around terms like *public morals, good customs*, and *national security* were vague, leaving it to the judgement of the different versions of the classification boards. Yet there was an emphasis on defining moral value underlying all the different decrees. For instance, the first decree under Onganía returned to 62/57 groups A and B and made clear that: "From this category [A] those films that are at risk of damaging the principles of Argentina's cultural tradition will be excluded."[24] And in 1968, the law denied classification to those films "which infringed against the national way of life or the cultural rules of the Argentine community."[25]

One year later, however, law 18.019 officially sanctioned censorship and provided a definitive list of six specific areas where the state could intervene by *cutting* scenes or *prohibiting* entire films, the first time outlawing films was endorsed. The law gives a strong mandate for the state to interfere when films justify "unacceptable behavior" by (1) representing adultery or offending the family and matrimony; (2) justifying abortion, prostitution, and sexual perversions; (3) incorporating lascivious scenes that upset morals and good customs; (4) defending crimes; (5) denying the duty to defend the nation and the right for the authorities to demand it; (6) jeopardizing national security, affecting relations with friendly nations or hurting the interest of fundamental institutions of the state.[26] The list supports film critic Laura Podalsky's argument that "legitimate" culture under Onganía was aligned with national, Catholic, and family values, and "false" culture with foreign, antireligious, and antifamily tendencies. Hiding behind a dualistic definition of the film project was a strong and clear agenda to regulate the content of Argentine films produced so that it aligned with legitimate culture.[27] What had been developing for over ten years had finally and officially become a uniform standard for judging all films appearing on national screens.

Law 18.019 created a final version of the Classification Board with a general director and adjunct directors who were all named by the Ministry of Education and Culture as representatives of the government. Moreover, it states that the INC needed to abide by the law by submitting to the Classification Board national and coproduced scripts, subordinating the INC's work to the Board, which was separate. The film industry was completely removed from the work of classification. From this point forward, everything screened in national theaters needed an official certificate authorized only by the Classification Board. While there were modifications to the law throughout the years, 18.019 had the greatest impact on the way film was exhibited in Argentina until

1984, when it was officially repealed under law 23.052. All mention of the international quality of Argentine films was reduced to focus instead on the local exhibition of films and the implications for local audiences.

The law matched well with the 1976 coup, when new guidelines were developed to ensure its interpretations were implemented correctly. However, by the early 1980s, debates about the role of censorship began to surface in newspapers, magazines, and public panels. Open criticism of and discussion on the topic of censorship was circulating, and opinions were being voiced publicly. In an article published in 1981, when censorship was under real scrutiny and debate about its role was at its height, Miguel Grinberg wrote a journalistic piece that detailed the process of classification that both the Classification Board and the INC followed.[28] He explained that two certificates were given, one by the Classification Board with a rating ranging from "appropriate for all audiences" to "prohibited," and the other, a certificate given by the INC for exhibition. The Classification Board had a limit of thirty days to classify the film, and its distributor/producer could then appeal the verdict. Once the film was prohibited twice then the case was closed, at which time only an appeal in court was allowed. When cuts were required, the distributor/producer was responsible for making them and resubmitting the film for classification.[29] Each time the film was classified, a sum of money ranging from US $400 to $900 depending on the length of the film, was expected for the task.[30] Thus the censorship process became a money-making endeavor for the state. The economic-based argument was one of the reasons that Tato boasted in 1975 that with the prohibition of thirty-four films the country had saved $300,000. "When we reach two hundred banned films, [the communique adds], we can expect to save for the nation amounts on the order of US $1,500,000.00."[31] During the time when law 18.019 was in effect, a total of 725 films were affected. This included the films that were released with cuts, prohibited, or those that were never released commercially.[32]

THE BÓ-SARLI PRODUCTIONS AND THE CENSORSHIP CONTEXT

Productions during 1957–63

From its beginning the process to implement full legal censorship arguably put pressure on independent producers like Bó-Sarli, who struggled with the new measures imposed on their pioneering film shots of female bodies, which pushed the limits of what local screens could exhibit regarding sexuality. One may even wonder whether the laws developing to control onscreen appearances were trying to keep up with the duo's experiments. Significantly, their work fits seamlessly into the historical framework of censorship's centralization from 1957 to 1984. From their first production, *Thunder among the Leaves*, they experienced a form of oversight. It was finished in February of 1957 but not released until one-and-a-half years later, a time frame typical for most of their films. Law/decree 62/57 limited the possibility of release at home as the film did not receive category A status. Sarli was obliged to travel with it to the Karlovy-Vary International Film Festival to present it abroad before it premiered nationally, already setting in motion one of the perceived characteristics of their work that emerged later, as a commercial enterprise meant for international audiences. Such delays in release were not uncommon. *Las aguas bajan turbias* (*Dark River*) in 1951–52 experienced a similar delay when director Hugo del Carril was accused of being a communist for working with a script based on the novel *Río Oscuro* (*Dark River*) by the imprisoned political writer Alfredo Varela. Yet in the case of *Thunder among the Leaves*, the film set a precedent for how Sarli-Bó films would be treated because of their one constant feature: the displaying of Isabel Sarli's body and bodies in general. The film was finally released on 2 October 1958. After the INC attempted to cut scenes, it classified it as "restricted for those under the age of 18."[33]

The biggest obstacle Bó-Sarli faced, however, was Penal Code 128. Any citizen could denounce those who "publish, produce or reproduce books, writing, images or objects that are obscene and those who expose, distribute, or circulate them."[34] Violation brought with it a prison term of fifteen days to one year. The public prosecutor de la Riestra claimed that *Thunder among the Leaves* was "attacking morals and good customs."[35] For some reason Sarli's nudes were more offensive than nudes from Europe. For instance, both *Hon dansade en sommar* (*One Summer of Happiness*, Arne Mattsson, Sweden, 1951) and *Sommaren med Monika* (*Summer with Monika*, Ingmar Bergman, Sweden, 1953) were playing in Buenos Aires without any problems. The films had inspired Bó to include a controversial nude swimming scene similar to the one in *One Summer of Happiness* in his first feature with Sarli. Sarli even attests to Bó taking her to see the avant-garde foreign films in preparation for her role in *Thunder among the Leaves*.[36] While the two Swedish pictures had no issues playing in the capital region, Sarli's were different. Her body was considered too "ostentatious," and that made it "provocative" for the audience.[37] In the case of *The Shad Fishermen*, their follow-up film, the INC did not delay its premiere; but, like its predecessor, one week after it appeared onscreen it was seized and under court restriction not allowed to play in theaters for infringement of Code 128.[38] The producers of both the first and second feature faced criminal charges for distributing obscene materials.

Given that the first two experiments were tied up with the courts, their third one, *India*, was handled differently. *India* was a film about a criminal who flees to the jungles and comes across an indigenous tribe. He falls in love with Ansisé, the chief's mixed-race daughter. The example of *India* demonstrates that while legally there was no indication of the practice of preproduction manipulation by the INC through decree 62/57, control was already taking place before it became the law. Bó consulted intensively with INC Director Emilio Solezzi to ensure that the film would not experience delays once it was completed. During the production of *India* it became clear that the problem was not nudity per se, but Sarli's body itself.[39] Maká women were allowed to appear topless. Playing a mixed daughter of the Maká people's leader, Sarli had to wear a minidress to cover her body (fig. 2). As the diva herself attests: "The authentic indigenous women could show their breasts but not I."[40] The threat that Ansisé's body poses is evident. She is positioned differently from the indigenous women, hiding her *mestiza* or white breasts under cloth while the others expose their indigenous intimate body parts in an anthropological and ethnographical spectacle. The fully clothed Ansisé only reveals her nude body during the bath scene in color under the Iguazu Falls (fig. 3). The waterfall scenes were tolerated because they were deemed of aesthetic quality. However, the sexualized images had to be hidden under red concentric circles that both concealed the spectacle of the skin but most importantly highlighted the underlying nudity of the star in a technique that marked its self-conscious extradiegetic bright-red psychedelic loops in a scene shot in color. The combination of all elements destabilizes the body of the star, as a white or *mestiza*, female nude body, although she appears in brownface. On the one hand Sarli is exceptional because her body, unlike the bodies of the Maká women, is deemed both desirable and threatening. Although her face was painted in brown makeup, her body bears the mark of her whiteness, and her sexuality thus must be covered. Unlike the Maká women, who are documented in their "natural" state, Sarli's body is sexualized and performed as a spectacle. An exception is made for the scenes of natural beauty that were

FIGURE 2. Ansisé, in the foreground in this still from *India* (1960), wears a dress to cover her breasts, while the Maká women in the background appear topless.

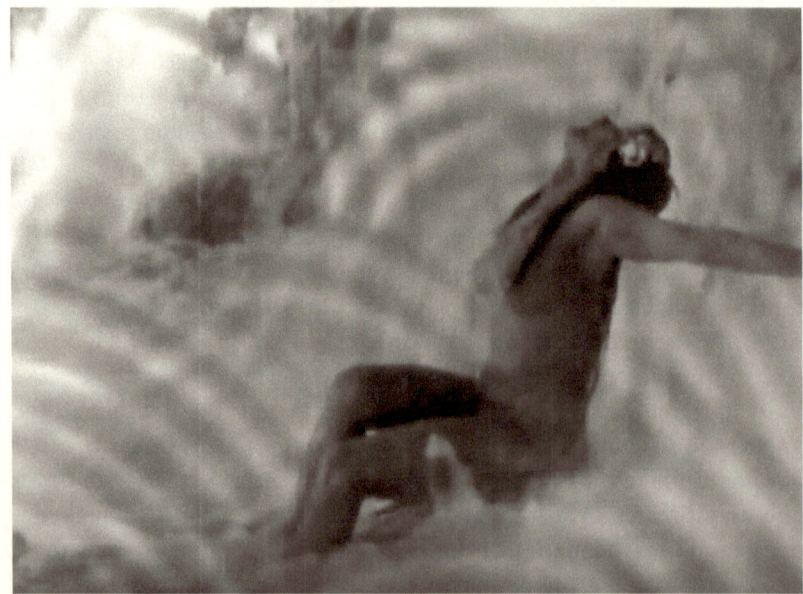

FIGURE 3. Ansisé in Iguazu Falls is nude but masked behind red concentric circles to create a dream-like sequence and hide Sarli's provocative body.

deemed in good taste. In the waters of Iguazu Falls, the natural landscape motivated the director of the INC to allow the scene to remain in the film, but the scene was risky. Even if the aesthetic value were equivalent to that of earlier foreign models, the national examples needed more restraint. Nevertheless, despite the cautious consultation with the INC, others did not deem the concessions enough, and *India* was denounced as offending the judgment and good morals of Argentines under Code 128.

While the first three films were seized by the courts, *India* was released a month and a half later by Judge Luis María Ragucci, due to not finding sufficient cause to prosecute its actors, director, and producer.[41]

This initial period of the Sarli-Bó collaboration represents their first attempt to work within a system that was seemingly more open but had at its disposal structures that inhibited certain images from being seen in public. Bó's films did receive special treatment, and the INC imposed a clear direction for the duo to follow. Court proceedings were effective at hindering the full exploitation of Sarli's appeal and delaying the release of most productions. In the end, they won all cases filed against the first four films. On the other hand, the negotiations in the case of *India* and Bó's practiced restraint in *Heat*, *The Girl Ass-Keeper of Ypacaraí*, and *Favela* exemplify how he was trying to make films within a legal framework, one that was beginning to shift and change. Despite their concessions, the Bó-Sarli pair were already categorized as problematic. While they received A-list status for some productions, they were experiencing prior censorship when legally this was not the norm. Both *Heat* and *The Girl Ass-keeper of Ypacaraí* received A category ratings. The latter placed fifteenth in the productions for the year of its release in 1961, allowing for funding and a prize for cinematography to be awarded to Julio Lavera, both contentious moves in the industry.[42] In the case of *Heat*, Sarli does not bare her body, given that the duo still had two films stuck in court proceedings (*Thunder among the Leaves* and *The Shad Fishermen*). Nonetheless, a complaint was filed before the courts for the scene in the film, which shows Bó brutally beating the sea lions on the island, a practice he claims still existed at the time.[43]

From the beginning Sarli and Bó were a hit in Argentina, but they were also not making any money because of all the court challenges that kept their films off the screens. These somewhat financially failed experiments of their early filmmaking ended with Sarli working on a project titled *The Female* (Leopoldo Torre Nilsson, 1962) and Bó returning to his soccer films with *Pelota de cuero* (*Leather Ball*, 1962), which he stars in and directs, a break from the pair's shared ventures and the headaches of being challenged at every turn.

Productions during 1963–66

The tightening in 1963 through law 8.205 produced an outcry that culminated in a protest against the looming threat of censorship. Reactions by the press, the film clubs, and critics motivated meetings, debates, roundtables, and interviews with authorities. In January 1964 in the Presidente Alvear Theatre, many filmmakers and artists gathered to express their discontent with the new law. Auteur-director Torre Nilsson, who had personally been through the prohibition of a film with the unreleased *The Tigress*, gave a speech about the problem and impact of censorship.[44] He asked a full theater of supporters:

> What has made the state, national sovereignty, and economic stability worse: a supposed noxious cinema or the parades of tanks on the streets, the quarrels of the ministry, or its unscrupulous negotiations?[45]

In the same speech, Torre Nilsson asks: "I want to know whether cinema has begotten as many delinquents as unemployment, hunger, misery." He suggests that the true enemies of the state are: "those who do not know how to use the pen or the paintbrush but instead glorify fire and scissors."[46] As head of the Generation of 1960, Torre Nilsson was leading a young group of filmmakers to fight against censorship.

Bó, arguably censorship's most affected and individual opponent, was conspicuously absent from the protest. And yet, at this time he was busy traveling and filming abroad to resume the early coproduction work that characterized their cheap films. From their first feature and throughout *The Shad Fishermen* and *India*, official and nonofficial coproductions with Paraguay, the duo established a trademark that branded them as transnational. A film like *Favela* shot in Rio inspired similar collaboration. The second phase, when they returned from their independent projects to work again as a duo, showcased productions like *Lujuria tropical* (*Tropical Lust*, 1964), coproduced with Venezuela; *The Impure Goddess*, shot in Mexico, and then *The Lioness* shot on Brazil's Paquetá Island.[47] The association with Colombia Pictures International and Pel-Mex began to generate more coproductions and work that took the pair outside of Argentina. One wonders whether the clear shift toward the exterior was solely because of their interests in expansion or whether on some level they had no choice but to try their work abroad, to ensure that the productions they wanted to make were seen. While they had a vested interest in remaining within the nation where their base audience was strong, they also continued to venture outside because the limited possibilities in Argentina were becoming more and more difficult to navigate. Very little is known about how censorship impacted the Sarli and Bó's careers in Argentina during the 1963–66 period of decree 8.205, but it is certain that they did continue to expand the more international aspects of their cinema.

While Bó and Sarli were seeking to capture a more international audience, their content was being rejected at home. For instance, *The Shoemaker's Wife* received such bad reviews that Bó was inspired to write an open letter to the press questioning their motives and their favoritism or preference for foreign "bad" films rather than local ones.[48] Even such a seemingly innocent film was deemed controversial. The comedy was about a young vixen who marries a shoemaker in a small town. He gives her all that she desires. The naïve depiction was exhibited in San Juan, Argentina, in its full uncensored version in 1965. It featured a nude Sarli in a few scenes; but in the censored version she was wearing a bathing suit and underwear in the contentious shots. The San Juan city council closed the Renacimiento Theatre for five days and fined its owners for not exhibiting the proper version of *The Shoemaker's Wife* with the cuts that the National Classification Honorary Council had required for an exhibition meant for an audience over eighteen years old. The League for the Protection of Minors, one of the family leagues advocating for censorship, had classified the film as prohibited for those under the age of twenty-two.[49] At this point there was more breathing room for producers as required cuts were not yet confiscated by the censors.

But what is clear in this example is that both sides of the censorship debate had their own tactics: one such strategy by the National Classification Honorary Council was to delay the classification of a film, thus leading to a fine for any screenings without the obligatory certificate and confiscation of the film. Likewise, producers and directors such as Bó had their own schemes. They released films before they were classified in order to create a scandal and attract bigger audiences once their films were classified and allowed to screen. While law 8.205 set a standard, it was still flexible enough to provide an out for directors who wanted to challenge the status quo.

Productions during 1966–73

After 1966 the laws were clearly becoming more intrusive, and consequently Sarli-Bó's work was kept under a watchful eye, regardless of where it was shot. There is a correlation between the censorship inflicted on the individual projects and the boundaries that the films were pushing. In part, the freedom of expression explored in the films existed because Bó-Sarli's work fit within the international wave of youthful sexual nonconformity that was garnering a newfound audience, particularly abroad. Films such as *Naked Temptation, Meat, Fuego, Naked on the Sand,* and *Fever* became huge successes within Latin America as well as in the sexploitation markets in the United States and Europe. The accolades garnered outside of Argentina encouraged the couple to take more risks and be more daring, as did the demands by their distributor Colombia Pictures International. At home, however, the opposite was happening; the bold scenarios, audacious subject matter, and enterprising sketches became a clear point of contention with the authorities. The pressure from both sides explains the development of dual versions of each film. While at first the negotiation with authorities like the INC and the censor boards was more on a film-by-film basis, as the laws were tightening it made sense to make concessions before the films were submitted for review. The hot and cold versions typical of early sexploitation, in which hot meant more nudes and sex, whereas cold meant less skin, is inverted by Bó in his description of what he terms "impure" and "pure." Playful with the paradigm set in the Global North, Bó describes the cold or covered-up versions as "pure," whereas the hot ones with the original scenes were "impure."[50] As Fernando Martín Peña explains, Bó's terminology uncovers an essential prudishness on the part of the creator.[51] Alternatively it can relate to the mischievousness of an auteur who had to play with the censors' ire to screen his work.

More importantly, the period marked by decree 16.955 (1966–68) was characterized by delayed film releases and, in one case, a premiere taking place abroad before it could take place at home. Earlier films such as *Naked Temptation, The Mayor's Wife,* and *My Father's Wife* all took one whole year to be released. The more contentious ones that followed under law 18.019, like *Fuego, Tropical Extasy, Fever,* and *Bewitched,* took much longer. For instance, *Bewitched* was made in 1969 but not released until 1976. In the story, Leandro, an entrepreneur who exploits his workers, is married to Ansisé. She is an indigenous woman who was taken away from her kin and is now obsessed with having a baby but never gets pregnant. About this film, a journalistic note chronicles a meeting between Isabel Sarli and the director of the censor board, Ramiro de la Fuente. Notably flustered, Sarli explains that they "didn't prohibit my latest film, *Bewitched*, but they made so many cuts that we can't project it."[52] Apparently, "the baths [scenes] are scandalous."[53] In 1966 Bó was detained because he accused the censors of taking bribes. He had been trying to get the certificate to screen *My Father's Wife* for seven months.[54] After being told to cut a posterior shot of Sarli entering the Iguazu Falls, Bó defended himself by citing an example in *Zorba, the Greek* (Michael Cacoyannis, Greece/USA, 1964), which reveals shots of Anthony Quinn's buttocks and was shown uncut in Argentina.

On the other hand, *Meat* had a relatively timely but heavily censored release within a year of being made. In this story, Delicia works at the local meatpacking company. On her way to work she is brutally violated by Humberto, a cruel worker, given the name of "El Macho." On 20 September 1979, ten years after its original debut, a new screening of the film showcased the whole uncensored version for the first time in Argentina (fig. 4). As the text in the ad highlights, this was "The Unveiling of Isabel Sarli": "as you had imagined her, now you can see her." Many thought *Meat*'s rerelease meant a loosening in censorship restrictions, but one month later *Insatiable* was given the harshest judgement of all, as it was banned outright. It was the only "sexy" national film to be banned altogether, though 116 foreign films suffered the same fate.[55] *Tropical Ecstasy* took nine years to be released and *Fever* only two.[56] However, *Fever* had its own problems. The controversial scene with the horses engaging in coitus caused the INC to take away the funding given to directors from the ticket sales. The pair protested the decision with a hunger strike on the Plaza de Mayo in front of the president's house, la Casa Rosada.

The case of *Fuego*, Sarli-Bó's most screened film, presents yet a different example. *Fuego* was prohibited from the beginning. Armando Bó had four sessions with the censors, and in each they demanded new cuts, so much so that the story was unintelligible. The film included:

> Sexual perversions, lascivious scenes, or ones that upset morals and good customs . . . a film with scenes with high erotic content, lesbianism, and unfettered passions that can produce conflict for minors.[57]

Instead of negotiating a censored premiere in Argentina, Bó debuted the film in New York. When it finally played in Argentina in 1971 with two missing scenes, it had already spent twenty weeks in New York and

FIGURE 4. Advertisement for *Meat* (1968) upon its rerelease with previously censored scenes, *Heraldo del Cine: Semanario Internacional Dedicado al Espectáculo*, no. 2494, 13 September 1979. Courtesy of the library at the Escuela Nacional de Experimentación y Realización Cinematográfica

garnered an international audience that continued to bolster the pair's fandom. The intricate history of each film is only scantily told in these vignettes. But there is one such case that gives insight into the complexities of how censorship worked and its many layers for producers and directors to work through, a story that is told by one of the files in the censorship archive.

THE CASE OF *INTIMACIES OF A PROSTITUTE*

Within this context, the case of *Intimacies of a Prostitute*, Classification Board file 504/72, offers a meaningful example. *Intimacies of a Prostitute* was shot in 1971 and finally released on 2 May 1974 as *Intimacies of a Nobody*.[58] The time line spans a very important change in government, a shift that meant the return of Juan Domingo Perón after an eighteen-year exile in Spain. While reconstructing what actually happened to the film is almost impossible since only parts of the file are accessible, using primary materials (the partial file, DVD of an eighty-six-minute version of the film, film laws, and press coverage) helps understand the span of film censorship and how the Bó-Sarli vehicle represented a challenge to these different historical moments. The file on *Intimacies of a Prostitute*, the only one remaining of the Bó-Sarli films, sheds light on three specific periods of film censorship in Argentina. First, the full implementation of law 18.019 under the directorship of Ramiro de la Fuente, the lawyer and ultraconservative Catholic who served from 1963 to 1973. Second, the period of shifts at the Classification Board under the directorship of Octavio Getino, whose mandate from the INC was to change the process of censorship and help develop and implement a new law for film classification that repealed law 18.019.[59] Despite the more liberal environment, the film was not released during Getino's directorship. It still took *Intimacies of a Prostitute* another year to be released under the third period, when Horacio Bordo served as interim director until Tato replaced him in August 1974.

Intimacies of a Prostitute follows the usual formula of the Bó-Sarli duo—a mix of melodrama, socially conscious cinema, and erotic elements where love always triumphs. The film begins with a voice-over of the protagonist, María, telling the story of her difficult life as a sex worker and offering a confession of her intimacies. After being exploited in her hometown by her stepfather, his friends, and her employers, and motivated by her boyfriend, Cholo, she moves to the big city to find work to help pay for her ailing mother's treatment. In the city she encounters the same abuse from men and turns to sex work with the help and guidance of a friend, who in the end will help her see the value of her work as a prostitute. Cholo joins her and becomes her pimp, further exploiting her. She experiences much misfortune and is even imprisoned. After her release she returns home to a very sick mother. Upon seeing María and discovering she is a sex worker, her mother dies. Determined not to be exploited anymore, María chooses to travel throughout the country with Cholo.

In a very progressive vein, the narrative acknowledges that many things need to be done to help prostitutes: laws need to change and society must understand their circumstances and accept the valuable work they do. In Patagonia María meets a rich landowner, José Luis, who falls in love with her and wants to rescue her from her hardship. Even though she marries José Luis, Cholo is not willing to give her up. In the end José Luis and Cholo fight and Cholo falls off a cliff to his death, leaving María and José Luis free to live happily ever after. Despite the reestablishment of heteronormative sex at the end, the story challenged the moral codes expected in the cinema at the time.

INTIMACIES OF A PROSTITUTE'S CONVOLUTED PATH TO BEING RELEASED

The partial file shows that *Intimacies of a Prostitute* was first given to the Classification Board to review on 10 July 1972, at which time it was categorized as prohibited. The results from the first appraisal initiated a process of negotiation, which began with a consultation between Bó and the Classification Board on 1 August 1972 and resulted in a reclassification on 5 December 1972. However, a letter from the Council dated 11 December 1972 changed that status to "restricted for those under the age of 18" pending the following detailed modifications:

> cutting the scene of the coitus with the store owner, suppressing the lesbian scenes in the jail, the word "dyke" and the shot where she begins to take off the apron of the other inmate, suppress the scene showing the sexual organs of the man in the light blue housecoat, [remove] nude coitus with the protagonist moaning in the washroom, [remove] coitus in the marshes, [remove] shot where the protagonist walks toward the lake, opens her nightgown, kisses on the breasts in the stream, and [remove] bath of the protagonist naked in the trailer.[60]

The letter by de la Fuente explains that the film was viewed in three versions and that the first two could not be authorized. He concurs with the Council that this new version became permissible once it was cut accordingly. He states:

> They [referring to the cuts] are so numerous that it becomes difficult, if not impossible, to list them all in the usual way. On the other hand, the similarity of some with what has already been authorized leaves as its only guarantee of control the fact that these [cuts] remain in deposit, as will be noted in the certificate.[61]

Both letters underline some of the intricacies of the process and the objections the film received. The Council was separate from the director of the Classification Board and could potentially interpret the law differently, though the director had the final word. As a matter of fact, that occurred in this case: de la Fuente overruled the use of the word "dyke" since he felt it could be used for an audience over eighteen. Nevertheless, he did add further cuts: "The shot where one can distinguish the sex organs of the man in the light blue housecoat; the part where the protagonist, walking toward the lake, opens her housecoat; and other shots that remain in the deposit."[62] The aforesaid highlights another problem: some cuts remained with the Classification Board and others remained with the director of the film. The implication of the Classification Board's power to retain the excised remains complicates even further any attempt at piecing together a history of this film because the remnants have suffered the same fate as the files.[63]

While limited, this portion of the file accentuates the scenes that were seen as challenging the law and the ideological morally-based censorship that was being put in place. At the end of the file there is a two-page list of the "dialogues and observable scenes" in the film. While the list referred to was definitely composed after de la Fuente left (which we can conclude because the title of the film differs from the one used in the de la Fuente part of the file), it hints at some of the scenes that were in the film before the cuts. A comparison between the two-page list and the eighty-six-minute version available today on DVD shows some clear inconsistencies between the final version and the original. What was cut was what was seen as the excess of sexuality. The sex shown in the film was cut to the point that certain scenes showed nothing, and others only insinuated sexual acts, resulting in the excesses and intimacies of the sex act being radically minimized. The final cut produces a very awkward version of the film, with many scenes seemingly interrupting its narrative cohesion and exposing the very act of cutting and censoring. As a result, there are clear gaps in the narrative and style that go beyond the cheap aesthetics of the Bó-Sarli pair. As has been noted previously, the cuts performed by the censors, who were not necessarily filmmakers (as with de la Fuente), exposed the censorship apparatus. At times one wonders whether parts of this were done deliberately by Bó to divulge the censorship that was taking place.

There are some patterns in the censorship that need further fleshing out to better understand what may have been considered offensive. Primarily, the frontal nude scene of the man with the light blue housecoat is a problem for both the Council and the director of the Classification Board. The married man in question is María's ex-employer, meaning that she continued to see him in her sex work. Despite this clear violation of the prohibition of representations of adultery, the censors' problem with the scene has more to do with male nudity itself. While both José Luis and Cholo appear nude in parts of the film, you never really see intimate segments of their bodies. However, María's nude body is shown in its entirety throughout the film. The camera captures all her intimate parts and does so for all angles. The opening of the film and the later scenes of María in the water during her time with her new husband José Luis clearly show her breasts, pubic areas, and buttocks, albeit only momentarily. Although María appears completely nude in the water and her whole body is visible, the water's constant movement as she swims around makes it difficult to actually contain some parts of her body, especially her pubic area and buttocks. There are clearer and longer shots of her breasts. The documentation refers to two male nude scenes that were eventually cut from the film: the first of the male actor in the light blue housecoat with a shot of his penis and the second of Cholo's buttocks when he is raping María near the end of the movie. Both scenes in question are cut in an awkward way in order to avoid exposing male bodies. The discrepancy and hypocrisy about what are permissible for both male and female bodies exposes an inconsistency in the application of the law by whoever was doing the cutting. The current version available still does not include the original male nude scenes.

Moreover, the documentation reveals a particular problem with the prison scenes, when María meets a woman with whom she has sex. By building into the narrative a same-sex scene, *Intimacies of a Prostitute* ventures into the popular genre of women in prison films, in vogue in the late 1960s and throughout the 1970s. Clearly the scene in question was offensive, because from a Catholic perspective it could be argued that it violated three of law 18.019's principles: it was "offending the family," "justifying . . . sexual perversions," and "incorporating lascivious scenes that upset morals and good customs."[64] In the current version the scene is absent, and what is left of it lasts barely a minute. Yet in the documentation, it seems to be the film's most contentious part. In Diego Curubeto's *Meat on Meat*, a documentary about Bó-Sarli's censored material, Curubeto features a clip from the scene, proving that Bó kept the scene in his own archive rather than submitting it to the censor's deposit. Given the documentation, I suspect that the Classification Board itself further cut much of the same scene. To recreate the whole original, one would need access to clips in both archives. In the final released version, the sex is hardly visible, only insinuated and awkwardly executed. The Council does express much concern about the topic, suggesting to "suppress lesbian scenes in jail," as a general note.[65] De la Fuente does not particularly mention the scene, but it is clear that he makes necessary cuts to the film in general, cuts all too obvious in the fragmented eighty-six-minute version. The actual encounter, which features a woman kissing María on the shoulders and peeling off her uniform, is interrupted by a suspicious guard's arrival. The sex continues, but it is only heard as background during a shot of a wall. The lead-up features a conversation between the two, interrupted various times by a cutaway to a fight scene and a flash-forward to the actual sex. The sequence looks as clumsy as it sounds due to its many cuts, leaving a very fragmented scene. The file has allowed for reading how censorship was enacted during de la Fuente's stint as director of the Classification Board, who took it upon himself to make edits he deemed necessary in interpreting the law, independent of the Council.

On 14 December 1972 the film received the official classification certificate from de la Fuente. This version runs for ninety minutes, four minutes longer than the current version on DVD, an important point as studying the work of Bó and Sarli is always complicated by the many versions that existed and the few that are still available. Nonetheless, on the certificate in the file, de la Fuente's signature is missing. There is a gap in the documentation of what happens after the certificate is authorized, since the film was not released until one-and-a-half years later.

A HICCUP IN THE SYSTEM

After Héctor Cámpora came to power and democracy brought the return of Perón to Argentina in 1973, a liberalization of the INC and the Classification Board also took place. Peronist filmmaker Hugo del Carril was named director of the INC, but his commitments abroad meant that classical filmmaker Mario Soffici acted in his place until his return. On 8 August 1973 Octavio Getino took the directorship of the Classification Board for a period of ninety days.[66] In this time he restructured the Board and replaced the leagues, which made up the Council, with others, involving instead psychologists, psychoanalysts, sociologists, film critics, and directors in the classification exercise.[67] The Classification Board then allowed the release of many films previously prohibited for political reasons, such as *State of Siege* and *The Devils* (Ken Russell, UK, 1971) and others for moral reasons like *The Decameron* (Pier Paolo Pasolini, Italy/France/West Germany, 1971) and *Last Tango in Paris* (Bernardo Bertolucci, France/Italy, 1972).[68] During Getino's period, the Classification Board classified rather than censoring films, and he set up experimental public classification sessions where the public decided if the film was suitable for all, or for those over fourteen or eighteen.[69] When Getino's term was coming to an end, he had a falling out with the minister of culture, which terminated his position. However, Getino continued to work with the government as adviser on film legislation until the death of Perón on 1 July 1974.[70] Tato was made the head of the Classification Board after Perón's death in August 1974, the same month when President Isabel María Estela Martínez de Perón signed the new film law proposed by the INC and others, which would in fact be shelved. After the death of Perón, the activities of the Left and the Triple A, a right-wing state violence group that was responsible for the disappearance of thirty thousand people, became more commonplace. The country entered a political crisis that led to the military coup of 25 March 1976.

To return to the film, the gap between the certificate issued by de la Fuente and the next document, a letter by Getino dated 1 September 1973, spans almost a year. The delay suggests that in the end *Intimacies of a Prostitute* did not get the final approval from the Classification Board. In his letter, Getino gives Manuel Augusto Padilla, the assistant director of the Classification Board, the authority to classify the film. Padilla's letter dated 13 September 1973 states that "the lesbian sequence performed in the women's prison, due to its harsh realism and its content and prolonged duration, infringes on some of the dispositions of article 2 of 18.019."[71] Article 2 outlines the six areas that must be avoided in film. He also explains that to achieve immediate classification the Board must follow the current rules as stipulated by the government, meaning that, given the law, flexibility is minimal. Therefore, the lesbian scene still presented problems even for this new, more progressive leadership with a liberal agenda, which was already permitting films to be released that had previously been banned. The objection to the lesbian scene affirms the fact that sexuality was not a priority for the ideological Left. Moreover, it also suggests that nonheteronormative sex was still unacceptable. Its inclusion in *Intimacies of a Prostitute* and other places like *Fuego* was a challenge to societal norms.

During the same period, on 11 September 1973 in *La Gaceta*, a film trade magazine, Getino publicly warned "Not so much eroticism."[72] Apparently, he had been inundated with erotic films for new classification; out of the seventeen films he received, nine were "objectionable and bordered on pornography."[73] His argument is based not on the moral standards of the law but on the fact that the changes he was making to the Classification Board were enduring real criticism from important organizations. Therefore, classification of all newly made erotic and pornographic films justified the work of those trying to stop the changes from occurring. Getino even spoke for fifty minutes at a conference explaining his strategy. In other words, in order to change the law and eliminate censorship altogether, he needed to apply questions of freedom *judiciously*. In the end, he didn't think that films selling sex contributed to his more serious political cause. He also pointed out that Penal Code 128 was still in effect, and even if he were to release all pornographic films people could denounce them in court for being "obscene." His public condemnation of films that were selling sex took place precisely in the time frame when Bó-Sarli submitted *Intimacies of a Prostitute* for reclassification.

Bó responded to Getino's and Padilla's remarks with a letter asking for the swift classification of the new version of *Intimacies of a Prostitute*, which had some new cuts but had also included some scenes previously eliminated. The letter implies that while the Classification Board still existed as an overriding body there was, at least perceptably, more freedom to express what appears onscreen. Bó's instincts were correct; on 18 September 1973 both Padilla and Getino classified the new version as "restricted for those under the age of 18." However, its new classification was not enough for the film's release since no certificate was apparently given at the time.

Interestingly, the documentation on the actual release of the film is not present in the file, but from the press notes we can surmise a few things about its ultimate premiere. On 19 March 1974, an article explained that distributor Columbia-Warner changed a word in the name of the film from *prostitute* to *nobody*. The INC gave *Intimacies of a Prostitute* an

A certificate on 23 April 1974, and finally on 2 May 1974 the film premiered at the Normandie Theatre and in nineteen other small theaters in the barrios or outskirts of Buenos Aires in a ninety-five-minute version that does not exist today. *Intimacies of a Prostitute* was approved under Horacio Bordo as temporary head of the Classification Board and Mario Soffici as the director of the INC, two months before Perón died and three before Tato took over the Classification Board.

In the final version, the change from *prostitute* to *nobody* (*prostituta* to *cualquiera*) is a significant one. *Cualquiera* literally means "anybody or no one," but in slang terms it is a euphemistic way of referring to a hussy, tramp, woman of ill repute, or whore. In the first scene the character explains: "My name is of no concern, actually they are my intimacies, the intimacies of a prostitute who is courageous enough to confess." Her dialogue employs the word *prostitute*, and the character emphasizes that her identity is not what matters but instead what counts is the value of her story and the need to assert her voice. It is important to note that while the title was censored, the opening statement was not, which makes one wonder, Why make the change in the first place given that her profession is never kept a secret? Like the Sui Generis song where the censor "does not name her," the film title attempts to erase her specific identity. On the one hand, she becomes a *cualquiera*, a nobody or a María (a very common female name that may also imply a nobody), with a generic story, an erasure of identity that one might argue foreshadows what happens with *los desaparecidos* (the disappeared), those who were murdered during the 1976–83 dictatorship without any explanation of their whereabouts. On the other hand, the film presents "intimacies," a story about a specific sex worker, and a specific film, which underwent an incredible journey through different intimate moments with various censors until its ultimate release. The title change adds an extra layer of complication for the critic who is trying to piece together its intricate film history.

At the beginning of the film, the credit sequence where the actual title appears also leaves traces of a convoluted process. The title shot, with the edited name, is worthy of some reflection. The final word is covered over by a black mark beneath the red letters of *cualquiera* (fig. 5). This is an ingenious, if not also openly resentful, way of dealing with the title change on Bó's part—it is quite noticeable that he had to cover over the *prostitute* by blacking it out and then adding the new name. In fact, the technique both emphasizes the word *cualquiera* and draws attention to the censorship. In other words, it reminds its viewers of a technique

FIGURE 5. Opening credits for *Intimacies of a Prostitute* (1974), reflecting the censorship of the title from *prostituta* to *cualquiera* (nobody)

commonly used to hide what may not be shown with a black strip, clearly referring to the act of censorship itself, of refusing to show the intimacy onscreen. More problematic however, is that the title sequence appears after a medium shot of Sarli, tilting down toward her feet and showing everything that is in between. The title appears right below her pubic area, and it too emphasizes the same bodily part that was cut on a male character and barely seen on the female in the movie. Her pubic area is also covered by the letters of the title. With its cuts, *Intimacies of a Prostitute* still embodies the contradictions of the period and the convolutedness of showing sex onscreen at a time of tightening regulation.

THE *PAUTAS* AND THE DICTATORSHIP

The official guidelines for film production or *Pautas*, as they were called, were released on 4 May 1976, just over a month after the most brutal dictatorship rose to power in Argentina. The new provisions, which were meant not to add stipulations to the existing laws but to reinforce their true spirit, were based on law 18.019, and thus clarified any ambiguity in the legal framework. The media covered the release, which involved summoning film producers to the INC for a reading of the new directives. Portions of the manuscript were released to the press. The whole dossier, housed at the ENERC, contains the original documents by the Secretariat of the Press and Dissemination signed by army officials responsible for the department. Two distinct areas can be highlighted in the dossier: (1) the strengthening of moral values that underlie all laws relating to film production and (2) the directed focus on the youth in the guidelines, all of which indicate clear assumptions about what constitutes good taste in moral and cultural terms.

At the foundation of the guidelines are core values maintaining the same Christian morals that inspired previous laws. The call begins by touting the fundamental ethics that are central to society: order, industriousness, hierarchy, responsibility, suitability, and honesty.[74] In regard to sexuality, two specific points are made. First, there is a call to eradicate stimuli based on "sexualism" and violence. The word *sexualism* referred to the natural "instincts" of males. Most of the Bó-Sarli films operated under the assumption of the violent nature of male sexuality, clearly violating the first principle. Second, there is a clear indication that all terms and images that are obscene, lewd, shocking, or appealing to erotic or double entendre must be limited.[75] Both stipulations became obstacles for the Bó-Sarli productions since their basic topics and themes could easily be rejected.

The *Pautas* advise future projects to abide by the clear rules stipulated by the government. The warnings were meant to orient the film business and lead its practitioners toward more cohesive productions with values that aligned better with national priorities. They also made a promise to fund more films via scripts, but these films needed to follow the prescriptions outlined here. The *Pautas* warned that if films were already in production that funding or "serious mutilation" could be at risk.

A separate memorandum was released on 10 November 1976, specifically geared toward guiding the films made for a youth audience. The call encouraged youth films to align with adult ideals and promote intergenerational dialogue based on collaboration, faith in the future order, and confidence in authority; all values antithetical to the 1960s and 1970s youth movements. The aim was to "encourage maturity, commitment to the normative, responsibility, generosity, order, and virility."[76] Clearly, the appeal to the youth accentuates how the new power continued to see film and media as a potential for maintaining a structure of authority and keeping the manipulated masses within normative moral standards. Aimed at young people prior to the dictatorship, the solution was meant to fix the problem of youth: to restore the hierarchy so that youth only reproduced models set by their elders, not questioning the status quo or the power of authority figures. The message delivered to the young reinforces the underlying assumption that censorship functioned to protect and defend those who were incapable of making decisions for themselves.

Tato's own testimony exemplifies the same patronizing attitude not just to youth but to everyone:

> The cinema that I want [is] positive, clean, decent; a cinema that is cultural, not only industrial. . . . Argentines, in reality, are not mature enough for certain things, and movies can be bad for us. I speak of course about a lot of Argentines, not all. In any case, it's not about defending he who is mature, but those who are less mature. It's not about attacking a right but about defending the people who do not know how to do it.[77]

While young people were the clear target, the rules affected everyone; the state made sure to control people's choices regarding the content of films.

In the change that brought the dictatorship to power, Miguel Paulino Tato was the only official to survive the transition. He held his position until 21 September 1978, when Alberto León, a conservative lawyer and member of the Central Commission of the League of Fathers, took over the Classification Board. While not as severe as Tato, León led one of the darkest periods of film production in Argentina, but he also began to open up practices from 1979 until the downfall of the dictatorship, which brought a new future with a different law. The majority of the films made between 1976 and 1983 were light sexual comedies featuring provocatively dressed women, sexual innuendos, and local stars like Jorge Porcel, Alberto Olmedo, Susana Giménez, Moria Casán, Adriana Aguirre, and Graciela Alfano. Many were produced by Aries Producciones. Althugh the sex comedies may have offended the rules set by the *Pautas*, productions were considered acceptable because they represented repressive, misogynous, and even violent tendencies that were for the most part complicit with the regime because everyone knew their role in the hierarchy. Although on occasion the Classification Board did repress some of these teasing films, they were generally meant for domestic audiences with local content that had very little exportability.[78]

In the case of the Bó-Sarli productions, by the time the dictatorship had arrived, some other films had yet to be released like *Bewitched* and *Tropical Ecstasy*, which premiered in 1976 and 1978 respectively.

Both debuted during the dictatorship, many years after they were made, but with countless cuts to the originals. *A Butterfly in the Night* was another Sarli-Bó production made between October and November 1975 and released in a heavily censored version on 5 September 1977. Bó-Sarli made three other films during this period of authoritarian rule: *Insatiable*, *Last Love in Tierra del Fuego*, and *A Madcap Widow*. The first spent years under review before it was finally banned on October 1979, and it never premiered as long as the dictatorship was in power and Bó was alive. The League of Decency in Rosario issued a public communiqué against the film, which shows the type of displeasure that it generated:

> It is inadmissible that in our country films such as the one mentioned can be made, in which the main character plays a nymphomaniac and resorts to such a poor story in order to exhibit all kinds of immoralities. . . . We are surprised that the censors have not prohibited other films inexplicably being exhibited, and which even receive subsidies.[79]

The film was released on 23 September 1984 and seen for the first time in its entirety when the law changed following the end of the dictatorship. According to an ad for the screening: ". . . And censorship cries, cries, cries: The public said yes! The only Argentine film that, prohibited by the courts 'in safeguarding public morals,' could not be exhibited, not even with cuts or mutilated!" After the fact and after Bó's death, censorship becomes a selling point, promoting the scandalous nature of a story that has finally been freed (fig. 6).

The last two films ever made by Bó-Sarli encountered fewer complications for their release: *Last Love in Tierra del Fuego* made in 1978 premiered the following year, and *A Madcap Widow* was made and debuted in 1980. Could these seemingly easy releases imply there had been a change in direction? Curiously, *Last Love in Tierra del Fuego* received a credit from the INC and was considered to be the most complicit with the authoritarian regime. It tells the story of an actress, Isabel Borja, who remembers her past life as a star when she retires to Tierra del Fuego and then becomes a teacher. It acquired a status of complicity with the military junta when critics began to question the final scene, where its star appears as a teacher in a classroom and the class goes outside to raise a large Argentine flag. However, while clearly appeasing the authorities, the scene can also be read somewhat ironically. Argentina's top-rated and international erotic sex star, who was infamous for baring all on the screen, becomes the role model for a new obedient youth.

FIGURE 6. A poster for *Insatiable*, found in the newspaper *Clarín*, from its first release in September 1984 after Bó's death. Courtesy of the Museo del Cine Pablo Ducrós Hicken

Within the context of the *Pautas* and their emphasis on young people, the irony couldn't be clearer.

The case of *A Madcap Widow*, at first seemingly as straightforward as their penultimate film *Last Love in Tierra del Fuego*, is again embroiled in controversy. *A Madcap Widow* had been eligible for a funding credit after the Censor Board had reviewed the film, but the INC denied them the credit after viewing the final product. In a letter dated 28 August 1980, the INC denies funding to the film based on the fact that the film does not contribute

> in cultural and artistic ways given its inconsistency in cinematographic quality, as well as the abundance of situations and dialogue lacking in discretion and loftiness, bordering on bad taste, that does not serve an objective or positive example for the community.[80]

Throughout Sarli and Bó's career and until the very last film, they were accused of "bad taste." The controversy around *A Madcap Widow* occasioned their last threat to leave the country for good. In a press conference on 11 September 1980, they declared that they would not make another film together in Argentina, a promise they ultimately kept. Bó fell sick with cancer and died the following year. Their twenty-five-year-long filmmaking partnership had come to an end.

Two years later, Argentina's transition to democracy brought Raul Ricardo Alfonsín to the presidency. He appointed Manuel Antín as administrator of the INC. The film director and later founder of the Universidad del Cine selected film critic Jorge Miguel Couselo to head the Censor Board. Together the two proponents of democracy drafted the version of the law that was finally accepted on 20 February 1984, annulling law 18.019, dissolving the Classification Board, and devising a rating system to replace the practice of censorship. The newly elected executive power proclaimed the following in defense of new law 23.052:

> It forms an essential part of a democratic conception of society, the idea that men have autonomy to choose and develop their own life ideal, so the State must abstain from pursuing behavior that does not affect others' rights or society as such.[81]

Such a declaration heralded the end of an era of state control, initiating a more robust classification system that would ideally encourage new and innovative filmmaking practices without stifling creativity.

This chapter represents the first step in a process needed to reevaluate the complexities of censorship throughout this period of film history, when Armando Bó and Isabel Sarli were struggling to obtain screen time in national film houses. Reading the case of *Intimacies of a Prostitute* clearly shows the intricate nature of the exercise of censorship, a practice defined by different laws outlining what was permissible and what was prohibited. Judgment, however, lay in the hands

FIGURE 7. Isabel Borja, dressed in Argentine colors, proudly raises the Argentine flag at the end of *Last Love in Tierra del Fuego* (1979), with the schoolchildren in the background.

of the individual censors and the boards tasked to make such rulings. The *Intimacies of a Prostitute* file further demonstrates how even in moments of more liberal interpretations of the laws, certain topics and images were still seen as threatening to the public good. It shows that censorship was a private exercise shared by many *willing* participants. So many, indeed, that claims of an artistic authorial stamp on a film are almost impossible. Yet in the case of *Intimacies of a Prostitute*, its filmmaker left behind certain traces that make reference to the violent act of the cut, in the end giving Bó as director *some* authorial control. The body ends up being the victim and the focus of a convoluted history that preferred to hide intimacy because it was considered dangerous to the public good.

On another level, the historical process unmasks a genealogy of certain disciplinary affects that the state was working hard to sculpt. A variety of forms of power work in conjunction with the force of affect, "intensifying, multiplying, and saturating the material affective processes through which bodies come in and out of formation."[82] The excessive state apparatus determined a set of onscreen values and controlled morality by stalking and structuring a system to survey and keep them in check. The seeming arbitrariness of the process becomes clear in the example of how Sarli-Bó were limited by it. However, its lack of transparency suggests that there was more happening beyond just the regulation through laws. The films were systematically singled out from their first production *Thunder among the Leaves* to the last one projected in public, *Insatiable*. Was it purely because of their contentious content? Or were there other reasons beyond the legal parameters guiding the censors' scissors and revulsion? Were there different competing affects at the core of the rejection of or displeasure with the Sarli-Bó work? Was it purely just the rejection of public display of the sex, or was it the actual bodies that were performing the sex and other controversial activities? The next two chapters seek to answer these questions, arguing that onscreen bodies produced certain affective relationships offensive to the state and the censors, regardless of who was at the helm.

CHAPTER 4

Collective Working-Class Male Bodies

Flavia Forkel: What are you doing here?
Guillén: My work.
—*Thunder among the Leaves*, 1958

WHY THE LENS OF LABOR?

There are various ways of approaching the concept of labor in film, whether through its presentation of different types—material, abstract—or the self-conscious role an actor's body plays in his or her work, or even the promise of labor as affect. This chapter will engage directly with how the different meanings layer throughout the Sarli-Bó films. The main factor is the gendered male classed body as it performs and enacts manual labor, an abstract concept that promises specific types of affects (particularly the negotiation between belonging and not belonging for male bodies), and that on some level but not exclusively, refers to the political movements based on worker rights that continued to simmer after being muzzled in 1955. By returning to the first feature film, *El trueno entre las hojas* (*Thunder among the Leaves*, 1958), where Bó, through the collaborative work of his scriptwriter, makes the object of work an explicit topic that later implicitly permeates the whole Sarli-Bó oeuvre, I will begin to define the social aspects of their cinema that were both within classical genre specifications and differed from those. Labor, in the pioneering movie, is tied to a new niche audience that the duo enticed, giving the "simple" man access to the star.

The body of the common worker, who falls in love with the excesses of the main protagonist, exposes the dirty faces and greasy hands of capitalism and exploitation in its negative sense. An emphasis on lower-class laborers shares the stage with the new cinema movements developing in the late 1960s; but differently, *Thunder among the Leaves* shows nostalgia for a time when hard work was the means and foundation of society, and more specifically for males, that propelled one to noble ends. The film emphasizes not the Fordist mass-produced labor of assembly lines generally associated with Perón's urban followers, although in *Meat*, for instance, the reference to factory work frames the narrative. Instead, Bó-Sarli showcase work produced in and with nature, one with a more artisanal and nostalgic attachment that in many ways had been lost in the industrial system that was well entrenched in the second half of the twentieth century.

With the advent of the successive dictatorships since 1955, any opposition and its early class-based ideals, along with other leftist movements that foregrounded the worker, continued to be a threat. From the pair's first film together, there is already an appreciation for manual and repetitive hard work that is honest and not exploitative. While the connection to capitalism is never fully disavowed in the films, it is also never completely embraced. Alternatively, I suggest that the Bó-Sarli proposition coincides with their own art, films that are part of a system of exchange within capitalism but clearly positioned outside its industrial framework, functioning within postnational networks that connect to new but niche markets at home and around the world. Over time, the films continued a formula that still functioned on the margins of the film industry, both abroad and domestically. In many ways, the material work emphasized in their cinema is the nostalgic precapitalist and abstract work of the past: more artisanal, handmade, and less manufactured, but also repetitive, cheap, and formulaic descriptors equally applicable to the products of the Bó-Sarli brand. Hitherto, suspended moments in the time frame of the simple melodramatic narratives provided a space from which to think about a specific audience, a sex onscreen spectator that Bó-Sarli built up as an ideal worker and voyeur. The worker was their base, although in the late 1960s their films became popular with women and then in the 1970s with intellectuals who delighted in their camp aesthetic.

I will begin with an analysis of genre in *Thunder among the Leaves*. The film was Sarli-Bó's first foray into the erotic cinema they were to produce, but it contained elements of melodrama borrowed from earlier classical examples and realism from the newer neorealism that was influencing filmmaking throughout the continent. Two melodramatic precursors, *Prisioneros de la tierra* (*Prisoners of the Earth*, Manuel Romero, Argentina, 1939) and *Las aguas bajan turbias* (*Dark River*, Hugo del

Carril, Argentina, 1952), served as earlier models with marked differences worthy of further exploration to better comprehend the nuanced shifts that the post-Perón era brought. Nonetheless, melodrama as a lens fails to fully capture the intricacies in this film and its unique imaging of the male body in the process of hard manual labor, a body that is clearly inscribed in the spectator, who watches the sexualized star within the context of a changing Argentina.

To place the body of the worker at the center of the chapter is to argue that underlying the legacy of the Sarli-Bó productions is an affective mode of bonding that highlights the group and not the individual, whereby the worker's body created affects in the minds of specific spectators. These affects led to potential positions of outright rejection or the possibility of belonging to a community of already established but highly contentious workers. The two sides of the political spectrum each had their own moral and ethical positions that revolved around questions of masculinity. Manual labor first introduces a male body that has been politically rejected and is trying to make its comeback within a historical moment of turbulence.

Only by studying the relationships between work and leisure in Bó-Sarli's cinema, two seemingly opposing values that complement and counter each other, can the appreciation for the sex onscreen happen. By starting with the male worker who makes a quiet comeback, I begin to explore the anxieties of a society grappling with a changing masculinity caught between work and leisure, a masculinity defined by its interaction and relation to the female body. The relationship is highlighted, for instance, in *Carne* (*Meat*, 1968), where the shift between assembly-line work develops into assembly-line sex and continues in the affective and immaterial work of the female body in its position as a sex worker. All the references home in to the body as the center of inquiry to understand the intersection of class and gender in the affective relationship that multiplies onscreen and in the theaters. While the female body of the worker is never truly at the heart of the current chapter, women's labor is a voiceless presence in key examples (*The Shad Fishermen*, *India*, *Favela*, *The Girl Ass-Keeper of Ypacaraí*, *The Lioness*, *Meat*, *Naked on the Sand*, *Tropical Ecstasy*, *Ardent Summer*, and *Last Love in Tierra del Fuego*). The Fordist assembly-line work in *Meat* features acts of women performing work in a world clearly dominated by the violent macho. The film refers to work and gender to expose the problems of a masculinity of belonging. The immaterial and affective labor of the sex worker provides a second example of female bodies in labor.

THE TENSION BETWEEN MELODRAMA AND THE QUESTION OF LABOR

As popular culture became mass culture through the advent of industrialization, popular expressions had at their very foundation issues relating to class, even when class may be renounced. The history of melodrama in Latin America can be traced to popular entertainment, serial literature, radio, and television, as scholar Ana López explains.[1] Early scholarship on melodrama develops from Peter Brooks's historicization of the genre in French theater and literature. Brooks describes melodrama as an excessive mode based in moral conflict that arises from the end of a cohesive society, due to the breakdown of the traditional Sacred and its institutions, with the arrival of the modern sensibility.[2] Film critic Thomas Elsaesser adapts Brooks's ideas into its development in film, particularly in classical family melodramas of the 1940s and 1950s with the unit as the new space of patriarchy and capitalism. As a new site, the home registers the negotiation in the conflict of industrialization and uncovers the problems of alienation in the modern workplace. Elsaesser envisages the underlying issues of class and a consolidation of bourgeois power against the remnants of feudalism, where the ideological conflict of the modern sensibility is exercised into emotionally loaded family situations.[3] For Elsaesser, melodrama's sense of style through an elaborate mise-en-scène, excess of gestures, and heavy presence of music dwarfs any depth of content and exposes the female as its target audience.[4]

In Latin America, national cinemas began to fill the void that Hollywood could not fill after the development of sound. Hollywood's failed attempt to adapt the technology to the linguistic needs of Latin America provided an opportunity for nations to use their national characteristics and songs to develop their own industry through the genre of melodramas in the 1930s, such as the *ranchera* melodrama in Mexico and the tango melodrama in Argentina.[5] In the case of Mexico, López argues that the cinema in general, and melodrama in particular, became a place from which to negotiate new roles in a changing, modernizing, postrevolutionary society.[6] The creation of a new class of urban poor whose "willpower, roughness and illiteracy became insistently visible in the formerly feudal national landscape" allowed melodrama to resolve the tensions found in society and serve a socializing function by teaching new habits and codes of behavior.[7]

Like in Mexico, melodrama in Argentina replicated the same characteristics by focusing on the popular classes. Historian Matthew Karush helps to elaborate the genre's adaptability to the different context. Karush finds in melodrama the perfect vehicle for perpetuating the national myth that the collective had upward mobility, a myth that appears in the early days of film, music, and radio productions. He contends that the class-consciousness, most famously associated with Perón in the 1940s, was not his invention but a deeply ingrained myth at the foundation of the nation that was clearly articulated in the basis of melodramatic popular culture found in the new media before Perón consciously took up the mantra. In his chapter on the rise of the barrios, Karush shows how the political parties, barrio associations, and advertisers of a new consumerism in the 1920s downplayed class differences and instead spoke about upward mobility, respectability, and modernity to appease any working-class solidarity that persisted.[8] And yet class tension during the first years of film production depicted in differing expressions of popular culture served as the raw material for what soon became known as Peronism, a movement that essentially polarized the nation in the decades to come.[9] When in power during his first two terms, Perón insisted on depoliticizing class conflict and instead emphasizing social harmony. Thus, he ultimately betrayed Peronism's roots in a class-based politics, showing how it was better suited in the opposition rather than as a party in power.[10]

While the question of class was basic to classical Argentine melodramas, melodrama's commercial necessities encouraged a conformity that reinforced the idea that the long-suffering poor are the authentic Argentine citizens. Seen from such a perspective, melodrama systematically depoliticizes social conflicts and transforms them into stories of personal journeys, a formula used time and time again in the history of cinema. More recently, in postdictatorship middle-class films such as Oscar winner *La historia official* (*The Official Story*, Luis Puenzo, Argentina, 1985), the same formula repeats itself and extols the "virtues of individual self-realization."[11] The representation of work results in a similar fate as it folds into melodrama's tendency to reduce the political into the personal, and in conforming to the status quo as the material conditions of work altogether disappear.

A clear melodramatic model of the construction of work can be found in earlier socially conscientious examples such as *Prisoners of the Earth*, made a few years before even Perón had garnered any political presence. For Peronist critics like Octavio Getino, *Prisoners of the Earth* was the most important film of the 1930s and conveyed "a dimension effectively Latin Americanist, a circumstance not very common until then—nor seen later—in national cinema."[12] Romero's production tells the story of working conditions for the *mensúes* (descendants of individuals in the Christian missions) in the yerba maté (a traditional South American infused tea) fields, as well as an ensuing rebellion.[13] The film opens with theatrical music and shots of the sweeping, foreboding, and infinite clouds that had become the trademark of classical cinematography, to situate us in the jungles of northern Argentina. Then a cut shows a couple kissing.[14]

While *Prisoners of the Earth* tells a collective story about "blood and alcohol," as the introductory titles inform after the credits roll, the personal love story takes precedence over the collective tale. And thus, while the main elements of class consciousness had been present since melodrama's early days, what is clearly absent in films such as Romero's, and others up to and including the early 1950s, is the presence of workers in their material conditions of work. *Prisoners of the Earth* has a few shots of the working environment, but the emphasis on work is missing, with a contrasting focus instead on the relationship between Andrea and Esteban, essentially the private lives of the film's laboring protagonists. Nor are there any real problems if either stops performing their work at any time in the film: work falls to the backdrop, as it becomes a socially trouble-free context. The melodrama here takes precedence over the collective tale, and labor is only a pretext for the story's romantic plot.

A later example, Hugo del Carril's *Dark River*, replicates a similar account in the yerba maté–producing fields in the Alto Paraná, but unlike the 1939 film, it marks a shift that takes place after the influence of Italian neorealism. In *Dark River*, the conditions of work are featured more prominently alongside the dramatic love story between Santos and Amelia. Clara Kriger explains:

> And although Hugo del Carril does not construct scenes of masses, it is unusual to see in fictional cinema of this stage a group of workers that strive, are frightened, sweat, and rebel in unison.[15]

Kriger's words explain the move from 1939 to 1952, by acknowledging del Carril's unique posture on work during Perón's time. In her foundational *Cine y peronismo*, Kriger examines the first period of Perón's government, its policies, and the films produced. She concludes that during Peronism, films never showed class conflict in any definitive way, a claim similar to Karush's. Exploitation and problems of class were seen as something of the past—unnecessary after the fulfillment of class harmony under Perón. Del Carril, a public Peronist, followed a formula in a powerful film that validated the regime. Yet while neorealism influenced him, there are striking similarities to *Prisoners of the Earth*. Film scholar Ana Laura Lusnich's comparison of the book to the film shows the distance *Dark River* takes from the contemporary historical moment but sees the film as a point of transition between Argentina's past and future.[16] She explains:

> Finally, the film shows great distance from concrete historical reality. For it constrains bad labor conditions to work, alludes to the explicit mention of *yerbateros* [a maté seller or producer] and companies, highlights the role of unions as a positive resolution, displaces the role of the exploiter as one who belongs to a neighboring country and who has come to Misiones, supported by foreign capital.[17]

The distancing that takes place in *Dark River* has clear political consequences that align del Carril with Peronism and its worker movement based on nationalism, also being careful not to offend or critique the contentious regime.

Both stories develop in a distant past, a premodern era, separated from the present moment and from any association with worker discontent.[18] In *Prisoners of the Earth*, both protagonists die, a rather tragic ending to a film that began with high-angled shots of hopeful yet threatening clouds. Alternatively, *Dark River* presents a symbol of hope for a better future with the successful escape by the couple to the south, where the *mensúes* are empowered by the unions. The workers are clearly exploited by a despotic landowner, unlike in the earlier film, where the boss is somewhat congenial and not entirely despicable, even though he is still a foreigner. Del Carril's film captures a consistent position when it comes to class. The promise of class harmony at the end is inevitable and even desired. Nonetheless, in keeping with the general form of melodrama, both films eschew class as an issue because in the one case the rebellion is suppressed, and in the other, the unions save the protagonists from the disaster and everyone moves to another location, where the class structure stays the same.

While the question of work in the 1952 film appears to be more at the forefront and is shown as the work of the collective, the melodrama and romantic love between Amelia and Santos continue to be the driving force of the diegesis. For instance, performance of work emphasizes not hard labor but the quantity of work. In a sequence one-third into the film, the long workday appears through shots of different activities in the field, featured by a montage sequence edited through a series of dissolves emphasizing the length of the collective action, and displaying workers in the totality of work and its strenuous result. The arduous activity unites the two protagonists, culminating in an onscreen kiss. The romantic moment interrupts the work, and despite the heavily surveyed environment no one notices the couple's liaisons that distract them from their tasks. Del Carril's narrative employs leisure to disrupt the abstract conception of work the film constructs.

Prisoners of the Earth and *Dark River* both present slightly dissimilar versions of class conflict. In the first example, class struggle is a persistent, unproductive threat that is finally eliminated as the rebels are crushed. In the second, the laborers win and leave the appalling working conditions of the plantation to go to a better unionized environment in the south, a more concrete Argentine reality and space. *Dark River* offers a future escape from the harsh conditions of yesterday through the mobility of the working class and the choices they have moving forward in a Peronist world. The beginning of the film emphasizes the greatness of today versus the atrocity of the past through a voice-over narration typically adopted by neorealism when the film is meant to carry a specific politically motivated message. Despite such differences, both films end with a reestablishment of order in a situation where class is not reconfigured or emphasized, but harmony is the driving force. As long as unions exist, workers' interests are defended; in the one case, class is evaded, whereas in the other, there is no need for any worker protection as the problem undoubtedly remains with the rebellion.

My discussion of the two films is paramount to understanding what comes after the fall of Perón in 1955 and in Bó-Sarli's debut as a new erotic team in *Thunder among the Leaves*, which in many ways borrows from the two early antecedents as another example of melodrama. Yet the film offers a new conclusion unique for melodrama and remarkably unlike the others. It is not surprising that Paraguayan author Augusto Roa Bastos, whose social concerns formed the basis of his own fiction, wrote the film script.[19] According to media releases, *Thunder among the Leaves* was based on the author's story "The Minister's Daughter" from the book carrying the title of the film, but that short story title does not exist. Literary scholar Marcos Zangrandi suggests that Bó may be referring to "Those Dark Faces," about the daughter of a deputy who is raped by the workers of an hacienda.[20] Roa Bastos's unique initial contribution to the script establishes a new collaboration that kindled the careers of the author along with Bó and Sarli. Moreover, many of the patterns established in Sarli-Bó's first feature became a formula that continued onto the second, *The Shad Fishermen* (1959), also scripted by

Roa Bastos.[21] As I show, the two initial collaborations establish an aesthetic and ethic regarding work that begins as an important motif and quickly enriches the formula adopted in most of the duo's films, even those without the contribution of the foreign author.

Thunder among the Leaves is about a logging operation deep in the Paraguayan jungles at the border with Argentina and Brazil, reproducing onscreen the same place of worker exploitation as *Dark River* and *Prisoners of the Earth* but within a different industry. (The place became a central shooting locale for Bó-Sarli productions.) Historically, the three films register the colonial and then capitalist foreign drive to exploit natural resources in the region using *mensúes*. Just like its antecedents, it is set "long ago" in a distant past, dissociating itself from the current political situation. Since there is a clear setting in Paraguay through accents, spoken Guaraní, and other references, the film detaches itself even further from the political context of Argentina.[22] While none of the three examples examines class conflict in depth, owing to the adoption of the melodrama genre, Bó's is harsher in its depiction of the exploitation of the workers in an undefined era and provides direct and revelatory messages about the realities of the act of work.

Melodrama continues to imbue the film as a genre through music, clear demarcations of good and evil, and moments of excess. However, the main story is about worker exploitation without being reduced to a love plot as in the other two film examples. There are female actors, cast from the Maká tribe in Paraguay, that appear but speak no lines and take on only secondary roles. The female protagonist is Flavia Forkel, the owner's wife, played by Isabel Sarli.[23] She arrives onscreen after forty minutes and has a secondary role. Originally, Sarli was not expected to be a main feature in the film. Sarli's name was not among the starring credits, but after the crowds began to flock to the cinema to see her scandalous nude appearance, she became its main draw. Moreover, her desire for Guillén, played by Bó, is not enthusiastically reciprocated in the film, and in the end she is a victim of the revolt. The melodrama, which normally relies on the relationship between the two protagonists to drive the conflict, is relegated to the background and secondary to the social commentary about work during frightening and exploitative conditions. This notable shift was perhaps owing to the development of a different audience than that targeted in the family melodramas of the 1940s.[24]

While *Thunder among the Leaves* follows a recipe established by its antecedents, material labor performs a more prominent role than for instance in the socially conscious *Dark River*.[25] In part, the shift it marked is attributable to the new trend of neorealism born in the postwar years of the 1940s and 1950s, which developed into two very distinct movements in Argentina: the bourgeois criticism found in the artistic, more aesthetically conscious films of the Generation of 1960 that were driven by the auteur-director, with Leopoldo Torre Nilsson as its most successful intellectual example; versus the more gritty neorealism practiced by the Santa Fe school at the Film Institute of the National University of Litoral, with its founder Fernando Birri and his notable documentary *Tire Dié* (*Toss Me a Dime*, Argentina, 1958). The latter version of neorealism eventually led to different expressions with similar ethics that branched out ultimately into the Third Cinema of *The Hour of the Furnaces* as its most internationally acknowledged example, all of which became part of the New Latin American cinemas. While never credited for its social contribution, Bó's first film was an intermediary between *Dark River* and the film movements that were developing in the region, yet quite different from the social commentary and intellectualized examples of the new cinemas. His popular aesthetics, simple politics, and the discovery of a new star never allowed Bó to take the political path of his counterparts. Instead, he stumbled onto a new niche market with the exposure of the female body.

Even though realism was underpinning the vanguard movements as a clear break from melodrama, particularly the documentary film expressions pertaining to the New Latin American cinemas influenced by neorealism, the films did still indulge in what Laura Podalsky calls an "archive of emotions."[26] The new cinemas disdained emotional manipulation as conscious political engagement became easily aligned with the rational. Nonetheless, there is a clear position in both Italian neorealism and the New Latin American cinemas that detail "what to feel and how to frame the story of those feelings."[27] The politically active group rejected melodrama outright as genre because of its industrial mode. Yet with a different end in mind, class struggle was still framed in melodramatic terms of good versus evil.

Numerous archival sources lay the foundation for the desired affect, referencing for instance the sentimental novels of the formation of the nation that Doris Sommer discusses in her classic seminal study.[28] For Podalsky, the historical reference of affect surfaces in the documentaries that defined the movements; the close-ups and facial gestures featured in the films gave them a sentimental and moralizing tone just like the romances from the nineteenth century. She eloquently argues that the socially conscious new cinemas of the 1960s used affect that extended beyond the melodrama centered on the love story between a couple. The close-ups of the begging children in the infamous train scene in *Toss Me a Dime* contrasts the plight of the poor with the mobile, well-dressed bourgeoise women sitting comfortably on the train discarding their excess dimes. Emotion or affect mobilizes the spectator and "instantiate[s] a new understanding of reality."[29] Referencing Cuban filmmaker and theorist Tomás Gutiérrez Alea, Podalsky sees the political work done through visceral jolts and emotional appeal, a dialectical tension that is meant to propel the spectator into new ways of knowing and understanding.[30] By rethinking the continental history of filmmaking through the lens of its affect, Podalsky invites her readers to see the multilayered genealogies in which aesthetic and industrial tendencies branch out and converge in the many expressions of realism in Latin American film of the period.

Similarly, film philosopher Elena del Río turns to the affective-performative in films to explain a process of becoming through a Deleuzian lens that is missing in genre studies, which has more to do with stabilizing meaning and knowledge rather than liberating it.[31] Like Podalsky, del Río finds the use of genre as an analytical tool both limiting and frustrating. For instance, inquiries such as Linda Williams's have connected genre to the body. Her key study on melodrama describes it as a "filmic mode of stylistic and/or emotional excess . . . with 'lapses' in realism, by 'excesses' of spectacle and displays of primal, even infantile emotions, and by narratives that seem circular and repetitive."[32] Expanding Clover's definition of horror imbued with violent rapture as a low body genre, Williams adds comparable excitable genres to the mix, like pornography's orgasm and melodrama's weepie, ones that cause similar bodily reactions.[33] She describes the perverse pleasures of melodrama as masochistic or a downward thrust to a diminished or suffering body that produces a nostalgic tone of coming "too late."

Del Río argues that it is difficult to consign the affective-performative to stable and well-defined generic paradigms.[34] Melodrama, thus, cannot explain the contradictions that are taken for granted in genre studies. Instead, she seeks those "heightened affective moments" to "shift the emphasis from the organized body, slave to morality and representation, to the ethical and creative potential of the expressive body."[35] Del Río's reconfiguration of a poststructuralist reading offers a way through ideologically contradictory moments that melodramas offer but genre is incapable of addressing other than as an ideological impasse. The problem is that such moments, couched as purely liberating within a narrative that may seem very closed and limiting, produce an uncomfortable instability. Affect can offer a new point of departure to look at how labor and leisure function in similar instances, ones which I argue can liberate emotions in new and exciting ways. These emotional responses are not clearly defined in one way or another yet do offer excessive traces impregnated with a charge in a given historical context. I do not propose to know what the audience thought about particular intense flashes, but I do wish to explore the very repetitive nature of affectively charged scenes that produce a potential liberating connection to the spectator.

Thunder among the Leaves fits nicely within a certain tradition and history. This first feature marking the origin of the Sarli-Bó collaboration can be read as a product of the changes that were taking place in society and film culture (the outlaw of Peronism and the dangers of labor movements, the decline of the studios, and the influence of neorealism). The position of his newfound commodity, that of the sexualized star, was to quickly develop in the films, making them more overtly melodramatic with the use of Sarli, whose affective work grew to become that of a diva unleashing instinctual urges upon her presence. And yet *Thunder among the Leaves* leaves a mark on the Bó-Sarli oeuvre, whereby work, material and then immaterial, takes on a strong current that inevitably leads the emotional appeal to a particular type of spectator. What I argue here is that work, mainly experienced through the male body, is as important as leisure, which will come to encompass both sex and love, in forming a complementary to the dialectic to allow the popular Bó-Sarli films to infiltrate into a niche local market and eventually an international one.

THUNDER AMONG THE LEAVES AND HARD MANUAL LABOR AS AFFECT

The sequence appearing during the opening credits of *Thunder among the Leaves* consists of: (1) a close-up of an axe slicing the trunk of a tree, (2) a tilt up the towering base before the camera tilts down to capture the tree's collapse to the ground, (3) cut to a medium shot of bodies working hard and sweating, together showing labor and its product. Then the following text is superimposed on the images:

> In the mysterious heart of America, nature and man set free their centuries' old sorrows. At times it's man versus man . . . large country estates and factories, ranches and maté plantations, plantations and sawmills, built on the effort of sweat and human suffering, staking out the wild land. . . . There was . . . a handful of unruly men. They endured and fought for the conquest

FIGURE 8. *Thunder among the Leaves* (1958) begins with a man working.

of something infinitely more precious than gold or silver; their freedom, primary passion of men and goal for their invincible fate....

The titles on the screen set up the story of Paititi, a harsh and forsaken logging operation in the jungles of Paraguay from which no one ever escapes. Just after the opening sequence, an old man, half naked, wearing the loose trousers of a gaucho, chops with an axe (fig. 8). All of a sudden, he hears the voice of his boss calling him to his imprisonment. The first images highlight the repetitive nature of the task of work and the slowing down of time on the screen. By focusing on the actual work and the male body performing it, the film, in documentary fashion, constructs a recurring scene that substantiates the narrative claims of exploitation. Work, from the first shots, is tied to enslavement: the fight goes beyond the material efforts of hard labor to incorporate a more humane struggle against the capitalist foreign landlord.[36]

When work is not happening in *Thunder among the Leaves*, the laborers use their free time to organize how they are going to overthrow the overseas owner. Once they achieve their goal, they decide to stay and take over the logging, believing that in the end the work performed through a collective body has value. Interestingly, *Thunder among the*

Leaves is more about an occupation of the sawmill by the workers than about a process of unionization, as in *Dark River*. The nostalgic and utopic vision of workers who value their function as an act of pride and re-conquer it for themselves in tactical fashion, like the filmmaking entrepreneurship developed by Bó-Sarli, inspires a utopic vision of the material task of labor seemingly in line with the recent wins for working-class politics that Peronism had brought. However, a connection between the movement and the film will prove more complex and nuanced beyond their representation in film. While Roa Bastos may have inspired the original emphasis on work, its continued presence as motif suggest that either Bó was a supporter of such views, or he and Sarli stumbled upon an audience and formula that appealed to the masses.[37]

If *Thunder among the Leaves* isolates the material act of working, the other Sarli-Bó films, most of which were not produced in collaboration with Roa Bastos, also highlight similar concerns through important documentary-like shots of workers in action who repeatedly interrupt the narrative. In some instances (*The Shad Fishermen*, *The Shoemaker's Wife*, and *The Mayor's Wife*), the titles refer to different jobs or roles performed by workers. Following *The Shad Fishermen*, the narratives become more melodramatic as Sarli takes on the predominant role, with their intention of incorporating erotic elements as their overriding trademark. The increasing presence of the female star does not, however, erase or negate invasive moments of labor. These have an affective effect and complicate the seemingly simplistic, melodramatic, and even folkloric plots that drive the stories. Images of bodies performing tasks of labor add a social dimension to the productions, isolating Bó-Sarli films from other comedies featuring sex, which will dominate during the late 1960s.

Many examples of suspended time through performances of labor throughout the movies isolate specialized yet artisanal tasks: shad fishermen, sea lion hunters in *Heat*, basket weavers in *Favela*, market vendors in *The Girl Ass-Keeper of Ypacaraí*, shoemakers in *The Shoemaker's Wife*, reed cutters in *Naked Temptation*, fruit farmers in *The Hot Days*, fishermen in *Tropical Ecstasy*, loggers in *Bewitched*, ranchers in *Fever* and in the harsh Patagonian environment of *Ardent Summer*, and an entrepreneurial kiosk owner in *A Madcap Widow*. By inserting and dwelling on particular moments of labor, the films all stress the difficulty of the work and its repetition in actions (fig. 9). In all examples listed, the workers are mainly males commonly identified with the working class. The performance is of very specialized artisanal trades enacted on

FIGURE 9. Documentary-like images of work in *The Shad Fishermen* (1959) and *Naked Temptation* (1966)

a small scale by individual entrepreneurs, making reference to premodern practices in local, often-isolated communities. From such a perspective, labor contributes to the aspect of nostalgia the films reinforce, an ethic that ties back to the foundations of Argentine popular culture, discussed by Karush, one on which Peronism had likewise capitalized and which melodrama reinforced, yet one that an affective lens can nuance.

THE SPECTATOR'S BODY INSCRIBED

Moving beyond labor as merely representational requires us to focus on the repetition and on the dialectical relationship it shares with leisure—not what it means within the plot or what it represents in an individual movie but on the affects it creates that allow for possible connections. Like the interruption of leisure discussed in del Carril, the affective events become obvious only through the act of repetition. It's important to rethink why labor continued to be ever present in the Sarli-Bó films despite the increasing role of sexuality. *Meat*, for instance, solidifies the connection between labor and violence that leads to the problematic leisure of the workers. However, the nudes, which made Sarli an instant sensation, are likewise moments of the affective where the star's body exceeds the frame of the shot to create what cannot be fully articulated, a connection to her audience, whether the relationship tipped toward lust/desire or its opposite, displeasure or disgust. The onus in this case is on the observer, another leitmotif whose origin can similarly be found in *Thunder among the Leaves*. That is the place of the spectator, who consumes the female body through the star, and is fully inscribed in the diegetic moment on the captured celluloid.

To return to the performance in *Thunder among the Leaves* that solidifies Sarli as a sensation, the water scene similarly highlights the glaring look of a common worker. In the original script, Roa Bastos described the bath as one with a "white bathing suit" without any mention of the nude.[38] The draft emphasizes "a sensation of absolute nakedness," a feeling that displaces the actual nudity. The Paraguayan author intuitively included that affect as important, but Bó, as ultimate auteur who overrode the written script, scribbled in pencil in capital letters above the typewritten words to describe further instructions: "NUDE." Bó's visual attention rather than Roa's literary focus does not explain the specifics of the scene but instead emphasizes: "comes to a close-up shot of a pair of eyes that are seen excited by Flavia's bath" (fig. 10). The only instructions imposed on the script by the director focus the camera on the spectator

FIGURE 10. The spectator as a worker in *Thunder among the Leaves* (1958)

or voyeur within the text. Arguably, the nude scene is the most crucial point in the film, and yet instead of elaborating what it will look like, Bó's addition does not detail the visual construction of the nude reveal but describes the shot of the man watching. We can read the move by Bó also intuitively as attention to the affect of the shot, the experience of the spectator rather than the scene being observed. The shift allows a rethinking of the possibilities of the infamous scene from plot to affect. The witness, another example of the common worker, becomes an iteration of the spectator in the text as he enjoys the performance that Flavia provides. By incorporating the leitmotif of the spectator within the diegesis, Bó firstly identifies and prioritizes an audience. However, pushed further, Bó discovers or even invents an affect that exceeds the screen. The shots of Flavia during the scandalous scene, swimming leisurely nude in the river, undoubtedly contrasts with the hard, exploitative work the men in Paititi perform, and adds a dimension that will be ever present in the ensuing productions, juxtaposing leisure and its opposite, hard labor.

Sarli's nude debut in *Thunder among the Leaves* made her an instant star and triggered another idea: her character's leisure is always unknowingly disrupted, mostly by workers' eyes that happen to fall upon the excesses of her nude body. She embodies the escape from the harsh reality that only leisure in and through the cinema can provide. In many ways, she founds an archetype that follows throughout her career and goes on to define the starlet. The first incorporation of bodily reveal plays with the myth that Sarli did not know she was being filmed naked. Supposedly the naïve actress was told she would wear a skin-coloured suit, as confirmed in the original script written by Roa Bastos, but when asked to perform in the nude she refused to appear exposed. Bó tricked her by telling her that he shot the scene from afar on a hill and that nothing was visible in the staged shot. When he used the telephoto lens, he was able to capture a closer image of her bare breasts. Nonetheless, the other scene with Forkel's hallucinations of Flavia opening up her blouse and showing her breasts (which appears in the script but does not explicitly mention the flashing of the breasts) and the angle of the shots in the infamous river scene leaves doubt about the original explanation, as I discuss elsewhere.[39] The scene in the river marks the birth of an innocently nude diva meant to be devoured by the eyes of hard-working men.

The same archetype of the voyeur reappears in other Sarli-Bó films: the local kiosk owner and his sidekick friend break in to watch Flor Tetis bathe in her own backyard in *The Madcap Widow*, first behind trees, then after climbing up to get a better look. In *Ardent Summer*, the gaucho and farmhand, shielded by a tree, watch the captured woman Bárbara enjoying her pleasure in the open field. In *Insatiable*, the workers stand by gazing as one of their coworkers indulges in Carmen. In *A Butterfly in the Night*, the three friends take shelter behind reeds as they stalk Yvonne when she bathes in the river. All these examples, and many more like them, highlight not only the leisure of the star, Sarli, but also the workers' leisure in the act of watching as she enjoys her body, indulging in the delights of her sexuality. In some, she is masturbating (*Fever* and *Ardent Summer*), in others she is having sex with a man as in *Insatiable*, but in most she is simply enjoying the beauty and freedom of her body in the water.

The voyeur has a long history in cinema, particularly in the portrayal of sex onscreen, with early examples like Russ Meyer's first feature *The Immoral Mr. Teas* (USA, 1959), released after Bó's debut with Sarli.[40] Critics have described the careful limit delineated by Meyer between the voyeur and the nude women that he watches.[41] As Elena Gorfinkel explains, sexploitation "allegorizes their own condition of reception through the trope of the erotic spectator caught up in the act of consuming sex."[42] But the distinction is made between seeing and doing sex: the women are out of bounds. In the early films, Sarli was always

FIGURE 11. Spectators watch the water scenes from afar in *A Butterfly in the Night* (1977) and *A Madcap Widow* (1980).

out of bounds, but these evolve into the "roughies," where sexual contact happens. What remains nonetheless, in the Sarli-Bó features, is the consistent onscreen identity of the actual voyeur (fig. 11). Generally, the consumer of nudity and sex is the worker. Although Bó teases with other voyeurs such as the accomplished and well-off entrepreneur in *Fuego*, normally the spectator is a common worker finding enjoyment in the liberty of watching an expression of female sexuality.

In all of the cases, sex means leisure, a time-out for the worker, who relishes in the act of watching and enjoying the sex "onscreen," behind the barriers that separate him from the star. The close-up faces, from the debut of a modest-looking man watching from above the cliff into the water below to hiding behind windows, among bushes and reeds, or up in trees, belong to workers, always very humble, everyday people. These are onscreen nonprofessionals and professionals, included as spectators in the script, a technique that helps to insert within the diegesis a metacinematic audience that Bó was trying hard to entice, one who identified with that very first and then later repeated faces. This is the everyday working-class male associated with the Peronist movement, who in the story is able to catch a glimpse of the exceptional movie star, entranced by her sexual excesses and beauty—and in some cases, he may even manage to win her love. From the first nude shot that Bó himself clearly writes into the script, he plans the scene with a specific spectator in mind. One who makes an appearance and is meant to substantiate the scene but more importantly also teach the movie-going audience, mainly of proletariat workers, how to see and interpret the many nude scenes. From the initial movie, Bó brought into the conversation a new protagonist but also made clear that the woman on the screen was a worker too, one who was performing an essential function for the common man.

THE CYCLE OF LEISURE AND WORK OF AFFECTIVE BELONGING

Do you know why you are so famous? Because you make movies for the people, for the masses.
—Isabel Sarli, 1999[43]

Scholar Zangrandi establishes a cause-and-effect relationship between the initial erotic charge produced by Sarli's nude scene in *Thunder among the Leaves* to the eventual uprising of the workers, comparing the affect created in the diegesis to that of the abuse of the proletariat woman, which instigated the rebellions in *Dark River*. According to Zangrandi, both scenes sparked the upheavals that eventually end in tragedy. However, a shift from the melodramatic framework to one considering affect suggested a more complicated version of the eruption that the scene generated. Within the narrative, the rebellion had begun before Flavia even set foot in the lumberyard. Like *Dark River,* this film features an evil boss who is foreign, unreasonable, and unfair. It is Guillén who sparks the rebellion after suffering atrocities in the workplace. Guillén, a literate city dweller and foreigner, brings with him ideas from abroad. Both films justify the agitation of the exploited, including the Indigenous population, who are shot at when they demand compensation and situate themselves from the point of view of the worker, unlike in *Prisoners of the Earth*. Guillén, who sees the inequalities taking place, helps the subjugated to unite in rebellion.

Rather than reading the moment of bodily exposure as only one of cause and effect, we can shift to emphasize the potential created by the onscreen sexuality of the female body. The suspension of time is both the catalyst for the ensuing revolt and an opportunity for the female body to enjoy her communion with nature and create a potential affective charge. Thinking about the onscreen reveal through affect produces a relationship to leisure that exceeds a lineal pattern of recognition. Performance of work and leisure are at the forefront of the affective, allowing for unconscious reactions that lead to emotional appeal beyond a static recognition of melodramatic excess to one of multiple and endless possibilities.

To return to a representative reading of the film, the solutions posed in *Thunder among the Leaves* differ from the two examples of similar melodramas. The question of Guillén's foreignness, determined by a clear and distinct Argentine accent, is problematic. The specific location of the shooting was in a region of Paraguay, which nonetheless is multinational and at the crossroads of Argentina and Brazil. In a conversation with Flavia Forkel when she claims that he, Guillén, is different and doesn't belong to their class, Guillén responds, "I have won the privilege of being part of them." When she asks what he has in common with the others, he says: "Suffering, they are my brothers, I am learning to be like them, to be dignified by them. . . ." Flavia's point of view is that of her husband; she sees no value in the people or in their work. For her, the workers can be discarded because their lives do not matter. There is a clear class- and race-based distinction between Flavia and Guillén and the others. Guillén, who obviously is an outsider, describes the workers as follows:

> They are debased by slavery. Those people are strong and pure like the earth, it would have been beautiful to live in human dignity, but here we live buried alive. We tear trees with our teeth for the sawmill, and in those trunks instead of sap there is human blood.

He honors and values them when describing them as a group: he belongs to the group. The injustices here are called out in a very general and vague way, unlike in the new cinemas that followed, and yet they are thus appealing to the same emotions of ethics, perhaps through a melodrama of exploitation but also through an affect of belonging.

The final scene of the film shows the fellowship between the humble outsider and the other workers from the region, reconciling Guillén as a foreigner yet acknowledging his role in the uprising and securing him a future in the company and group. After the boss drowns in the water, Guillén exclaims:

> We have triumphed. Our greatest victory is having discovered that united we are invincible. We must remain strong and united more than ever. Here or anywhere. Is it not true, comrades?

All the workers respond with a resounding yes. And Guillén asserts: "We are going to show that work is a good thing when it is not tainted by fear and hate. Work done by friendship and camaraderie." One of the local workers says: "It is true what Guillén says, there is no need for escape, we are going to stay here and confront what may come. The sawmill is a piece of our land and we have reconquered it from the bossy gringo with our sacrifice and our blood." The complexity of the final dialogue in the film is thanks to the authorial efforts of Roa Bastos, who asserts the Paraguayan voice of its interlocutor, one that does not need to be overridden by the literate Argentine Guillén.[44]

While Guillén's efforts and intentions are well defined throughout the film, in the end it is about all the people who work together to conquer their work and humanity. The discourse on labor provides the concluding words to the film, followed only by a shot of Guillén overlooking the water and remembering Flavia, before he joins the rest of the group, in a clear act of accepting the invitation to be a part of the collective. In this instance, and unlike the other two example films, to take the company from the demanding foreign boss is an act of true camaraderie, showing a more complicated relationship than the dialectal one between work and leisure as one of cause and effect.[45] What wins out in *Thunder among the Leaves* is the act of work as a noble male-centered pursuit. It sets a standard that is not completely lost in the other Bó-Sarli productions. Work and leisure are inextricably linked to each other, providing a new potential masculinity, one that films that feature sex can easily and naturally address.

The trio's first collaboration provided a complex negotiation between working male bodies, female sexuality, and workplace exploitation. The same ethic about work repeats in the rest of the films. As an ever-present specter, work materializes through different forms. *The Shad Fishermen* exposes the harsh conditions in the fishing community and the cruel actuality of labor, a continuation that reinforces the contribution by

Roa Bastos. But as Bó takes on a more active role in the scriptwriting, authoring more than just the images, the echo of bodies in the process of work persists. For instance, the severe contrast between exploited workers and a self-serving authoritarian can also be found in *The Lioness*, *The Hot Days*, *Bewitched,* and *Ardent Summer*. The authoritarian is always toppled by the workers or by Sarli's character. Alternatively, the star's preference or love for a worker rather than the more refined or wealthy husband appears in *Sex and Love*, *Heat*, *Ardent Summer*, and *Fever*. Other films simply embody work as a noble end in itself that saturates the narrative in its representation of the everyday: *India*, *Heat*, *The Girl Ass-Keeper of Ypacaraí*, *The Shoemaker's Wife*, *The Hot Days*, *Naked Temptation*, *The Mayor's Wife*, *My Father's Wife*, *Meat*, *Naked on the Sand*, and *Tropical Ecstasy*. Finally, the performance of labor appears as a simple and necessary means to improve one's lifestyle, which leads to certain sacrifices in the case of *Favela*, *The Shoemaker's Wife*, *The Mayor's Wife*, and *A Madcap Widow*. All of the examples take the act of working as a generally positive endeavor and show the power of the worker or the liberated woman when confronted with difficult, exploitative environments. The male body overcomes challenges and wins back his dignity or endures. In another but equally thought-provoking example, the meatpacking plant workers in *Meat* demonstrate the assembly-line Fordist work that explicitly ties work to sex at the level of the narrative. As the only example of a factory work setting, *Meat* complicates the working masculinity alluded to in *Thunder among the Leaves*.

FROM ASSEMBLY-LINE WORK TO ASSEMBLY-LINE SEX IN *MEAT*

If *Thunder among the Leaves* shows the unionization and overthrow of an overpowering foreign boss to create a more inclusive work environment where all hard-laboring males belong regardless of race or nationality, *Meat* situates itself differently to feature conflict between workers and violence at the workplace, inviting a reflection on industrialized work and its psychological effects and affects in the setting of a slaughterhouse/meatpacking plant in a small town, suburb, or *villa miseria* (shantytown), as Losada argues.[46]

The laborers in the film jointly work to produce beef for local and foreign consumption, Argentina's most important exportable product at the time.[47] It is no coincidence that relationships between workers fall within gendered identities. Delicia is on the assembly line and becomes the target of a male colleague, part of a *machista* culture that conflates the flesh produced in the work environment with the meat as leisure. The "leisure" here is not like the leisure elsewhere, where pleasure can be assumed to be part of the female role, and bodies enact their own affects separately through the act of doing or watching. Instead, it is an exploitative act of violation against a female coworker, whereby the behavior of assembly-line work becomes conflated with assembly-line "play," in a vile, twisted sense of the word. The matter of belonging can also be dissected along gendered lines, leaving a questionable place for women in the factory but also for men in such a setting.

On the one hand, *Meat* fits within the US sexploitation shift from "nudie cuties" to "roughies" taking place in 1964.[48] The roughies were deemed a more "mature and realist-inclined sexploitation" that represented the unleashing of male sexual psychosis and female alienation.[49] Moreover, rape was prevalent in sexploitation, and after 1964 the male voyeur became deviant, enacting a sexualized fantasy based on an instinct for control. In contrast, in the Sarli-Bó films the male voyeur had violent inclinations and was a more active participant from the beginning, even if that role shifted to his social circumstances, as in the case of *Thunder among the Leaves*.

Rodolfo Kuhn calls Bó's filmmaking moralistic and grounded in a sense of guilt. He claims that Isabel's characters either die or regret their actions.[50] While the argument may be valid, the moralistic aspect made the films more consumable for both a Catholic public and a censorship apparatus that was well-entrenched in the Catholic traditions. The case of *Meat*, arguably the Sarli-Bó film with the most ties and obvious references to Argentina, demonstrates a recipe that blends both work and sexuality issues through a moralistic story about a worker who cannot control his macho instincts. Cultural identifiers such as the accent used, the context of the meat industry, the tango songs, and the presentation of the maté together allude to the nation. Likewise, Delicia is part of that representation. In the final half of the film, when Delicia is repeatedly raped by different men, she wears a light blue skirt, a matching sweater, and a white scarf tied around her neck, the exact shades of the Argentine flag's national colors. The judgement on the crimes of kidnapping, locking in a refrigerated truck, and repeated rape, an act committed against meat/Delicia/Sarli/the nation, is clear. But the more subtle and curious reading comes with what the film posits in regard to work and gender, sexuality, and class-based identities at their intersection, a proposal that differs from the merely class-based ones in *Thunder among the Leaves*, and where Bó-Sarli's films evolve in their social proposition.

Meat continues the aesthetic of documenting work in its realistic site as the paradigm established in *Thunder among the Leaves* and followed subsequently. Near the beginning of the story, after the credits, Delicia arrives late for her shift, thus having to apologize to her supervisor. The assembly-line scene with all the workers handling the meat has authentic sounds and footage of employees performing their tasks. Credits show that the scenes were shot at the meat processing plant Frigorifico Cóndor S.A. – Dipano S.A., but the disclaimer tries to ensure that viewers disassociate the company from the violent story that ensues. The scene begins with a pan through the factory of nonprofessional male and female actors performing their regular duties, until the camera zeros in on a group of women professional actors. Beginning in the factory, the close-ups of meat and then the shots of the workers handling the beef are made more authentic through sounds produced in the environment. The film itself never judges its images of authentic work, only registering them in cinema-verité fashion. Thus, they function like a documentary to bring the real into the film without evaluating that reality. The scene featuring the work in a meatpacking plant makes references to the real politics behind such environments, their workers, and the question of food, more particularly beef.

Two clear representative examples of beef and its industry are relevant to the analysis of *Meat* in the Argentine cultural archive: a scene from the simultaneously produced *The Hour of the Furnaces* and the foundational short story by Esteban Echeverría titled "El matadero" ("The Slaughter Yard," 1871).[51] "The Slaughter Yard" chronicles the battle between Unitarios (liberals, city- and trade-based, with European ideals, representing civilization) and Juan Manuel de Rosas's Federales (of the countryside, regional autonomy, associated with barbarism and the Argentine gaucho), two opposing political forces who represented contradictory ideals during the formation of the nation in the nineteenth century. The story criticizes the ruthless violence of the workers in a slaughter yard as a slick, refined nobleman from the city comes across it. The encounter between conflicting political camps results in brutal torture of the Unitario and his eventual death. The story emphasizes the clear barbarism of the workers, referred to in the text as the *chusma* or rabble, associated with the rural place of a slaughterhouse. A reference to the gauchos and its *criollo* culture of meat contrasts with the civilization of the Buenos Aires-based flaneur with more refined tastes and customs, mainly associated with the city's educated elite. While the details of the canonical short story concerning questions of race, gender, and class have been analyzed by literary scholars, the culture relating to the slaughter of meat and its influence on those who work in such environments makes it relevant for the analysis of Bó's film.[52] The ethical, ethnic, and gendered identity of the masses is clear in Echeverría's story. It is no coincidence that the purely masculine space of the slaughterhouse, excluding "respectable" women, mainly mothers and wives, inversely comprises the "other" violent, ethically dubious, lower-class, and racially defined women in an early projection of the nation-state.

The same year that *Meat* was made, Getino and Fernando Solanas finished the first part of *The Hour of the Furnaces*. The film, a long time in the making, made Third Cinema a viable praxis for Argentina and the rest of Latin America, one that called for the return of Peronist politics. A crucial scene takes place at a slaughterhouse. The innovative montage sequence attributed to the novel aesthetics of the new cinemas intercuts images from the slaughterhouse with advertising products, lifestyles of wealth, and intertitles providing clear political messages. The vanguard sequence in the form of an advertisement clip is brilliant; it interlaces many ideas about workers, the reality of work in the nation's main export industry, contrasting sharply with a lifestyle of leisure sold to the working class through advertisements of foreign products that invade the nation. In relation to Bó's fascination for work and leisure, the intertitles explain the images by suggesting the exploitation that happens from abroad for working-class individuals as a form of violence. This provides a clear message about how Argentina is not benefiting from its exports and working people are not making as much money as they did in the past, identifying and questioning the metaphor of "rich country but poor people" with a final title that references the external debt. Aesthetically, the scene juxtaposes contrasting shots to shock its spectator. Through the use of peaceful and tranquil music, which coincides with the beautiful images and advertisements showing "attractive" Caucasian people and their leisure lifestyles, the violence of the slaughterhouse suggests a similar underlying violence to the seductive images. Although there is no doubt about the sequence's political message, *The Hour of the Furnaces* does underlie other issues that are relevant in our reading of *Meat*. Male workers are the ones who enact the violence in the slaughterhouse onto the defenseless cattle, documented pointedly with a close-up shot of the cattle's shaky eye as it meets its death. The violence of the scene displaces gender, as does the whole film, to concentrate on class issues that were in line with the movements and beliefs of the Third Cinema generation of filmmakers and activists.

Both examples, Echeverría's short story and Getino and Solanas's documentary, show the explicit violence and its implied class-based nature, whereas *Meat* adopts a more deliberate function, one that alternatively emphasizes the gender lens missing in the others. An earlier scene inserts violence as the central problem of the film. The scene begins with the whistle that signals the start of the work shift at the factory. Then there is a cut to a shot inside a walk-in refrigerator with Delicia examining her clipboard and her boss instructing her on what to do to ensure the beef is properly checked for external consumption. When the boss leaves, Delicia begins her inspection, and the suspenseful music accompanies shots of the hanging carcasses that obscure Delicia's body from sight. She quickly becomes aware that she is not alone; someone is watching her through the corpses. Hunted like prey, she runs but is unable to escape. The predator finally catches her and proclaims what became a trademark phrase for the film, "Carne sobre carne" ("meat/flesh on meat"), and then throws a carcass on the ground, followed by Delicia, then forcing himself on her body. When he is done, he leaves her on the meat (fig. 12). She picks herself up and cries, surrounded by the carcasses in the background.

The scene establishes a crucial correlation between beef and Delicia. First, Delicia is prey to the predator that is El Macho much like the cattle sought for slaughtering; but secondly and more importantly, the connection between meat as the product of work and Delicia as product not consumer will dominate the rest of the narrative. It is not only that she identifies with beef but also that she is associated with it by her male coworker whose name clearly fixes his gendered and sexist position. From the perspective of El Macho, he wants to empower himself imposed onto the meat that is Delicia, and thus why he rapes her continually in the very same work environments where the product is prepared and delivered: the refrigerator in this scene and the truck later on. The scenes of violence historically have an antecedent in Echeverría's "The Slaughter Yard." Not only does the story refer to the culture of violence in the countryside but also to the popular masses who are overcome by the barbarism of violence implicit in the preparation of the meat. While *Meat* can be seen as a modern-day version of the story, the narrative adds a more blatant layer of gender and places the film squarely within a working-class environment that makes the simple parallel a problematic

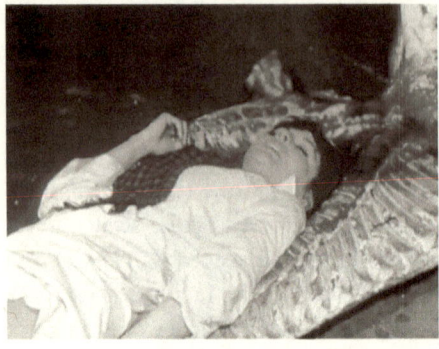

FIGURE 12. Delicia on a carcass equated to the meat or flesh in the workplace, in *Meat* (1968)

one, and where the balance of work and leisure coincide as in *The Hour of the Furnaces*.

The underlying culture of beef generally emphasizing questions of class and race in the other examples registers differently in *Meat*, where work, specifically the Fordist assembly-line work also featured in *The Hour of the Furnaces*, clearly divides along gendered lines. The film is not about the relationship between worker and boss but the relationship among workers themselves, mainly the male-female divide. The division of gender in *Meat* displaces earlier reflections about class struggle in *Thunder among the Leaves* and *The Shad Fishermen*. In many ways, the clear class consciousness in *The Hours of the Furnaces* comes to be problematized by the violence on gender that *Meat* enacts. To understand the gender and class implications and their intersection in the film, I turn to the history and politics of meat in Argentina as it relates to a culture of masculinity.

The politics of food consumption has clear origins in Perón's administration, the first to use food, more particularly meat, as a symbol for propaganda in establishing its own vision for the nation, continuing the tradition set by "The Slaughter Yard" but giving it new meaning. Perón manipulated the idea that beef, as a luxury item, had been unattainable to both migrants from the countryside and common workers in the cities. The ideal past of the gaucho, represented by the unrestricted access to wild animals and to free and abundant beef, had become a distant nostalgia during "the consolidation of big estates, the establishment of foreign meatpacking industries, and the emergence of a network of commercial distribution of food."[53] As real wages rose 62 percent from 1945 to 1949, so did the physical volume of grocery store sales, by 40 percent.[54] People were making more money and using their newfound wealth on food.

Simultaneously, the administration instituted policies that made the attainability of beef a renewed possibility for people. The Peronist state supported meatpacking companies with subventions and subsidized beef sales in major cities. They opened municipal markets where food was sold at reduced prices, sponsored consumer cooperatives, and the Eva Perón Foundation developed *proveedurías*, stores that offered groceries at lower prices. Behind the supportive policies was the discourse that the popular masses now again had access to the luxury of meat in a nostalgic return to the abundance experienced by the gaucho. While seemingly a simple idea, the politics of beef had many different facets, as Natalia Milanesio asserts in her article about food consumption. First, it aligned with the nationalist agenda that dominated Peronist politics, and second, it also had links to an underlying masculine culture of beef.

Before Perón, the Argentine beef industry was devoted to ensuring large, high-quality, and inexpensive beef quotas for exports to the detriment of local consumers. For instance, from 1910 to 1920, 90 percent of beef production went to Britain.[55] The political left criticized the export practices by local businesses, claiming that it was contributing to the dichotomy of "the rich country but poor people," a critique appearing in *The Hour of the Furnaces*. When Perón came to power, he challenged the traditional dichotomy through the policies mentioned as well as imposing a price ceiling, closing illegal abattoirs, and fighting black markets.[56] Furthermore, when thinking about the traditional staple of *asado* [grilling], a food practice that is linked to the gaucho and cooked in the open air by males outside the domestic space of the kitchen, one cannot ignore the gendered implications of meat. "By securing beef for the internal market, the Peronist administration symbolically recovered the historical sustenance of national masculinity."[57]

Although over time the Peronist vision shifted away from promoting solely beef in its food policies, the connection the state made between food, its most representative class of workers, and meat as a luxury item had effects that would still be relevant in 1968, when both *Meat* and *The Hour of the Furnaces* were made. *The Hour of the Furnaces* is an obviously Peronist film. Beef, as a national product consumed by the local popular masses, associated with the masculinity of the past, serves as the backdrop for *Meat*, which addressed more directly its gendered characteristics than the class one found in the Third Cinema example.

In *La vida en las fábricas*, Mirta Zaida Lobato studied, from a sociological point of view, the worker's life in Berisso, a town in the greater La Plata area in the province of Buenos Aires, where US-owned meat-processing plants Swift and Armour had operated for years. Lobato argues that the factories were a battleground after the fall of Perón. The instability of work, changes in political subsidization, a drop in prices of meat, and diversification of the consuming countries ensured that the long-fought battles won during the Perón era relegated the workers to a difficult and precarious position yet again.[58] The political tensions occurring during the Perón period within the different ideological positions staked by workers became whitewashed by the common threat that Perón's fall meant to any worker talking about rights. Yet Lobato's focus on the female worker explains her multiply marginalized position in the work environment:

> The formation of a class identity, of a national identity, and of a political identity was also intersected by the difference of gender. Women of lower classes were subject to a sometimes not very subtle domination. Subaltern groups found it difficult to find ways or words to express their ideas because in the factory, in the union, in the political parties, and in sum, in society, their voices were scarcely heard . . . and their necessities were silenced. . . . [T]he mechanisms of deliberation and decision were based on maintaining inequities and their exclusion, although not even through formal exclusion. . . . [T]he tensions in the factories, in the union, and in society gave way to a competition between different publics that helped to disseminate discourse that questioned privilege of the few—in terms of class—and also in the mapping of the differences in gender.[59]

The silencing and muzzling of female workers exist in both the story and the documentary, both of which put aside gender issues for class ones. In the case of "The Slaughter Yard," the female worker is an even more primitive and despicable figure than her male barbaric counterpart, and in *The Hour of the Furnaces* she is absent, altogether written out of the story. Defiantly, *Meat* features the role of women in the workplace. An early scene follows the documentary moment described when the female workers engage in a conversation about marriage, children, and work. The women show a very skeptical position when it comes to all three. Sex means having children and marriage means more children. All three have to do with the curse of being tied to reproduction. Work is a necessity for feeding the many children that sex brings.

While Delicia is quiet when it comes to the topics discussed by colleagues, as she is inexperienced, she insists that she loves her boyfriend Antonio and will marry him once he receives a promotion in the same meatpacking plant. Sexuality here is positioned differently than the reproductive function that the women complain about. In the case of

Delicia, it is part of the naïve embrace of love as an abstract concept. With rape and violence, the fantasy world created by Delicia changes, displacing the reproductive function associated with the female body in her original fantasy and affirming the experience of the other women workers about sex. The double standard becomes exposed: for the female worker sex is more work (children); for the men it is "leisure," or the expression of a violent masculinity. In the scene, the women share a work environment that entails complaining about work as a necessity. Work for all the women is an obligation, as in the case of Delicia, whose grandfather is sick and unable to make a living. Her friend wants to leave the hard labor of the factory to sing a tango, another endeavor not suited for a woman and historically associated with sex work. When the friend follows her dream, she encounters a violent pimp who steals her earnings. For women, there is no pleasure of nobility in work; it becomes a mere means to a given end.

The film shifts from the work of the females to the "play" of the males. While the women regard work as a product of reproductive responsibility, the sexual rape in the second half of the narrative is problematically attributed to the "leisure" side of the dialectic. In the scene preceding the rape, a group of men gather over a communal *asado* to devise a plan to abduct and later violate Delicia. Ironically, the friendly and connective social event of cooking food in the open air, always an already masculine space, motivates the violence and harsh masculinity that ensues, just like in "The Slaughter Yard." But the twist comes in the gender and class identity of the victim, where a lower-class female replaces the elite male of the story. Classifying the rape as leisure is highly questionable, as Delicia does not enjoy the sex or violence. She clearly resists from the beginning by screaming, pushing, and kicking the three men, who physically force her into the truck. They lock her up in the truck and move her to a new location where she waits for each of the different workers to enjoy themselves at her expense. She continues to resist throughout the encounters with words, psychological manipulation, or by spitting, kicking, screaming, and hitting. In an assembly-line act the workers receive their share of the "meat" that is Delicia, a privilege they acquired through a purchase from El Macho.

The production-line Fordist work ethic materializing in *Meat*, unlike any other in the Bó-Sarli productions, extends to the violent sex that happens. The scenes that make up the second half of the film take place in the back of El Macho's truck, the same one that delivers the beef packed at the plant. The transportation vehicle that moves the company's product to other national and global locations is the very place for the multiple rapes from six different men entering the space in a production-line fashion. The men desire Delicia and see her as pure "meat," in a replication of the work environment in the factory. What I mean is that it is no coincidence that the workers, who are an integral part of the production and distribution of meat for the factory, replicate the performance in the act of Delicia's rape as an act of assembly-line rape. Delicia's clothing, matched with the national flag, adds another layer of signification, perhaps unveiling a need to reappropriate into the nation the highly commodified and international star.

Inspired by the meat they had just eaten in the male-centered, ritualistic *asado*, and claiming a sense of national ownership of the commodities—both Delicia and the meat they produce—the men ironically create a sense of belonging that is based on male brutal violence, much like the foundational short story. The workers do not see Delicia as an equal worker or as an empowered human being, they all coalesce in one expected masculine identity, that of the macho or original orchestrator of the whole adventure. The juxtaposition of Delicia against the carcasses in the plant uncovers El Macho's treatment of Delicia as a product or a thing that can be consumed. Correlating sex and meat is clearly intentional as the film was marketed with such connection in mind, a legacy that continues to this day as Sarli's body is used to sell the country's dying but most renowned export.[60] Yet the highly problematic pairing of the woman's body and meat hides many issues about work and leisure, as I have discussed.

The truck in *Meat* both covers and exposes the degrees of each encounter, showing that while on the surface the different forced rapes were all the same from one clear, male-dominant position bragging of the conquest, what happens inside is a more nuanced scene expressing a multitude of possible masculinities.[61] For instance, the third encounter with Josecito exemplifies his struggle between what is expected of him by the other males and what he knows is right and just. He refuses to rape Delicia, even though he desires her. He, unlike the others, sees her as a human being and declines to force her to be with him. When he exits the truck, his struggle continues, as he rejects the men's celebration and excuses himself from the group. He says he should hit El Macho but he cannot bring himself to confront the bully and the overall expectation of masculinity. Another position is played out by the fifth encounter with a gay man. The character is quite aggressive before entering the truck; outside, he plays the part of a hyper macho man. When he enters, he tells Delicia that he can't bear it any longer because he desires her boyfriend Antonio. While the character is a caricature of homosexuality through his very feminized demeanor, he clearly represents the divide between his homosexual identity in the truck and the one he performs outside of it. The scenes allow for the development of differences found in the closet, a variance that changes the discourse on acceptable masculinity.[62] The many possible identities that exist behind closed doors all coalesce into one of a macho man outside the truck. Masculine identity, seen through this lens, has nothing to do with being but instead is reduced to a question of belonging. The community of workers needs to belong to a masculine identity, which in the end can be disconnected from people's true desires and feelings.

Meat is a cautionary tale about the dangers of the industrialized assembly-line work ethic and its effect on male and female workers. Like *The Hour of the Furnaces*, it shows how workers become alienated from the production of the commodity they produce as it adopts an abstract value that can easily be transferrable to another human being, in this case a vulnerable female. Work and violence create a sense of superficial masculine belonging that differs greatly from the utopic labor-collective belonging of *Thunder among the Leaves*.

The film leaves the audience with many questions about who in the end does not belong. Is it the workers in a Fordist work environment? Is it the female in such a vile milieu? Is it the love or violent sex on the screen? Or is it the filmmaking process itself? The film comments on each and all of the mentioned topics without leaving a definitive message. But one thing is clear: the assembly-line work ethic defies work, lifestyle, amorous relationships, and the filmmaking process itself. In the end, what wins out is the more artisanal and personal—love, sex, and work. Masculinity as defined in the films is based on a certain type of labor, the same type of sex and love that also described the rest of the Sarli-Bó productions.

AFFECTIVE AND IMMATERIAL WORK: THE FEMALE BODY OF THE SEX WORKER

In *Meat*, the reference to the working female body as a prostitute comes in the figure of Delicia's friend, who sings tangos in the cantina, a profession historically associated with sex work. The first man who enters the truck after El Macho tells Delicia that what is happening to her is due to the ban on brothels. Films like *Meat* integrate the laboring female body into secondary narratives, whereby primary positioning is generally relegated to the male working body. Instead, the female body, mainly belonging to the star, relates a different story about leisure, albeit quite problematic as in the case of *Meat*. However, these two seemingly opposing tendencies converge in the immaterial and affective labor performed by the female sex worker.

Prostitutes are central to the story lines in *Intimacies of a Prostitute* and *A Butterfly in the Night*, stories about the lives and challenges of a protagonist who works selling her body. The films *My Father's Wife*, *Naked on the Sand*, and *Tropical Ecstasy* also reference sex work, though it is not necessarily at the forefront of the story. Similar to *Belle de Jour* (Luis Buñuel, France/Italy, 1967), the main character of *Bewitched* goes to a brothel herself as an act of rebellion against an ineffectual, distant, and loathing husband. In all of the examples, prostitution is a profession like any other that one can leave behind, despite some difficulty, as the baggage that it brings seems to haunt the protagonist (*Tropical Ecstasy*) or tempt her back to its more exciting lifestyle (*A Butterfly in the Night*).

The topic of prostitution nicely merges the two variants in the films discussed here, due to its status as a nonmaterial affective form of labor. Issues of work and class in the case of this chapter, and gender and sex in the case of chapter 5, merge through the subject of sex work. In *Tropical Ecstasy*, the protagonist leaves her life in the city for the onerous work on the beach, a better alternative to the violent existence in the brothel. In *Intimacies of a Prostitute* and *A Butterfly in the Night* the protagonist's position is elevated: she is able to leave the profession by marrying a wealthy man. In both films, marriage offers an escape, mobilizing the lower-class prostitute to the higher-class status of wife but limiting her to its constraints. These become objectionable for Yvonne in *A Butterfly in the Night*, when she chooses to leave the comforts of a heterosexual relationship to return to the streets in Paris.[63]

Prostitution, however, embodies the site where gender begins to infiltrate into the affect of labor. A challenging topic among feminists, sex work inserts female empowerment into the discussion of sex, one that cannot be limited to the melodramatic discourse about a victimized woman. While it is true that issues of trafficking may indeed pose a real threat to women in the profession, women still have the choice to seek prostitution as a real alternative mode of earning a living. The debate was synthesized in the sex wars of the 1980s, encompassing prostitution, pornography, and controversial practices such as bondage/discipline or sadomasochism that pitted anti-porn/anti-prostitution factions alleging exploitation of women and male violence on the one hand against their sex-positive sisters, who recognized empowerment of women to choose different sexual options. This is mainly a feminist battle taking place in Anglophone countries.[64] Regardless of the debates, the issue of sex work as an act of labor recalls the control or surveillance of women's bodies, which has no simple solution.

A more nuanced look at sex work can be found in *Sex and Danger in Buenos Aires*. Historian Donna Guy studied prostitution in the Argentine capital from 1857 to 1936, when the law of social prophylaxis passed. Law 12.331 banned prostitution and made prenuptial medical examination for men compulsory. Guy argues that social control of sexuality was directly linked to questions of family, nation, and citizenship. Municipal authorities, police, and doctors were all responsible for the social control of women's bodies.

While Guy's scholarship ends in 1936, she briefly discusses the continuation of the same discourse into the Perón and post-Perón eras. She argues that once the general was in power there was a different pressure that heightened the tightening of sexuality. New anxieties arose, as males dominated more spaces, such as that of the labor union and political parties. While the press interpreted pro-prostitution actions as those in line with a policy against the church, such as the legalization of divorce in 1954, for Guy it was clearly in line with earlier practices. Advances in medicine and the "new threat of homosexuality" helped to open up the bordellos in a desperate attempt to ironically "save the family."[65] The efforts of Perón to make prostitution safe and accessible to his male followers failed because he was unable to do so before he was overthrown.

Cristiana Schettini rightly points out there is an epistemological hole left behind in the research about prostitution practices between 1936 and 1994, when the debates about the unionization of prostitutes began to take hold.[66] A historical exploration of what transpires after 1936 remains unexplored, but Guy does set up a Foucaultian analysis that clearly stakes out the different sides leading to the implementation of the new law, to show the interests at the heart of prostitution and the control of women's bodies. She reaffirms this sentiment: "The roots of Latin American authoritarianism are deep within gender relations and the politics of social control, and the civil liberties of even the most socially unacceptable men, women, and children must be protected lest their civil incapacity be extended to other members of the population."[67] What does it mean for women's bodies and their control when onscreen discussion of prostitution is highly censored, as happened with the name change required for *Intimacies of a Prostitute* and the highly manipulated version of *A Butterfly in the Night*, which has many blurry scenes that erase or obfuscate its visual clarity? The problem of social control is a lot more nuanced and can be interpreted through the sex-positive lens differently. What does it mean in such a context, where sex onscreen is highly controlled, to bring up the silenced, nonexistent profession and character of the sex worker?

Taken in pairs, the films *Intimacies of a Prostitute* and *A Butterfly in the Night* work to counteract each other. They present a strategy that can be found all over the Bó-Sarli oeuvre, an anxiety that exists about exposing/showing/featuring sexuality in its many forms, alongside its moralistic guilt complex. While in *Intimacies of a Prostitute* María eventually settles down with José Luis, choosing heteronormative marriage over life on the streets, the attempt to follow the same path in *A Butterfly in the Night* is fraught because Jorge (the José Luis equivalent) dies. There is another lover, Lorenzo, who tries to win her over, but Yvonne says to him: "And you, you can chain me up, and I don't want to be that way anymore." Her final words are "I'm leaving," before boarding a train to return to her life on the streets.[68] The liberating ending contrasts with the ending of *Intimacies of a Prostitute*, when her marriage to José Luis may offer a way out of the troubles the pair experienced with censorship.

Despite the differences in their plots, both films were unacceptable for authorities. Although the *Intimacies of a Prostitute*'s ending is in other ways liberating because María is finally free from the shackles of her pimp, Cholo, who tries to maintain control over her throughout the whole film, she needs to be married to validate her worth. In this way both films offer liberating narratives with contrasting endings. *A Butterfly in the Night* sets up sex work as a flashback to the past, while in *Intimacies* it is part of the present story, which encompasses more than just the difficulties of life on the streets. The film lobbies for the law and promotes an activism about the need for legal protection for women sex workers. In a scene between María and her wise friend Olga, a fellow sex worker who helped her learn her trade, Olga reminds her of her own fight for the rights of the worker. She recalls pleading with a minister:

> This is a profession like all others. Pass a law of prophylaxis where all of us who have chosen this sad path can protect ourselves. . . . But nobody remembered us, and how many well-heeled men lay in our beds? And the next day they were big shots who went around preaching morals to their public. . . . Phonies.

The film exposes the hypocrisy of those hiding behind moral discourse and unwilling to openly fight for the rights of sex workers, and contends that sexual exchange still occurs despite its illegal status. It also serves as a commentary on the morals underlying the censoring apparatus. More importantly, it positions prostitution as a job and the prostitute as a sex worker who also requires protection through legislation, a return to past laws.

Through sex work, the films arrive at the question of female labor. The bodies of prostitutes in labor belong on the streets. They are empowered to pick their own destinies, while at times they are hard-working bodies that have become cynical. Sarli's characters are scared, distressed, and anxious bodies that are being watched, labeled, and shackled by their circumstances and positions as workers and women. If what Elena Gorfinkel argues is true, that "the screen performer's physical presence is expropriated and refigured: re-edited, reframed, and re-temporalized,"[69] then work only becomes visible in an instance, as its failure, when it is side by side with leisure.

The films discussed in this chapter clearly spotlight work as a masculine pursuit, one that involves violence but can also lead to utopic collective well-being. Through work, Bó defines a specific audience, the working-class male, who is both voyeur within the films and also wrestling through different positions to mark new masculinity possibilities in society. He is grappling with the changing times but still needs to belong in a culture that has been historically *machista*. Female workers tend to be performing immaterial labor, a type of work that crosses over to ensure the pleasure of male leisure activities. The roles of women as victims and men as oppressors seem to be reinforcing a rather patriarchal paradigm. However, despite men's attempt to control, surveil, force, and define Sarli's body, she enacts other functions that make her portrayals onscreen of work as a sex worker rather slippery. Through the filmic form, the narratives tell other stories, presenting different options for female bodies that are simultaneously liberating and sexual, a tale for the next chapter.

CHAPTER 5

Affective Intimate Interludes

The Risky Female Body

BODILY MEMORIES

When General Juan Domingo Perón was overthrown in 1955, people rose up and bolted to the streets to protest the new authoritarian policies, especially the prohibition of symbols, signs, doctrine, and artistic works that were deemed to illegally propagate the outlawed Peronist ideology. Nowhere was the resentment greater than in Rosario, the third most populous city, where massive demonstrations erupted. One infamous example that occurred in the working-class El Saladillo, a neighborhood surrounding the American-owned meatpacking plant Swift, featured women's bodies. To protect a statue of first lady Evita from the destructive forces of the army, female activists tore off their blouses and shirts to expose their breasts in defiance of the overwhelming and imposing presence of the troops.[1] Historian César Seveso calls their action a "regendered transvestite version of the 'descamisados,'" the shirtless ones.[2]

In reevaluating the historic performance, one can even conclude that already by 1955 the presence of women's bodies in public display always produced an already gendered performed act. Suffragettes winning the vote less than a decade earlier, in the 1946 election, appropriated Peronist political methods through a new lens. To be a "descamisada" marked the gesture as already gendered, and regardless of how its staging is interpreted, one cannot erase the gender prominence that it implies.[3] More clearly, its sexuality as an act both materializes the body and emphasizes its difference. The evocative example serves as a reminder of the rooted connection between Peronism, women, and sexuality in public space. To think through this act as one that is only gendered, however, is to limit it to mere representation.

This chapter reflects on what the body could mean beyond identification and as a means of connecting to its audience on an affective plane. The "pornographic" bodily display the activists chose counteracts a normative ideal of women and challenges class and gender expectations at their intersection. To isolate the "pornographic" through the female body from that moment in Argentine history as it progresses through the work of Sarli and Bó in Latin America and beyond will require a multifaceted approach. The body creates an affectively charged disturbance that is both within representation and outside of it, allowing for and promising pleasure, pain, disgust, risk, and access to past memories and future possibilities.

In the previous chapters, I have built a case for contexualizing Armando Bó and Isabel Sarli's work within Argentine movements through a politics of the body that grew into a more complex philosophy of liberation in the 1960s better aligning with the sexuality crusades of youth culture. In so doing, I have argued that their films tie to the connotations of the working body, but a more obvious and a seemingly easier correlation can be found in their sexualized images. The corporeal presence of Isabel Sarli, the films' main attraction and the premise for the duo's marketing, drives the movies and the enterprise of their work. Their productions encompass two different thematic strands: first, that which references the political, realistic, and material world of their time as already outlined in chapter 4; and second, just as important, the emphasis on the excess of leisure and pleasure, more specifically in exhibition and enjoyment. The two angles are not exclusive; their cinema proposed a more open sexuality. This chapter will focus on what made them popular and famous throughout the Americas, showing how the central emphasis on the body, particularly Sarli's voluptuous form, will broach a notion of sexual pleasure that evolves from the everyday occurrence to a form of female empowerment seen through its liberation. The clear tension developed through stories of female violation, victimization, and oppression discussed in chapter 4 creates a myriad of conflicting possibilities that materialize in the content and plots of the films but are liberated through their form. The repetition of a structure that makes their work knowable to audiences only becomes more attractive through its difference, a difference that in many instances ironically happened with the nuanced cuts the censors instigated, adding to the experimental and individual aesthetic that Bó had developed from his first production with Sarli.

While this chapter does not trace a definitive path from objectification of the female body to its emancipation, it does focus on moments of both contradiction and grappling in the aesthetic creation of the films that help to define an implicit and explicit sexuality. As in the rest of the book, I argue that to limit their trajectory to one movie does it a disservice, since their oeuvre more holistically helps to understand the context of censorship and the political and social times that their films are set against: an assemblage of onscreen moments of sexuality, ideologies (Peronism), and trends (a mix of film influences: European art, classical Argentine, neorealism, and sexploitation cinemas) outlined throughout *Violated Frames*. My argument relies on what I describe as suspended instances of affective charges, or repetitions of emotional bursts that interrupt the already fragmented narratives. The jolts begin to define their work and create a familiar brand of images that draw in audiences by galvanizing a multiplicity of possible affective responses. The contradictory impasses expose the inconsistency of the cuts and the way that Bó, as both author in most cases and director in all, worked the state apparatus to ensure the release of their films. To isolate the female body from the narratives is to emphasize that it lives outside the film texts with clearly defined and autonomous displays that exceed the constraints of the story. As events, these instances communicate beyond representation, through an affective register achieved from the onscreen female body, thereby saturating it with a burst of emotional power that simultaneously sutures ("sews" into a series of shots) the spectators into the film and distances them. The films also reveal that like the bodies that fled to the streets in the moment of Perón's downfall, bodies do carry memories and can enact a projection of a future possibility. Both past and future notions go beyond the static notion of bodies, especially their onscreen counterparts. Sarli's repetitive yet different onscreen nude appearances are much more nuanced and complex, carrying a trace of the past to include various dimensions such as its physiology, the local site, the setting, its personal and cultural contexts, memories, experiences, codes, and norms to inflect a future projection, inspiring reactions that range from pleasure all the way to disgust. And, in fact, the displays of Sarli's body that I discuss throughout the chapter made it both offensive and dangerous.

THE AFFECTIVE FEMALE BODY IN TIME

Linda Williams's classic essay "Film Bodies: Gender, Genre, and Excess" offers important insight into the connection between what appears onscreen and the audience through the framework of what she refers to as "body genres."[4] By identifying melodrama, horror, and pornography as "low" genres that produce different bodily responses in the spectator, Williams sets up a paradigm that approaches affect through the structure of genre. While her early analysis is based on its oversimplification in genre, a concept that categorizes films into straightforward groupings, it does contemplate the relationship between the screen and the spectator, not as a set of reactions to specific films but more generally to archetypes. The basic idea that so-called low genres (more popular and easily consumable ones) are more likely to evoke a bodily reaction may indicate a bias toward generalizing popular audiences. Yet Williams's work becomes a useful tool for approaching popular film, not specifically pornography, nor melodrama, but films that push the limits of sex onscreen in a hybrid version of soft pornographic melodrama. Temporally, both genres reenact different moments of fantasy. In the case of pornography, the endless repetition of the "on time" and "now" contrasts with melodrama's pathos of "too late" or the loss of something, reenacting the fantasy differently.[5] Time forms the narrative structure of each genre.

As a hybridization of melodrama and a soft-core pornography, in the Bó-Sarli productions time functions differently from Williams's reflection on the categories. Instead, Elena Gorfinkel's though-provoking analysis of labor in sexploitation film better reflects what happens in the pair's films. "Authenticating a place, a situation, a certain mode of production, the women perform a listless in-between temporality, a dead time between work, which is also another kind of work, working for the camera."[6] Gorfinkel's discussion of time's relationship to labor in examples like *The Sin Syndicate* (Michael Findlay, USA, 1965) exposes a fissure that its mode of production enables but that furthermore subverts the façade of the film itself. To focus our attention on the question of time accords a broader understanding of the Sarli-Bó films themselves and provides another way of comprehending the soft-core images of sexuality.

Employing the Bergsonian project of the French philosopher Gilles Deleuze to theorize about the isolated images of sexuality, *Violated Frames* considers the concept of time on the affective plane. For

Deleuze, the movement-image lives in the present and repeats the now in much the same way that the actions of the Sarli-Bó films present movements through a linear and causal plot narrative.[7] Critics have complained about and condemned this very characteristic of the couple's movies. Simple acts that meld into each other and allow for the familiar and formulaic story lines have frustrated reviewers throughout the history of their experiments. The repetition of straightforward plotlines and underdeveloped characters explains why critics trashed their works. On the contrary, the body images that interrupt the narratives were seamlessly added whether they belonged to the stories or not, and created expectations, growing their fan base both at home and abroad.

The contradiction between the stories and these sexual moments could not be clearer. These more nuanced episodes are infused with an alternative conception of time, one similar to Deleuze's time-image, an image different from itself, virtual to itself, which is charged with both the past and the future becomes the central part of their work.[8] If the images of work, moments arguably referencing the past and future of possibilities, were found mainly in the bodies of the male actors, then what do the onscreen parallels of its main female performer propose? Since the defining feature of the films is its central star, exploring Sarli's seemingly repetitive appearances, performances, and the film aesthetics that mediate her body helps to assert that they actually are not movement-images but time-images that work to suture the audience to the Bó-Sarli brand. To isolate the sexual events, many of which are monotonous and featured as everyday occurrences like in Gorfinkel's example *The Sin Syndicate*, is to also acknowledge Sarli's onscreen body as a working body.

The moments in question are like the interludes that interrupt the narrative in classical Hollywood musicals.[9] The sexualized manifestations function in the same way as the *lucha libre* matches in the Mexican wrestling movies of the 1960s and 1970s.[10] Linda Williams refers to musicals to describe the sex onscreen of pornography as a "number." A closer look, however, suggests the Sarli-Bó "intermissions" are unique in their own right but also achieve the same goals as musical numbers. Whereas on the one hand they may highlight the spectacular nature of the film experience in all of its glory through performance, on the other they also show, in very intimate settings, the delights of water and the monotony of modest baths, showers, and dips, moments that link back to the working actor on the screen. And they spotlight female pleasure through the body's connection to nature. Like the musical numbers that serve to showcase talent or tell the story, the scenes end up becoming an important and crucial part of the narrative, although they are framed as something extraneous. Their seeming superficiality may signal their unimportance in the film, yet the censors' scissors easily cut away countless of these scenes because they found them highly offensive. The cuts left ellipses in the filmic sequence of events but also indicated that they were not so irrelevant.

A detailed analysis of such jolts finds that they are vital to the films and less gratuitous than may at first appear. As flashes of leisure and pleasure, transcending the mere spectacle, they are inscribed with memory of a past and the promise of a possible future by constructing an illustration of bodily enjoyment, one that exudes from the film and connects to the audience as affect. These affective resonances allow the female body to perform uncontained and freed in its excesses, even if that performance is not always credible. The pinup poses, the dancing, the water scenes, and the union of the female body to nature as a site of enjoyment are four specific recurring events that jolt the spectator and transcend the stories being told. Coherently, and as a continuous set of aesthetically similar episodes, they coalesce in repetition with a difference: they are distinct and progress with time. They feature the female body as excessively unruly and create a potentiality for future sexual norms. The body then becomes the site of unsettling, with a dangerous invitation reminding its audience of past histories and proposing future possibilities. The four jolts (poses, dancing spectacles, water scenes, and masturbation in nature) are all instances that create an affective network that through time functions to highlight the importance of the female body as sexual politics.

FIRST JOLT: THE POSE AND THE STAR

The early films set up a pattern by defining both Sarli's exceptionalism and stardom beyond the plots or narrative frameworks of each text. From the very beginning of their collaboration, when Bó highlighted Sarli's debut in *Thunder among the Leaves* despite her minor role, she has been constructed to fit the bill of a star.[11] Bó manufactures her onscreen appearance in three deliberate ways. First, her body draws in the male gaze inscribed in the narratives through voyeurs. Second is the medium shot that shows her breasts as her most prized feature. And finally, the shot-by-shot fragmentation of her body highlights her special attributes. All three substantiate the claims in Laura Mulvey's often cited psychoanalytic analysis of classical Hollywood cinema showing the dialectic between spectacle and narrative.[12] As a feminist theorist, Mulvey reveals how codes and conventions of narrative film construct visual pleasure through a "to-be-looked-at-ness" of the female lead.[13] She describes the process as "scopophilia" or pleasure in looking, identified with the onscreen male character.[14] Rodolfo Kuhn and others have defined Sarli's onscreen construction through such a lens, although Kuhn also outlines her contradictions.[15]

However, Mulvey's text analysis falls short in explaining the full extent of the sexuality as a more nuanced lens of the star begins to unfold. Sarli's exceptionality surfaces as she executes the expected dances and poses that have consolidated the careers of other vedettes, wearing elaborate costumes and performing specific gestures. Her favorite designer, Paco Jamandreu, molded ornamented dresses that highlight her body from early on in her filmmaking career, continuing until her final film made post-Bó, *La dama regresa* (*The Lady Is Back*, Jorge Polaco, Argentina, 1996).[16] Costumes fit for a queen always seemed to contradict the diegetic story because she generally played underprivileged characters in rural settings: humble farm girls, simple workers, and poor prostitutes.[17] For instance, in *The Girl Ass-Keeper of Ypacaraí*, the tight-fitting red dress does not match with the representation of an impoverished peasant. In *My Father's Wife*, Siboney performs in a dress too fancy and sophisticated for a sex worker of a small town singing in a local cantina; it seems too expensive for the cheap aesthetics of the film (fig. 13). And yet Sarli's offscreen, mundane, everyday existence constantly featured in the tabloids; her simple life with her mother, animals, and later her adopted children contradicted the extravagant lifestyles usually associated with big stars and found onscreen. It is precisely the tension between her exceptionality and her commonality that invokes one of the many affective moments for spectators bewildered by her sexualized and embellished onscreen appearance. A similar tension was strategically deployed by Eva Perón to appeal to a mass base through styled attire by the same beloved designer.[18]

We must look beyond Mulvey's theories to understand the generic conventions of the sexploitation genre, which can broaden our understanding of the Sarli-Bó work and place it in a more complex matrix of audience engagement with the sexual spectacle. Film critic Leon Hunt draws on the work of Tom Gunning, particularly his concept of "cinema of attractions," to examine onscreen sexuality. Hunt suggests that sexploitation stars have a distinctive relationship to the audience.[19] In

FIGURE 13. Siboney performing in a dress too garnish for a small-town sex worker, in *My Father's Wife* (1968)

reference to early cinema, Gunning describes the unique power or "harnessing of visibility" in the early days of film as "a cinema that displays its visibility, willing to rupture a self-enclosed fictional world for a chance to solicit the attention of the spectator."[20] Here, Gunning sees the attraction in the cinema's ability to show something, its function as exhibitionist. In focusing on this aspect, he is able to draw his attention to cinema's series of spectacles rather than its narrative continuity, whereby "theatrical display dominates over narrative absorption, emphasizing the direct simulation of shock or surprise at the expense of unfolding a story or creating a diegetic universe."[21] This distinction is what separates Gunning from Mulvey, who relies heavily on the narrative diegetic.

Throughout this book I have been arguing that while the narrative may bring glimpses of a specific politics, the fact that the films were heavily censored and developed through self-censorship makes it hard to keep the analysis solely at the level of the narrative. Moreover, it was not the narrative that attracted the spectators. For this reason, sex onscreen critics like Hunt and Eric Schaefer have found Gunning's theories inspiring because they propose an alternative.[22] Sarli's bodily moments that tease toward a possible sexual reveal can then be seen to fall within this exhibitionist characterization, what Gunning describes as an attraction like a roller coaster ride.[23] Hunt suggests Gunning's concept is equally applicable to striptease scenes in sexploitation or glamour film, where the look straight into the camera dissolves into a "wink" to the audience.[24] Thus, these moments are not necessarily tied to the diegetic story but function on another level that elevates them to become self-referentially exhibitionist, and they mark the exact instance when the star connects to the spectator. As Gunning explains: "The story simply provides a frame upon which to string a demonstration of the magical possibilities of the cinema."[25] Sarli's onscreen performances, thus, work as repetitive motifs that engage with the audience during these exciting spectacle events, stimulating visual curiosity and marking the main reason for going to the cinema to see her movies in the first place. The films create an affective network meant to entice viewers in new ways and produce a spectrum of possible reactions from complete enrapture to absolute disgust.

Beyond the present of the narrative framework, these flashes infused with affective possibilities generate a suspension of time that encompasses past, present, and future all at once. Timelessness seals a sense of belonging for the audience drawn in by the tension between the desired but mystifying star and the everyday simple woman. It allows for a continuity between films, leaving these moments as scenes that can be watched separately from the movie and live outside the space of the diegesis. This also makes the scenes easier to cut without necessarily interrupting the narrative flow. And yet they are crucial to the films and will provide opportunities for new readings.

The simplest example of what I am referring to is the pose, which has its foundation in a long history of visual art, photography, magazines, and films. For Sarli, poses continually interrupt the narratives and are always featured as extras that do not necessarily lead the story anywhere. For instance, *Insatiable* begins with a photographer taking pictures of a nude Carmen covered only by a boa. The cuts between the photographer snapping the pictures and Carmen's different poses result in Carmen looking straight into the camera, performing the wink that Hunt singles out. Her exaggerated moves with the medium shot highlighting her shoulders change to a pose of her head pulled back in different angles as she touches her breasts, smiles, teases with the boa, and then looks right at the viewer. The sequence is not important to the narrative as it has no direct relevance to the story, which is about a

FIGURE 14. Two poses from the opening scenes in *Meat* (1968): the first, one of many flashes of female nude statues that opens the film; the second, Delicia posing for her painter boyfriend

nymphomaniac and her adventures with different lovers. It could easily be cut or eliminated. And yet this scene draws the audience in from the beginning, which may explain why the film was prohibited. It exists outside of the narrative and offers a moment of suspended time within the story, as if we are looking at the different captured stills of the pinup. Another similar example is found in *Meat*'s opening, when static nude statues match the private moment of Delicia in a bedroom modeling for her boyfriend's painting (fig. 14). The sexualized posture of the nude female starlet with her head falling back mimics the female statues found in cities.

The poses in both *Meat* and *Insatiable* happen seamlessly and flawlessly within stories but are not essential to them. They contribute to creating a nondiegetic narrative of the star, and they can also be reproduced for further real-life exploitation as commodities beyond the film. Moments of posing create a repertoire of sex symbol pinups, as in *Naked Temptation*, when Sandra models topless with reeds, barely covered, to tease José María with a seductive smile, a famous shot still reproduced today in different versions (fig. 15). These shots recall the pinup made popular in venues like the first issue of *Playboy* in 1953. Indeed, Sarli featured in the American men's lifestyle and entertainment magazine as "the wild belle of the pampas," although her name was misspelled as Sarlis.[26] In the four-page exposé, the star is already framed as a simple working girl with a hand on her waist in a red dress and a fishing net as a backdrop, while she strikes her pose from the film *The Shad Fishermen*. She is presented as a humble proletariat woman, who resembles the "girl next door" with an

FIGURE 15. Sandra from *Naked Temptation* (1966) modeling topless with reeds, one of Isabel Sarli's most renowned images

added exotic element or otherness. By the time she appeared in *Playboy* she had already achieved star status in Argentina and other Latin American countries, mainly Paraguay.[27] Fitting the magazine's tourist gaze that foregrounded fashionable world resorts and enticing nightspots, the exoticization and rustication of stars like Sarli promises release from local taboos both social and sexual while at the same time downplaying the foreign for US audiences.[28] Of course, *Playboy* wasn't the only venue to showcase the bombshell. Her body and image appeared in the local and international popular press throughout her controversial career, with pinup shots taken directly from her movies that went onto have a life of their own.[29]

In one of her final films, *Last Love in Tierra del Fuego*, the pose is remembered more literally in the pictures of past images from Isabel's career. Real life and fiction coalesce, not only in the character's name, Isabel, with an ironic surname Borja (in reference to Argentina's famous elite author, Jorge Luis Borges, the antithesis of the couple's popular and populist work), but also in the pictures taken from Sarli's offscreen career that are used to construct Isabel Borja's fictional life trajectory. The promotional photos found throughout the story line of *Last Love in*

Tierra del Fuego relate to a past based on posing, like the real career of the star. The blending of on- and offscreen references helps to connect to the duo's history as well as create a bubble of timelessness, where past, present, and future fuse together. Yet the reason Bó integrated the earlier images and parts of home movies they had shot on their trips abroad into the narrative is because the film was heavily censored. Once Miguel Paulino Tato retired in 1979, Bó locked himself in the editing room to complete the film, adding the extra material. Ironically, by incorporating extra shots of poses and magazine photos that were featured in Sarli's real-life career, particularly during political times when more could be revealed, Bó was in fact battling the practice of cutting film. During this momentous celebration of the retirement of the harshest censor, he was reinscribing into the film what couldn't be shown earlier. By interweaving stills of poses, intertextual references to their other movies, in combination with excerpts from real-life star events, the present of the narrative takes on a rich assemblage of past memories.

SECOND JOLT: PERFORMING "BAD DANCING"

On the other hand, poses are embedded within more elaborate performances that allude to earlier genres and subgenres such as the *cabareteras* or Mexican brothel melodramas from the 1940s and 1950s that circulated across the Americas.[30] Mexican *cabareteras* and their successors, the sexier *fichera* films of the 1970s, featured different diegetic moments with musical numbers staged for an on- and offscreen audience. Another inspiration can be found in the US burlesque films of the 1940s and 1950s, which had their beginnings in theater and peep shows, featuring the female stripper. Sarli embraces the persona of stripper in her onstage performances in *Naked on the Sand*, *My Father's Wife*, *Ardent Summer*, and *Intimacies of a Prostitute*. They each are evidence of Schaefer's description of the burlesque genre, where the main feature is the female body, not necessarily its star. For Schaefer, the body in spectacle moves as a potentially socially disruptive force that challenges static and passive modes of looking.[31] He criticizes an all-encompassing analysis based on the conventions of film and argues that the contextual and transactional exchanges that happen in burlesque help to "open to a broader range of readings."[32] By providing an industrial and historical analysis, Schaefer shows that the burlesque film exhibits a "spectacle of the uncontained, undomesticated female body offering a sharp contradiction."[33] The same contradiction exists in earlier examples of *cabareteras* like *Aventurera* (Alberto Gout, Mexico, 1950) with their excessive performance of bodies "made of flesh and blood, a bundle of unrepressed instinctive desires," as Ana López reminds us.[34] Throughout this book, I have been arguing that sex onscreen in its many forms profoundly challenged national moral taste and official repressive apparatuses of censorship. In particular, Sarli's body had a clearly unsettling role. Unlike Schaefer, however, I suggest that not only did the films feature the body but also its star, since the two were inextricably entwined. The striptease performances offered another pleasurable event that exposed its full potential to disrupt as a body through Sarli's stardom.

In *Naked on the Sand*, Alicia performs a striptease for a male audience in the club. Her performance, highlighted by various camera positions, replicates earlier examples: the camera starts low on her legs (covered by a skirt) and then pans up her backside, stopping in a medium shot of Alicia wearing a golden coloured gown contrasting with her blue boa, while she moves her hips. She turns her head as shots of different male spectators in the club crosscut her performance. Her dancing continues when the camera fragments her body to zoom in on different details rather than the whole. The shadows in the nightclub help to obscure her body as she takes off her gloves, the skirt, then a spotlight on her midriff and buttocks showcases her thong. When Alicia removes her corset and exposes her breasts, she is left with only a bikini bottom. Her dancing happens in a trance, as she enjoys the music and claims ownership and pleasure in her own body. The close shots of her face and its enjoyment are intercut with specific body parts. Alicia's performance offers an exhibition of her sexual expression for a male audience, already seen in the film. Yet like the burlesque films it ends with a moment of self-excitation, where Sarli too enjoys her body.

The celebration of Sarli's body in performances like the one described in *Naked on the Sand* happened in part due to the conventions of framing typical of striptease scenes but also because of Sarli's credibility in her excitement and sexiness, which also happens naturally. Her face and movements based on positions found in the pose replicate in the onstage scene. The same, however, cannot be said of the dances she performs as part of a ritual in *India*, on the streets and in the theater in *Favela*, nor in a nightclub in *Heat* and *The Impure Goddess* (fig. 16). There her seeming control of her body exemplified in the striptease exhibition easily changes to evoke inexperience and naiveté in seductive dancing, aligning more closely with an everyday woman rather than the star.

Affective Intimate Interludes | 169

FIGURE 16. Concepción's bad dancing in *Favela* (1961)

Her fourth film, *Heat*, contains a distinctive dancing scene in public that reveals her inability to move her body confidently. Sarli's character, Magda, a shy college student who lives at home with her mother, meets Marcos, a hoodlum from the city's underworld. When Magda accompanies Marcos to a cabaret, she is purposefully left alone on stage and encouraged to dance.[35] She looks scared and naïve when suddenly thrust into the public situation beyond her control and in front of gawking male spectators. Yet she does not leave the stage but takes the daring path, accepts her fate, and indulges onlookers to perform a dance for them.[36] She embraces her spotlight and begins to move to the English rhythms of "When You Cha-Cha-Cha," by the Cha-Cha Boys. A close examination of the scene confirms its bad, mocking quality. The lackluster performance cannot be described as sexy. That is, the moves are present—suggestive poses and swinging hips—but Sarli is not connected to her body; the movements are contrived and inauthentic. There is no rhythm that bonds with the ethereal and light music of the tropical cha-cha number. One can blame Sarli's performative inexperience or even the lack of talent in her dancing. The bad quality of the dancing defines the parameters of the Sarli-Bó film project within a mode of production that was limited and cheap, financed with very low budgets, but there are other likely explanations.

At first, the bad dancing can be read as a form of parody, mocking the performative value of women's bodies. Furthermore, it exposes a

FIGURE 17. Ansisé's ballet moves in *India* (1960)

risky proposition that Sarli accepts in *Heat,* a given expectation for the female sex pinup or even just an embrace of the bad, campy quality of the productions themselves and her flaw as an actor. The bad numbers seen in *Heat* are repeated, for example in *India* where Ansisé, the daughter of an Indigenous cacique, performs a ritualistic dance (fig. 17).[37] As in *Heat,* Ansisé moves through space clumsily and swings her hips as the "indigenous" sounds of the drumming fuse with classically inspired music, matching the protagonists' own mixed-racial identity. The performer looks stiff, uncomfortable, and out of place. The bad dancing allows for self-conscious distancing. Whether its purpose was to create a glitch in the narrative or not, the bad highlights her distinction from the group she represents onscreen. Wearing brownface, Sarli is not at ease in an Other's skin or body. Her balletlike moves mixed with stiffly swaying hips emphasize the presence of the other in what is meant to be a ritualistic dance for a specific ethnic group. The self-conscious acts as both feature and demise of the star; that is, on the one hand she is built up as a celebrity through the various methods that have been described throughout this book, but on the other hand the deficient dancing highlights her imperfections and limitations. There is no doubt that Sarli is not a good dancer. When she is given the opportunity to feature her dancing her ineptness is exposed. Then why film those scenes in the first place?

The clear distinction between the types of performance confirms that Bó and the crew were capable of recording Sarli's onscreen sexiness through a framing that implemented the conventions of the genre. But it also corroborates that Sarli had control of her own body to communicate its sexiness and embrace its experience in ecstasy. So why even allow the dancing to be seen in its entirety, in a documentary-like, unedited, full body shot, if the goal was solely seduction? This question motivates better contextualization to posit the implications of what showing incompetence achieves. Sarli's inability to act was always a point of contention for critics, who may have seen the many virtues she had but couldn't forgive her awkwardness on stage. Bó incorporates moments of self-reflection in the stories to acknowledge her failures. In *Intimacies of a Prostitute*, the protagonist María explains, "They taught me to fake, love, and lie. I learned to dance. But in reality, it was only a pretext." For María, dancing is part of the job, a performance that must be learned. And as Sarli is the one saying the words, she explains that acting is also her work. In another example, the onscreen husband, Raúl, comments about Bárbara's onstage dancing in *Ardent Summer*: "you have to keep practicing, you do it better each time." But the performances are not Isabel Sarli's best execution. When shown in their full exposure and unmitigated by editing, the bad dancing highlights both Sarli's commonality, that which contradicts her exceptionality through costume and posing, and draws attention to the body as an actor.

Accepted techniques of spectacle are not what made her films unique as they tend to be interspersed in the narratives and not necessarily the basis of their signature. Furthermore, the scenes such as the one in *India* allow a peek into the uses and functions of the onscreen body as an excessive force and rather suggests the need to forge a new space for its female star, one that will distinguish itself from the traditional forms of staging but will also inscribe the tension between the everyday limitations of a common woman and uniqueness of the star. But most importantly, what is at the root of all the performances and those moments of suspension that can be easily removed from the text, and yet makes it its centering device, is the body itself. All the interludes insist on featuring the body. The conflicting and varied combinations between star and everyday mundane woman begin to form an excess of sensuality that rests on the protagonist's body both as star and worker, making way for another time-sensitive foray into the future of female enjoyment and pleasure. The duo teases the spectators with some conventions, but the repetition of the expected is at times interrupted with surprise, causing shock. Arguably, the most controversial and provocative scenes showcasing the diva's extraordinariness through the familiar happen in the water, with the starlet unrobing to fully expose her breasts in the early examples and the full-frontal nude scenes in the later period. The simple and artistic shots of everyday events in the water have won her the title of "the Clean One," perhaps the most important example of how the body is the main feature of the films. Water, through the many rivers, lakes, pools, baths, and waterfalls, not only echoes the repetitive form found throughout the Sarli-Bó oeuvre, but also it is here where the main affect occurs through its proposition about time.

THIRD JOLT: WATER AS TIMELESSNESS

Isabel Sarli's excursions in the water, the modest baths, showers, and dips, provided an opportunity to show off her indulgent body in simple moments of everyday life. In isolating the first nude water scene that sets the stage for all others, I attribute the groundwork for Bó-Sarli's success to the early pattern that they established from *Thunder among the Leaves* onward. The pattern creates familiarity but also generates certain expectations for the new and surprising. The growing international permissibility for nude female bodily images and the increasing limitations through censorship in Argentina added new possibilities globally, along with more risk locally. The water is where the bulk of the external conflict unfolds because its scenes are the most controversial parts of Sarli's work as an actor and Bó's as director, as well as arguably their most accomplished. The actor's stiffness and outside restrictions disappear in the water, where she is most at ease to play in the utopic playgrounds where the scenes are shot.

To return to the foundational reveal in *Thunder among the Leaves*, I show how its framing as a seamless instant of the capture, detention, and arrest of time is actually put together by a variety of cuts. Despite the frenetic nature of the editing, the soothing accompanying music allows for a suspension of time and a liberation of all possibilities. It is an example of Deleuze's virtual, images that exceed the present of the appearance into a temporal labyrinth. They reconcile a reflection on memory of the past with a future potentiality of the body. Through a repetition that recreates similar spectacles from film to film, the play between seeing and not seeing, the reference to past familiar scenes,

FIGURE 18. An instant when Sarli's breasts are revealed in the frenetic shooting of the infamous nude water scene in *Thunder among the Leaves* (1958)

and the difference that each film proposed by pushing onscreen norms, merge present, past, and future.

In the foundational scene, Flavia approaches the river on a hill through a shot from behind. She bends down as the camera pans up to an establishing scene of the environment and its lush surrounding forest, and a dissolve reveals Flavia splashing in the distance, followed by an extreme long shot of the riverbank. The quick dissolve, barely noticeable, confuses the spectator: Flavia seems to be the one watching the scene but quickly transitions to the actor performing in it. The jump-cut-like technique has a disorienting effect, making it seem more dreamlike. Its ellipsis plays with time, annulling it and perhaps setting the stage for future censored manipulation. A cut focuses on a closer perspective, and a medium shot of Flavia comes into view from the direction of the camera. Now she appears in murky water swimming toward us. She turns around, lifts her body slightly, and exposes her breasts (fig. 18). The cut to a longer shot shows Flavia enjoying the water, and then there is a tilt up to a spectator watching on the hill, an occasion described more thoroughly in the previous chapter. The point-of-view shot of Flavia from the distance is then interrupted with medium shots and close-ups that feature her breasts when she stands to expose them fully as she swims closer to the camera, alternating with longer views of the spectacle and close-ups of the spectator's face, in a continuous loop. The anticipation of seeing more of the star in her first exposé is juxtaposed with the point-of-view shots of a looming voyeur. The aesthetic choices that Bó made as a filmmaker were criticized by the press, and yet the nude scene is impeccably constructed to create temptation for a watching spectator both in the text and beyond it. The water and its idyllic backdrop offer the ideal vehicle for establishing a dialectic between seeing and unseeing, or to make on scene the once obscene.[38] The water coordinated with the editing easily entices and draws in the audience. The cuts and movement of the star allows for sporadic glimpses of her breasts, glimmers of a future hope of more peeks into what was revealed in the recent past seconds, to see what is only covered by the moving water. The whole scene is engulfed in harp-infused music that glosses over the frenetic visual cacophony created by editing and framing, made to seem more seamless than it actually is, and to coordinate the offscreen soundscape with the peaceful utopic environment in nature. All tensions and authorial choices coalesce in a series of moments of pure timelessness.

The aquatic setting provides the optimal environment for Sarli's spectacles because the movement in water simultaneously reveals and conceals the body. The tension between seeing and not seeing, within the description of the mentioned scene, will be at the center of all of their films, as will the location shots in pools, rivers, lakes, oceans, and bathtubs. From the first sequence in *Thunder among the Leaves*, the pair made Sarli's displayed body in water their main feature. In unison, the frolicking of the star in nature details intimate, mainly private moments, albeit mostly in public settings around different bodies of water that are generally interrupted by outside peering eyes. Many of the scenes repeat the observations described thus far within pools showing her swimming from different angles and through cuts that create a similar anticipation of being able to see her private parts more fully, parts that progress with risk through time to include Sarli's buttocks and full-frontal shots. From the original instance of an escape in the river, which offers a glimpse into a potentially explosive future, to the shower and bath scenes, mostly used to reference the now or an escape from the now, to the other drenched illustrations that cross story lines and fiction-reality distinctions, they all blend time through cinematography. The wet sequences have the power to be timeless as they repeat from one film to the next in a similar fashion and are not necessarily tied to the limits of each story. The images themselves live outside of the movie's framework, and thus they tell their own tale of the female body in leisure and pleasure during everyday junctures and as its roller-coaster struggle with censors' shears.

Shower and waterfall scenes, for instance, are a riskier version of the long swims in the water, presenting the possibility of revealing more of the body all at once. Their very nature ensured that they were handled differently. As early as *India*, a scene in a waterfall appears; however, manipulation in the post-production phase reveals the threat of full exposure. The dream sequence begins with a shot of Ansisé sleeping, followed by a cut that transports her to the falls, where she sits in the water completely nude with a flower in her hair. Another edit features an establishing shot of the waterfalls and the lake beneath it, and a pan to the right exposes Ansisé's naked body standing in ankle-deep water in an extreme long shot. Distancing is a technique applied to entice by *almost* exposing but simultaneously masking only through remoteness. Another cut moves closer to a long shot as she enters the water, and the camera again approaches with a movement that follows her and then pulls back to show the awe-inspiring setting. She climbs out onto the rocks to sit again in a poselike frame of the protagonist belittled by the natural surroundings. Throughout the rest of the film Ansisé is fully clothed in a minidress, unlike her Indigenous coactors, who were asked to appear topless. The scene was filmed before it was censored. Its artistic beauty meant that it was allowed to remain in the film but Bó had to add superimposed concentric red circles to further camouflage the threat of the fully uncovered female body, unlike their first scene from his pioneering film. The film continues the same aesthetic choices as *Thunder among the Leaves*: the chaos through editing and the harsh force of the Iguazu Falls gushing over the rocks contrasts with the nondiegetic gentle and whimsical music, which creates a sublime.[39] On the other hand, the waterfall scene caused the censors so much discomfort, given the potential to show all, that new aesthetic choices were made to cover Sarli's full visibility.

The everyday pleasures of the water are conspicuous in similarly impactful scenes in waterfalls (*Bewitched*, *My Father's Wife*), but also its simpler version in the shower. The latter are normal everyday actions that encroach into the narratives. For instance, in *Fuego* (1968), Laura is engaged in a conversation with her housekeeper in the shower, posing and exposing her breasts. Similarly, in *Naked Temptation* Sandra takes an outdoor shower. She lathers her body to a side profile of her breasts before exhibiting a frontal version. Both examples only serve as interludes to showcase Sarli's body. The shower delivers not a moment of jouissance for the character, unlike the baths, but it is a reason to show everyday activity and an excuse to feature the star baring all. Although in both cases the protagonist is the attraction for onscreen voyeurs, Andrea in *Fuego* and José María in *Naked Temptation*, they additionally preform the present as they enter the narrative as an everyday activity and take place as part of the action. Yet in the case of the waterfall in *India*, the scenes construct a more complex structure: it comes to the spectator in the form of a dream. The sequence in total has a timeless attribute produced by the initial sleeping Ansisé and the serene yet oneiric music that suggests a natural garden of Eden, in essence a timeless and immaterial space.

Countering the everydayness of the shower is the frolicking and pleasure found in bathtubs. As its own spectacle, it can be seen as an escape form the harsh realist fictions, but indoor baths also have a narrative function to drive the story. For instance, in *Ardent Summer* Bárbara submerges herself in a luxurious bath, enjoying the bubbles. She feels and caresses her body. The suds somewhat hide her private parts, but there are moments of unveiling of breasts that come with lingering close-ups and are crucial to understanding the sexualized nature of the scene. By playing in the water, Bárbara confirms the pleasure of the bath as a leisure activity, one separate from the rest of the story, differentiating the scene from the action. It is placed just after Bárbara and Martín marry, following his confession that he killed his wife. She tells him that she will never marry a beast like him, but he forces himself on her. The bubble bath scene in this case functions as an escape from the grim reality of violence that her captor imposes on her. The unbearable situation of Bárbara's imprisonment can only be compensated with the simple pleasures of a luxurious bath. It is through a bath that she begins her journey to emancipation in the film and begins to plan her own revenge and escape from her domineering abductor, Martín. The body gains its empowerment through the act of cleansing, in an event of pure enjoyment. As the story develops and the cruelty of Martín grows, Bárbara takes this time to afford the luxuries of the bath. Time in the film literally stops to foreground the action. Its capture creates productive results by progressing the plot. If the water scene in *Thunder among the Leaves* may have inspired the workers in their own revolt against the repressive boss, Bárbara's bath motivates her own insurgency against her despotic captor.

FIGURE 19. A medium shot of Sarli's breasts in *Bewitched* (1976), which recreates *India* (1960)

In addition, the water scenes allow for a continuation of stories from film to film. Pairing *India* and *Bewitched* more consciously highlights the continuity between the two movies. The water scenes enact a past, present, and future that coalesce to create virtual timeless moments. Ansisé returns in *Bewitched* as a victim kidnapped from her tribe by a new, wealthy husband. She is possessed by the legendary Pombéro, a Guaraní spirit.[40] The mythological figure embodies the physical haunting of an underlying trauma caused by her uprooting and her unmet desire to be a mother. The Pombéro possesses her body, and through him she kills all the men in her life; her husband at the root of the trauma, and the other lovers who follow. The interrelated narratives of *India* and *Bewitched* show the cohesion and looplike quality of the pair.

Bó deliberately constructs deceiving cohesion that in fact alters the original stories. For instance, *Bewitched*'s opening scene begins with a sequence of a majestic establishing shot of the Iguazu Falls to background music of a ritualistic dance found in *Thunder among the Leaves* and a medium shot of Ansisé topless, fully exposed, having forsaken her minidress in *India* (fig. 19). However, this time the scene appears without the red concentric circles that obstructed the spectacle. Ansisé's makeup, costume, hairstyle, and setting all refer back to the original, but in a cleaner, sharper full-color version.[41] The water scenes become the reference point for the past, as the contemporary Ansisé returns to the waterfall for pleasure and enjoyment. In the case of *Bewitched*, the

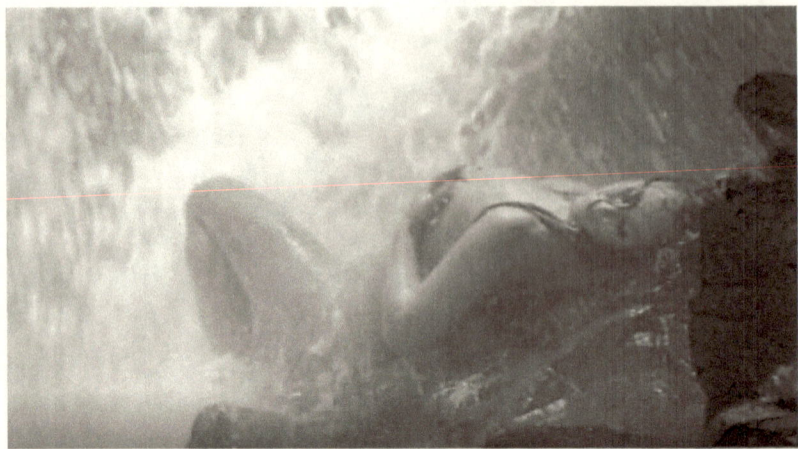

FIGURE 20. The waterfall scene in *Bewitched* (1976), a reconstruction of *India* (1960) but through a closer shot of the body

past of the film is *India*, although footage of the past comes from different Bó-Sarli films. What has happened is that new footage was created along with remnants from their other films to form an archive, even though it is new. For instance, in a scene when Ansisé's husband, Leandro, watches from a cliff as she plays in the water with her lover, Juan, Leandro remembers a moment from *India* and a superimposition ensues as the present-day Ansisé is replaced with a dissolve from the beginning of the film. As the two lovers frolic in the water, Leandro imagines the past with Ansisé posing topless. In a scene that follows, she returns to the falls alone and bathes among the rocks, a recreation of the infamous dream sequence with the concentric circles from *India* (fig. 20). The close-ups of her body this time, and the very act of clutching her breasts as pleasure, already carries out a different standard of onscreen permissibility allowed in 1969 when the film was shot, not possible in 1960 when *India* premiered. But these scenes were most likely the reason why the film took seven years to be released in Argentina.

In a later scene, Leandro describes to Juan how he met Ansisé. The description fades into a reenactment through a recreation sequence in sepia, seemingly from the past, which is the husband looking through the high grass to see Ansisé performing her ritual dance in *India*. The shot-reverse-shot setup intends to make it seem like the husband was present in the past, or in the original film itself, but the recreated images are of a crisper, clearer quality than the actual ones from *India*.

Through editing and montage, Bó incorporates the past of the film into the present of the story. Ironically, not only does Bó include *India* but he also does so with the same bad dancing scene that emphasized her body. The combination of using an assemblage of footage, some of which is newly created for *Bewitched*, allows for a reflection on time within the film and beyond it to reference other films through clear aesthetic choices. Instead of creating a sharp and linear definition of time, Bó-Sarli films annul time or arguably construct a circular conceptualization of time with added differences to their repetition, creating a role for memory. While superficially the reiteration of a formula happens at the level of the narrative, through the key water scenes the references to the past via their own movies allow for the infusion of time, returning to the past of specific roles, in addition to fast-forwarding to a present in the film narrative that changes that past and allows a glance toward a future possibility.

All of the water scenes bring a pause to the narrative progression of plot, even if the sequences are somewhat entwined in its development. The film can exist without the images, but by including them they add a dimension of time that helps the narrative progress in its sexuality. At the very moment of her exhibition, however, what matters more is that time is stopped to create a semblance of distance from the story and allow for enjoyment of the now of leisure. It provides an opportunity to explore the protagonist's body through the performance of the everyday and the camera's framing and editing, in line with sexploitation trends and features, and the method protects against censorship practices that may take place in some distant future and faraway room. Moreover, the endless water scenes deliver what is promised, anticipating affectively binding the spectator to Sarli's body. Seen separately from the individual films, the scenes provide another and parallel tale that stresses the natural environments where they are shot. In and through nature, beyond the simple nature-civilization dichotomy, the water scenes offer a moment of respite to highlight the aesthetic beauty of the topography and connect it to the woman's body. While seemingly neutral and naïve, they allow for successive clashing responses. The neutral water scenarios become more daring and perilous with actions that were deemed controversial as time progressed and as the protagonist becomes freer to express her bodily desires onscreen.

FOURTH JOLT: THE ECSTATIC BODY IN NATURE

On Valentine's eve in 2018, I attended a talk entitled "Assuming the Ecosexual Position," by Annie Sprinkle and Beth Stephens.[42] Stephens and

Sprinkle presented a funny, entertaining, ecofeminist journey through their work that included references to the many marriage ceremonies they had performed around the world with the earth, the snow, the sun, and more.

At the end of the presentation, I approached Dr. Sprinkle and asked her if any early films inspired her long career that began on the screen. I was mainly thinking of the nudist camp films and their 1950s revival, more so than the early sexploitation nudie cuties of the 1960s, because the former made stronger connections between the body and nature. But these examples were underground and historical, not easily available to a teenager in the 1960s. Sprinkle confessed that only one film ever inspired her. She had seen it with friends in a theater in Panama City when she was fifteen years old. She lived in the Central American isthmus where her father worked in the American Embassy throughout the 1960s. The film was called *Naked on the Sand*, she recalled. Not unexpectedly, the feature was a Sarli-Bó coproduction. Panama was one of those countries that had no filmmaking history, and the duo embarked on a collaboration at the height of their popularity.

As I was listening to both Stephens and Sprinkle discuss their ecofeminist performances, I couldn't help but be reminded of Sarli's own ritualistic sexual communion with nature, performed on the sand in this flick, and on the snow, in the water or forest, and elsewhere. By 1968, when the pair produced *Naked on the Sand*, their films had already reached all corners of Latin America and the sexploitation international circuits. In the case of *Naked on the Sand*, it was shot in Panama. A country with little experience in the filmmaking enterprise celebrated and promoted the choice by an already known commodity to feature its shores and tropical landscapes, spurring the imagination of curious teenagers like Sprinkle. The shots of Sarli rubbing her naked body on the sand took place on the same beaches where Sprinkle sunbathed and swam with friends. Seen through this lens, could Sarli also be an ecosexual?

From the initial stages, Sarli and Bó capitalized on the diva's connection to nature.[43] The bodily exposé in *Thunder among the Leaves* took place on a riverbank found at the juncture of Paraguay, Argentina, and Brazil, a beloved location for many other shoots that followed. The pastoral-like bond between the woman's body and water is not the only utopic natural scenario she explored. As a matter of fact, each film contains its own version of Sarli's ceremonial union to her environment. From the early examples on, the excess of establishing shots, flaunting the flora and fauna of the Americas, visually construct the same archetype. Subsequent to *Fuego*, the films all highlight other versions of harmony, but unlike the pre-1968 movies, these capitalize on female pleasure much like the performances in Sprinkle and Stephens's Love Art Laboratory.[44] Natural landscapes, such as the beach in *Naked on the Sand*, are a place where the female star can find solace and sexual gratification.

The once innocent and naïve communion with nature from the earlier productions developed into a more deliberate exaltation of the body achieved through female masturbation, whereby the environment becomes an integral part of the sexual experience, independent of the voyeur or any other onscreen physical partner. The scenes to which I refer encapsulate the tensions that have been at play throughout the book, but also add a new dimension of independence and liberation of the body. The most salient examples materialized in *Naked on the Sand*, *Fuego*, *Tropical Ecstasy*, *Bewitched*, *Fever*, *Intimacies of a Prostitute*, and *Ardent Summer*, where ecological landscapes not only tie the body to different open-air locales but also bestow alleviation or release for sexual urges. (*Sex and Love* would fit into this category, but the film has been lost, and the later films experienced so much censorship and self-censorship that the versions available today do not follow this trend.) A closer examination of key scenes discloses how the seemingly naïve exposure of the female body found in the early nudie cuties takes on a more sexual urgency where nature is the backdrop for climax or the search for that climax. Natural surroundings, a type of ecosexual communion with nature, may very well provide the exact place for the possible release of sexual desire, or the prolonged intensification of the "itch," in Leo Bersani's vocabulary.[45] The scenes construct an affective relationship that tends to highlight a more feminist and liberatory sentiment because Sarli's onscreen pleasure is uniquely found in masturbation.

The opening scene of *Naked on the Sand* revives many of the dependable archetypes discussed throughout *Violated Frames*. However, the beginning features for the first time a deliberate focus on masturbation, happening not only in water but also in other environments. The film begins with a shot of a bra on the sand and a pan up to find other clothing scattered on the beach, along with footprints that lead to a long shot of Alicia lying naked, all before the credits scroll onto the screen (fig. 21). As the star's name emerges in white letters, the camera zooms in over her distant image. The title hides her whole body to reveal its parts and her hands touching both her pubic area and her breasts, until a close-up of her face details the ecstasy she is enjoying in the sun. An

FIGURE 21. Alicia on the sand masturbating in *Naked on the Sand* (1969)

establishing shot of the landscape (the beach, the jungle, and the ocean) juxtaposes to a medium close-up of her touching her breasts.

The scene serves as a teaser to captivate the audience to watch the rest of the film. Yet what is most curious is that as the first example of the new trope in the couple's repertoire, it continues the clear tension between seeing and not seeing, identified in previous examples, but also unveils a new, liberated Sarli. For instance, their use of establishing shots sets up the environment but is paired with the close-ups of the star's body and her enjoyment as displayed on her face, without any acknowledgement of the presence of another. Sarli's sexuality acquires a more emancipatory stance, all undeniably within a natural milieu. The scene picks up much later in the film, when Alicia is found with sand all over her bare skin and fondling her breasts, and the camera zooms into a close-up of her face. Unlike the bells, fireworks, and rockets sounding in *Deep Throat* (Gerard Damiano, USA, 1972), Alicia's climaxing is seen on her face and it continues silently (fig. 22). It never seems to be fulfilled, like Bersani's itch striving for its own prolongation.[46] After exiting the water, she lies on the sand and rolls around, making love to the sand by herself. It is perhaps moments like these that inspired Roger Ebert to call Sarli the most narcissistic woman on the screen.[47]

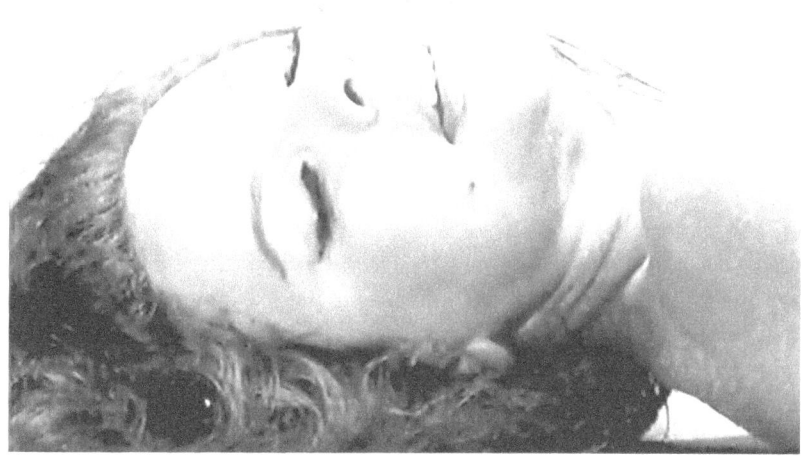

FIGURE 22. A close-up of Alicia's face shows as she reaches climax in *Naked on the Sand* (1969)

Both beach masturbation portrayals shift the interludes to a new sexualized level. As extraneous insertions into the narrative, Sarli's exposés become more about trying to achieve female pleasure than about appeasing a male observer in the text. According to Sarli's anecdote cited in the introduction, precisely at this phase in the late 1960s, more women saw her films. Whereas before she offered a naïve ambivalent reveal within nature, now her charges, jolts, or surprises take on a more personal, sexually satisfying connection to her environment. They still maintain their independence from the plot and thus their extraneous characteristic. However, if contextualized within sex onscreen history, they preserve Sarli-Bó's unique flare and signature happening within and through nature. To return to examples of earlier onscreen masturbation, the early sex hygiene films like *The Solitary Sin* (1919) quickly come to mind.[48] While the film has been lost and its reviews mention little about the plot, masturbation from early on was considered a shameful act, as the title suggested.[49] It wasn't until the Alfred Kinsey reports (*Sexual Behavior in the Human Male* [1948] and *Sexual Behavior in the Human Female* [1953]) that it was found to be universal yet at odds with publicly championed norms.[50]

The case of Russ Meyer's *The Immoral Mr. Teas* (1959), which is credited for starting the nudie cutie genre, proposes a stock character that is the common man of the "raincoat brigade."[51] In the film, the female body becomes an object of spectacle for the male voyeur. Dave Andrews concludes that Teas's peeping does not end in masturbation and that Meyer was not keen on making explicit self-arousal the topic of his film, as it was thus a possible threat.[52] Inspired by Andrews's analysis of the film, Elena Gorfinkel argues that Teas is a comic figure who is the epitome of a failed male sexuality as he circumvents the question of masturbation.[53]

The danger initially posed by burlesque films later becomes rather about looking and possessing through the gaze in the nudie cuties. In the late 1960s, the voyeur is gendered as female to "augment female display" in line with the rules of the genre.[54] Greater female subjectification and empowerment found in films like *Vixen!* (Russ Meyer, USA, 1968), *Barbarella* (Roger Vadim, France/Italy, 1968), and *Belle de Jour*, all films released at the same historical moment of the sexual revolution, show orgasm and pleasure for women as central to stories of female liberation.

The new phenomenon of onscreen female pleasure highlights masturbation as an important component, where the face becomes the visible sight/site of pleasure.[55] Masturbation spotlights a crucial aspect of autoeroticism, a notion well-defined in a film like *Barbarella*. The female no longer needs the male to achieve sexual satisfaction. In *Barbarella*, technology or a device leads to the orgasm. In the film the villain, Duran Duran, "plays the organ" while Barbarella achieves multiple orgasms with the aid of a mechanical electric instrument and through the representation of the crescendoing music. Barbarella essentially kills the machine as she continues to have multiple orgasms without dying, contrary to what Duran Duran expected. Ultimately the machine is conquered by the female's ability to achieve multiple orgasms without the need of a man, as Linda Williams validates.[56]

The reference to technology as an apparatus for achieving orgasm developed with the coming of hard-core film. The organ mutates into the vibrator and VCR in *Behind the Green Door* (Artie Mitchell and Jim Mitchell, USA, 1972). With the emergence of video, pornography infiltrated the private bedroom of its consumers to facilitate autoerotic fantasies.[57] Now the "raincoat brigade" from the movie theaters adapts to the exclusive viewing on the small screen, which opens up possibilities for women and a multiplicity of different audiences. Meanwhile, *Barbarella* and *Behind the Green Door* use masturbation as a narrative device, which gives independence to the women performing it in the absence of male actors, in line with newfound liberties for women won in the United States and worldwide. Yet female pleasure in these representations is thus achieved with a technological aid, in the confines and privacy of their homes. The excess of the orgasm is limited or confined to the home, where it can be controlled. The Sarli-Bó situation is different as it enacts the fantasy in the open natural world and links to the animalistic instincts of its public settings, liberating the female body from the enclosed space of the house generally associated with women.

The later films featured more daring sexuality through Sarli's characters, and masturbation is added to the collection of nude scenarios and encounters with male and female partners in shocking new ways. *Ardent Summer* takes a scene from *Fuego* and reenacts it as an example of female pleasure. In *Fuego*, the protagonist Laura walks to the snow fully clothed, falls to her knees, and begins to thrust snow down her blouse. She collapses to the ground and rubs her body on the snow, touching herself, a performance she enacts for Carlos, her lover. Female pleasure is only meant to attempt to heighten the sex between the lovers. In contrast, in *Ardent Summer* the scene plays out differently, more in line with the one in *Naked on the Sand*. Randomly, Bárbara exits the house covered only by a blue bath towel. She places the towel on the snow, lies on it, touches her body, and begins to put snow on her naked skin before rolling around on the frigid surface as if it were hot sand (fig. 23). The scene displays a moment of sexual liberation for its main character, an orgasmic orgy with the cold white snow. The example shows the more rustic nature of the Sarli-Bó films, where unlike *Barbarella* or the hard-core pornography that follows, the Latin American Bárbara presents an old-fashioned appreciation of nature. Water, and its frozen form snow, continue to ground Sarli's autoeroticism. There are no devices but the open air and the landscapes of the countryside. As a personal playground, the desolate and empty scenery provides the perfect location for the woman to experience her body in a surrealist bucolic sense, but also as she claims her own existence. All of a sudden and randomly, she appears naked to perform the scene that is unattached to the narrative. But importantly, after the two moments of pleasure, this one on the snow and the bubble bath, Bárbara enacts her own liberation from her authoritarian husband. She manipulates all the men and executes her plan for revenge. By the end, she shoots Martín in the open air as she looks straight into the camera and engages the spectators in her justice.

FIGURE 23. Bárbara on her towel finding self-enjoyment with snow in *Ardent Summer* (1973)

The most memorable Sarli-Bó sexual scene of female masturbation is found in *Fever*, released the same year as hard-core classic *Deep Throat*. What makes the scene a classic is that it perfectly brings together all the elements I have been discussing of the Sarli-Bó affective created through the female body: suspended moments of sex onscreen that can easily be eliminated by the censors; aesthetic constructions of beautifully crafted visual and aural communion of the body with nature; a reference to time fusing past, present, and future in a timeless ethereal event; and, through the content of the story, a push for a liberating form of sexuality that was and still is outside sexual norms. All coalesce in a shocking scene that highlights the role of the body in its most culminating expression. *Fever* is an absurdist or surrealist story about a woman who is in love with her dead lover. Believing he has been reborn in her horse Fever, she wishes to reunite with him. In an early scene, Sandra watches from the sidelines as two horses copulate, motivating what will follow. The moment of sexual union features the horse's penis penetrating the mare, a hard-core scene of animal sex as Sandra sucks her pinky finger in absolute delight and drinks a glass of champagne. The close-up

FIGURE 24. Visions of Sandra finding pleasure on the grass in *Fever* (1972)

of her face intensely watching chronicles the shift to the female as the new voyeur of sexploitation.

The scene between the horses reappears as a memory in the long sequence of self-pleasure that follows. The event uses the technique of superimposition to bring together three different instances: the past horse copulation scene witnessed by Sandra, Sandra's present lying in her bed during an evening storm, and a dream-like future of her running through the forest in daylight. The fantasy happens in a protracted long sequence, when Sandra runs nude in slow motion among trees, wearing a transparent long negligée until she arrives in an open field. Echoes of the horses neighing interrupt. Like the wild and instinctual horses, Sandra is dashing freely through the natural surrounding until she falls to her knees on the lush green grass, opens her negligée, and touches her vagina as she pants (fig. 24). An image of the horses copulating superimposes on her naked union with the grass (fig. 25). The sounds of the animals neighing overpower the backdrop as she pulls the grass that cushions her body, eats it, and uses it to masturbate until she is back in her bed with the vision of horses as the rain beating on the window interrupts her fantasy.

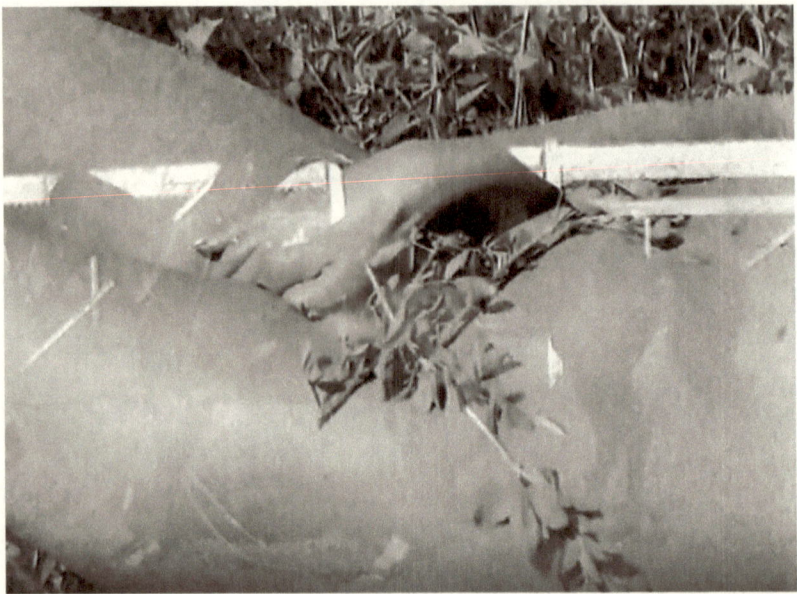

FIGURE 25. Sandra touching herself as an image of the two horses copulating is superimposed in the close-up in *Fever* (1972)

The scene has an experimental quality to it, achieved through the slow motion, the constant use of superimposition of different moments in time, and the empowering and folk-influenced music within a story about bestiality. Moreover, all the elements come together: the actual present act taking place in the house in private, the memory of the natural instinctive scene witnessed the previous day in the stables, and the fantasy of a future time when Sandra, almost horse-like herself, runs through the woods into a field. The beautifully assembled surrealistic scene serves as the perfect concoction of sexual female self-pleasure, natural surroundings, nonnormative sexuality, and instinctual animalistic desire, as well as the literal blending of past, present, and future possibilities. It aesthetically creates a very long moment of anticipation to the eventual masturbation that takes place on the grass and in the bed. The masturbation not only features the female body and its unique communion with the natural environment and its creatures, but it is also an onscreen instance of emancipation for Sandra where she is free to love the horse and herself.

All these examples of a communion with nature through the act of female masturbation suggest that the duo embraced the clichés of uniting nature and women to stage an occasion of unshackling the female body. The nostalgia for the past, the emphasis on the present moment, and the leap into the future all help to construct a timeless flash with an affective effect. The excessive use of establishing shots serves as a backdrop for a naturescape that takes on an overpowering presence in all of their stories. In combination with superimpositions and a spectacle of autoeroticism, the groundwork has been laid for an ecofeminism that allows the expression of an ecstatic, liberated female body in union with nature. To zoom in on the intimacy of masturbation makes it public, even if only through fantasy. Unlike its contemporaries, *Fever*'s public face is out in the open air rather than simply relegated to the bedroom. The connection to animals and the natural landscapes establishes an ecocinema that is both sexually and politically embodied and fastened to its places and locations. On the one hand, it emphasizes the idea of love and sex as the foundation of society, a utopian ideal typical in the 1960s' hippy world culture, and perhaps supplanting any true political criticism. But like the example of Stephens and Sprinkle, the Sarli-Bó films express a "collectivity [that] is routed through the personal, bodily connection to the planet and thus to each other."[58] Similarly they interlace the affective with the bodily and a sexual politics with an ecology linked to time. In their films, rather than being a prop to shore up masculinity, masturbation takes on a solely feminine quality through its star that celebrates a connection to nature through an ecological affective charge on the screen.

The spectacle of the female body does not disappear, but its excessive reappearance through a celebratory bodily communion reaffirms a different archetype, with the female at its helm and pleasure as the ultimate ideal. Rather than a possessive, stagnant version of "to-be-looked-at-ness," the Sarli-Bó vision veers toward an excessive connection with nature with room for multiple orgasms without the help of technology. In combination with the stories, the scenes would have made Sarli's body dangerous for those who did not agree with the daring project they were proposing.

ARCHIVING INTIMACY

The Sarli-Bó productions offer an opportunity to understand how pleasure and intimacy were defined in Argentina at the time. While the duo was influenced by early daring examples from European art cinema and later the sexploitation international market they had entered, they fit outside the perimeters of what was possible in Argentina. By isolating the interludes of female nudity and sexuality, one discovers a formal distinction in their films that makes their work unique and shifts away from traditional sexploitation. They offered an example heavily focused on Latin America that defined pleasure differently for both male and female spectators, focusing on the beautiful natural fauna and flora of the Americas as a primary ecosystem for pleasure. As the basis for an affective connection to their audience that underlay their whole enterprise and developed throughout the years of production, the infamous establishing shots of nature bond the female body to its landscapes. Incrementally and logically, the moments or jolts of sexuality began with the body's early exposure but soon grew to sexual encounters and eventually its own autoerotic pleasure, all of which remained within the liberated landscapes of Latin America's beauty.

It is no coincidence that the duo capitalized on the open grasslands, dense forests, sandy beaches, high mountain ranges, lush jungles, extravagant waterfalls, and all the different waterways that highlight the exceptional splendor of its locations. Place is important in their work to not only define their identities and that of their audience as Argentine or Latin American but also distinguish the region in all its glory. In doing so, they confronted the taboo of not only the female body and its sexuality but also its locality. Its position creates an affective connection that gives rise to new networks and pleasures, ones archived on the screen.

The archive that they left behind confronts many clichés through its own clichés, but also unsettles any easy way of looking, allowing for an expansion of different possibilities between the body and its environment. What began as a performative moment of the star, a confrontation between her bad dancing and the purely constructed pose, complemented by a moment of pure pleasure and leisure in nature, eventually became a sexualized form of self-pleasure. The growth that took place in their cinema was motivated by a changing market that permitted more possibilities onscreen. Sarli-Bó took on the challenge and confronted the taboo of the body as straightforwardly as possible, given the obstruction that censorship posed. By doing so and documenting intimacy, they created an archive of pleasure that integrates the personal, political, public, and private. Bringing together a possible Peronist reading with its focus on labor with the sexuality of the female body, they disrupt easy paradigms that juxtapose active males and passive females, the glamorous and the everyday, to move beyond familiar archetypes, proving that perhaps the answer to clichés is not their ultimate elimination, but better clichés. Through the affective dimension, Sarli-Bó created an archive of female pleasure that includes a timeless intimacy, showing anxiety about the onscreen sex moment because it was at risk of being cut.

Conclusion

*"You won with the censors . . .
They couldn't stop you!"*

In celebration of the fiftieth anniversary of the release of *Fuego*, the Buenos Aires International Festival of Independent Cinema (BAFICI) arranged for a first encounter between Sarli and independent cult film director and avid admirer John Waters, a meeting that was recorded and widely disseminated on social media. In that encounter, Waters reminisces about seeing all of the Bó-Sarli films in adult movie theaters in New York in the late 1960s and throughout the 1970s with Harris Glenn Milstead, who would later become Divine, a drag recreation of Sarli herself in *Female Trouble* (John Waters, USA, 1974). Waters explains that he also recreated shots from *Fuego* in his earlier *Pink Flamingos* (USA, 1972).

In their conversation, Waters and Sarli discuss censorship and the difficulty of releasing shockingly "bad" cinema. Waters identifies with Sarli's experience, being a pioneer in his own right. She reacts in articulate and clear English: "Here in our country they talked a lot against us . . . but now I can see all films with nudes. They criticized me . . . and now they do the same." In response, Waters congratulates her: "You won with the censors . . . they couldn't stop you!"[1] The exchange between two pioneering figures highlights the difficulty in making films that challenged onscreen norms, a struggle that diminishes with time as society accepts new paths forged by these early innovators. In many ways, what came after the dictatorship during the *destape* or unleashing in all realms of society that Natalia Milanesio describes was a stage for which Sarli and Bó's work set the foundation.[2]

Waters personally gives Sarli the "Buho" or Owl, the BAFICI award for her career and contribution to onscreen sexuality. It is not surprising that the Bó-Sarli films were revered by the trash fan and auteur in his own right. In many ways what Bó and Sarli did was inventive, and they were precursors to many contemporary gay directors, like Waters and Pedro Almodóvar, who is oftentimes compared to Bó.[3]

The encounter between the two icons of sexuality was the last public appearance that Sarli gave. On June 25, 2019, Isabel Sarli passed away from a cardiac arrest. In Argentina from north to south, homages were published in the press, on Facebook, and on Twitter. Coca-Cola Argentina posted a tweet of their infamous emblem in red and white, reading "Coca' 1935–2019" (though she was actually born in 1929), a tribute to the star whose nickname represented the love of the American beverage and whose figure replicated its early bottles. From Mexico to Tierra del Fuego, all throughout the continent, newspapers rushed to tell the tragic news. Internationally, her death was announced in Spain, Italy, and the United States: the *New York Times* published a tribute to eulogize her.[4] The work of *Violated Frames* acknowledges the important role that both Sarli and Bó had in the development of sex onscreen and their unequaled contribution to the media histories of sexuality in Latin America.

The pair developed a unique formula and used it to challenge acceptable norms throughout a long career beginning in 1956, when they first set out to make a film. With each new project, they pushed the taboo of appearing nude onscreen, and they dared broach other sexual topics, from prostitution to homosexuality and bestiality. The camp fandom of nonnormative spectators makes their cinema different. Their brand of social realism, with "bad film" aesthetics fit within a populist national affective mode but also reached far—into the adult movie theaters in New York, the Spanish-language movie theaters in other parts of the United States, Latin American nations, and other worldwide locations.[5] It draws a variety of audiences, showcasing:

> the power of the *grasa* [greasy, tacky, tasteless]. . . . It became an exotic toy of the upper classes for which the excessive mammary tentacles of Isabel Sarli were a gag in themselves without unraveling surrealist and "camp" keys, meanwhile any provincial recruit masturbated seriously in front of each frame that contained so much desirable meat.[6]

Violated Frames: Armando Bó and Isabel Sarli's Sexploits has contributed to the nascent field of adult film studies in two concrete ways. First, the book has proposed a way of exploring and openly confronting the loss of most of an archive that documented the censorship of all films screened in Argentina during a time of controlled regulation. The loss of this valuable resource has made the study of the origins of popular sex onscreen difficult but not impossible. Extensive archival research has successfully unearthed new documents that have helped to supplement the lost knowledge with creative methods for building upon its history. Second, this book reconstructs the history of sex onscreen in the context of Argentina and focuses in particular on the work of sexploitation couple Armando Bó and Isabel Sarli. The book represents an important step in incorporating the study of sex and the body in 1960s' and 1970s' Argentina, a project that ultimately spreads throughout the region.

Violated Frames has aimed to understand why onscreen bodies may have been offensive in the complex matrix of their contexts. By recreating the history of the Bó-Sarli films and allowing them to speak for themselves, I have illustrated the value of popular culture as it shapes how a society grapples with an issue as important as sexuality.

While Bó and Sarli played a crucial role in the international circulation of Hispanic cinema and sexploitation, most of the work is very much tied to the national context of its production. I have argued for the need to ground the study of the pair to local and regional contexts, because their cinema is a touchstone for understanding gender, sexuality, class, and censorship in Latin America during a time of internal political conflict. The pair offered an alternative to the Second Cinema movements such as the Generation of 1960 that were discarded as imperialist by the rising left-wing resistance to the Cold War politics of the North and the Third Cinema movements that resisted neocolonialism. They also exposed an archive of possible intersection with early feminist thought.

Through the kaleidoscope of their work, one can understand the development of a censorship apparatus in a long history that happened from 1955, when Juan Perón was debunked from power and exiled, until 1983, the end of the brutal military dictatorship. The Bó-Sarli trajectory is central to the study of the history of sex in Argentina as they challenged accepted public notions of sexuality and began to define its appearance on the screen. Since they were staples in many other Latin American countries and as their work traveled throughout the continent, they took on the same role more regionally. *Violated*

Frames builds a "bad archive" of onscreen sex and specifically reaffirms the value and impact of providing a lens in the context of the nation to historicize the body.

Time within the narratives and historical distance from the films allow for reflection about the invisibility of the female body in film history, which still haunts the present moment in the many activist expressions that have taken place recently. As the *#MeToo* movement and its Latin American counterpart *#NiUnaMenos* continue to grow and call out individual and state violence on women's bodies and their sexuality, the current public debate highlights just how bodies remain somewhat invisible. Such viral feminist campaigns against gender-based violence summon awareness of the systemic aggression committed on women's bodies and the historical role the state has played in the brutality.

Notes

INTRODUCTION

1. Jorge Abel Martín, *Los films de Armando Bó con Isabel Sarli* (Buenos Aires: Corregidor, 1981), 74.
2. The poem, "For the Argentine actress Isabel Sarli," was written in Beijing in June 1979 when Sarli and Bó traveled to China with their film *El último amor en Tierra del Fuego* (*Last Love in Tierra del Fuego*, 1979). See Néstor Romano, *Isabel Sarli al desnudo* (Buenos Aires: Ediciones de la Urraca, 1995), 209.
3. Martín, *Los films*, 48.
4. Romano, *Isabel Sarli*, 129.
5. Sarli was called "la Coca." The nickname given to her by her mother revealed her predilection for the American drink. Later her fans identified her with the original shapely Coca-Cola bottle because it reminded them of her curvaceous figure.
6. The nude scene in *Thunder among the Leaves* is generally lauded as the first in Argentine cinema. As Matt Losada points out, the film featured other nude Indigenous women, who are completely ignored, which begs the question whether similar scenes appeared before 1958. See Matt Losada, *The Projected Nation: Argentine Cinema and the Social Margins* (Albany: State University of New York Press, 2018), 175–76.
7. While Rodolfo Kuhn speaks about coherence in his book, which was not published until 1984, this quote came from a *Fuego* review from 1971 that I found at the Museo del Cine archives. See Review of *Fuego*, 1971, MS 41160, Armando Bó folder, Museo del Cine Pablo Ducrós Hicken archives, Buenos Aires.

8. Tamara Leah Falicov, *The Cinematic Tango: Contemporary Argentine Film* (London: Wallflower Press, 2007), 27.

9. The governments leading to Juan Domingo Perón's presidency, and throughout his time in office until 1955, instituted several policies to protect the national film industry, including the national screen quota, a loan program, and an import quota. See Falicov, *Cinematic Tango*, 28.

10. Upon its release, the film had its own problems with the censors due to the street lingo that it featured. See Rodrigo Fernández and Denise Nagy, *La gran aventura de Armando Bó: biografía total* (Buenos Aires: Perfil Libros, 1979), 107.

11. Octavio Getino, *Cine argentino entre lo possible y lo deseable* (Buenos Aires: Ediciones Ciccus, 1998), 39.

12. Getino, *Cine argentino*, 44.

13. Laura Podalsky, *Specular City: Transforming Culture, Consumption and Space in Buenos Aires, 1955–1973* (Philadelphia: Temple University Press, 2004).

14. All the sources cite the 50 percent agreement between Bó and Sarli as well as Sarli's crucial role in the business. Yet the agreement was not official anywhere other than in the contracts with Columbia Pictures. See Martín, *Los films*, 26; Romano, *Isabel Sarli*, 59, 158–59; Fernández and Nagy, *La gran aventura*, 129, 144.

15. Despite the commonly held belief that Bó discovered Sarli, it was actually Nicolás Bó, a Paraguayan investor in *Thunder among the Leaves*, who insisted that Armando use Sarli in the film. See Romano, *Isabel Sarli*, 35, 37.

16. In 1961–62, when all their early movies were experiencing legal difficulties due to nudity, they each went on to film outside the Sarli-Bó enterprise. Bó worked on *Pelota de cuero* (*Leather Ball*, 1962), another soccer film, which he starred in, cowrote, produced, and directed. When Sarli starred in Leopoldo Torre Nilsson's *Setenta veces siete* (*The Female: Seventy Times Seven*, 1962), she signed a contract that specified that no nude scenes would appear. Instead, it was an intellectual existential exercise about a prostitute and her circumstances. A few years later, it was eventually released in the United States under the title *The Female*, dubbed into English and with extra sex scenes. The additions sparked a legal suit against Torre Nilsson, who defended himself by saying it was the North American distributors who added the extra scenes. See Romano, *Isabel Sarli*, 73–75. In *The Virgin Goddess*, directed by South African Dirk de Villiers, Sarli, Bó, and Victor Bó star, but it is not a Sarli-Bó production; instead, the film was produced by Columbia Pictures.

17. Augusto Roa Bastos was exiled in Buenos Aires from 1947 to 1976. During that time, he began a career as a scriptwriter. *Thunder among the Leaves* was the first script he ever wrote, *The Shad Fisherman* the second. He worked with classical film directors such as Lucas Damare and René Mugica. He also wrote scripts for independent auteur directors Manuel Antín and Daniel Cherniavsky, as well as independent quickie directors Enrique Carreras and Alberto Du Bois.

18. *The Impure Goddess*, a Mexican coproduction, was based on Alfredo Ruanova's argument, and the script was cowritten by Bó and Ruanova. *Tropical*

Ecstasy was written and directed by Bó with José da Costa Cordeiro and Egydio Eccio.

19. Fernández and Nagy, *La gran aventura*, 215.

20. David William Foster, "Las lolas de la Coca: el cuerpo femenino en el cine de Isabel Sarli," *Revista Karpa: Journal of Theatricalities and Visual Culture* 1, no. 1 (2008): 1–5.

21. While the cinematographers were all experienced, the fast production schedules made it difficult to maintain continuity. For instance, without naming the film, Kuhn discusses a scene with a shot-reverse shot, the shot during the day and the reverse shot at night. See Rodolfo Kuhn, *Armando Bó, el cine y la pornografía ingenua, y otras reflexiones* (Buenos Aires: Corregidor, 1984), 16.

22. Kuhn, *Armando Bó*, 223–24.

23. Sarli met Paco Jamandreu in 1955, when she was crowned Miss Argentina and became his friend instantly. They started working together early on, although he is not necessarily credited in all of her films. See Jamandreu's testimony in Romano, *Isabel Sarli*, 188.

24. All the characters were to say the lines in English. They were written phonetically for Armando and Victor Bó, neither of whom could speak English. Instead of memorizing the English version, Armando began to recite the names of the soccer players from his favorite team, Independiente. Kuhn, *Armando Bó*, 20.

25. Kuhn, *Armando Bó*, 20.

26. *Last Love in Tierra del Fuego* was shot in 1978, but the censor Miguel Tato did not allow the film to be released. After Tato retired and after the successful retrospective of their films in April of 1979, Bó locked himself up to finish the film in the editing room, and he included footage from old films and the Super 8 footage from their trips abroad. It was released on October 11, 1979. The release was short-lived because an incident with a priest at a celebratory event meant that its run ended abruptly, one week after the event. Fernández and Nagy, *La gran aventura*, 255–57.

27. Fernández and Nagy, 21.

28. Kuhn, *Armando Bó*, 16.

29. Sergio Wolf, "Armando Bó con Isabel Sarli, el folletín salvaje," in *Cine argentino, la otra historia*, ed. Sergio Wolf (Buenos Aires: Ediciones Letra Buena, 1994), 80.

30. Wolf, "Armando Bó con Isabel Sarli," 82–84.

31. Kuhn, *Armando Bó*, 44.

32. Wolf, "Armando Bó con Isabel Sarli," 84–88.

33. David Andrews, *Soft in the Middle: The Contemporary Softcore Feature in its Context*, (Columbus: The Ohio University Press, 2006), 45–76.

34. Andrews, *Soft in the Middle*, 2–4.

35. Unlike Mexico, which had the Pel-Mex distribution agency, Argentina did not have an apparatus with oversight on distribution of national productions or a mechanism to help build coproduction agreements with foreign markets. There were attempts at building such an apparatus in the 1950s, and it was even given a name, Uniargentina, but it never amounted to anything. Independent producers like Bó had to work hard to build those relationships and

find the money for the coproductions. The funding came from independent investors, not the state.

36. Martín, *Los films*, 38.

37. Martín, 38–39.

38. Because Bó and Sarli were independent, there are no records about how much money the films actually made. In Argentina, they had so many problems with the censors that the films may not have recovered much of the investment, although they did have fans, mainly in the interior of the country. Movie posters made claims about how much money a film made in order to exploit it. Internationally, distributors paid them up front for the rights to show the film in a given territory. There were many individual private investors who financed such efforts. Columbia Pictures had the rights to their Spanish-language films. But the distributor of *Fuego* in English was a man who Sarli claims stole from them. They hired lawyers but were not able to recover the money lost. See Daniela Bajar, "The Impure Goddess: A Conversation with Isabel 'Coca' Sarli," in *Film Comment* (July/August 2010), www.filmcomment.com/article/the-impure-goddess-a-conversation-with-isabel-coca-sarli.

39. See Wolf, "Armando Bó con Isabel Sarli," 79–89.

40. Adrian Smith, "'The girl the whole world is waiting to see more of!' Isabel Sarli, and the Failed Attempt to Launch a New Star in 1960s Britain," in *Intensities: The Journal of Cult Media* 8 (January 2016): 95.

41. Smith, "'Girl,'" 96–97.

42. Romano, *Isabel Sarli*, 121.

43. Podalsky, *Specular City*, 205.

44. Podalsky, 205.

45. Kuhn explains that the reception of the duo varied depending on the public who saw it. In Buenos Aires, Kuhn was accustomed to going to see the films with intellectual friends. He describes people who engaged with the films, laughed, made comments, and so on. The irony is that the films received more participation from their audience than the political films of the "new cinemas," whose objective was to stop the film to allow for comments. When he went to a screening in Panama, he noticed a different reception. People took the viewing experience very seriously. They were annoyed with him when he laughed or spoke out. For Kuhn, the Sarli-Bó films are very Argentine as they show an Argentine moralistic perspective full of contradictions and simplistic naiveté. Kuhn, *Armando Bó*, 14–15.

46. Kuhn, 10.

47. Ebert watched and reviewed the pair's films. Currently, one can find one original review on the RogerEbert.com website. See Roger Ebert, "*Tropical Ecstasy*," RogerEbert.com, February 17, 1971, www.rogerebert.com/reviews/tropical-ecstasy-1971. He also made reference to their work when reviewing *La mujer de mi hermano* (*My Brother's Wife*, Peru, 2005), directed by Ricardo de Montreuil, in Roger Ebert's *Movie Yearbook 2009* (Kansas City, MO: Andrews McMeel Publishing, 2008), 383–84. See Roger Ebert, "Guilty Pleasures," in *Film Comment* 14, no. 4 (July/August 1978): 49–51, 80. In all three reviews Ebert speaks of Sarli as the most "narcissistic" actress in the world. She forms part of his "guilty pleasures" in 1978, and he was reminded of her films in 2008.

48. Victoria Ruétalo and Dolores Tierney, eds., *Latsploitation, Exploitation Cinemas, and Latin America* (New York: Routledge, 2009).

49. *Fuego* was dubbed into many other languages, and it was subtitled for the Japanese market. It was seen in Canada, almost all of Latin America, Japan, Hong Kong, France, and Italy. The Sarli-Bó team did a lot of groundwork to enter new markets, where Argentine film had never been seen. For instance, since there was no agreement between Japan and Argentina, there were lots of legal issues that needed to be worked out before the film could appear in its theaters. The formula for *Fuego* was going to prove groundbreaking. They adapted new strategies for different markets. For instance, in some cases they used English names, with the exception of Isabel Sarli, to disguise the film as a Hollywood production. The Italian movie poster for *Fuego* (*Conscenza carnale di una ninfomane*) lists Joseph Adams (Bó), Mary Jacobs (Alba Mujica), Bob Dunnigan (Roberto Airaldi), and director A. B. Greent (Bó).

50. Discussions about "the people" or the multitude bring into consideration the problems of thinking through populist politics and popular culture as mass culture. The issues mentioned here will be taken up in chapter 1; popular culture and populism overlap in the case of Sarli and Bó. See Jon Beasley Murray, *Post-Hegemony: Political Theory and Latin America* (Minneapolis: University of Minnesota Press, 2010); Michael Hardt and Antonio Negri, *Empire* (Cambridge, MA: Harvard University Press, 2000); Michael Hardt and Antonio Negri, *Multitude: War and Democracy in the Age of Empire* (New York: Penguin Press, 2004).

51. See the following newspaper reviews of *Fuego* for criticism the film experienced about its bad quality: Jorge H. Andres, "Retozos eróticos de Isabel Sarli en un perseguido film de Armando Bó," *La Opinión*, 25 September 1971, MS 41166, Armando Bó folder, Museo del Cine archives, Buenos Aires; "La muchacha que no era mala sino enferma," *La Nación*, 25 September 1971, MS 41168, Armando Bó folder, Museo del Cine archives, Buenos Aires. See Nayibe Bermúdez-Barrios, "Sexploitation, Space, and Lesbian Representation in Armando Bó's *Fuego*," in *Latin American Cinema: Local Views and Transnational Connections* (Calgary, AB: University of Calgary Press, 2011), for a critique of the stereotypes.

52. Review of *Fuego*, 1971, MS 41160, Armando Bó folder, Museo del Cine archives, Buenos Aires.

53. In one review, the critic says: "The common places are reiterated ad nauseum, the thrashed-over dialogues and the gratuitous expressions are reduced to the ridiculous. The lack of dramatic sense is memorable. The insertion of background music overcomes the limits of folly." See Review of *Fuego*, 1971, MS 41161, Armando Bó folder, Museo del Cine archives, Buenos Aires.

54. Bermúdez-Barrios, "Sexploitation, Space," 253.

55. Bermúdez-Barrios, 262.

56. Selling *Fuego* required work and the use of their previous collaborations. Relationships with distributors abroad existed, but each film had to be sold individually. Bó had to win over the distributors because many similar films were competing on the market in the late 1960s. When he arrived in New York with Victor, he tried to sell both *My Father's Wife* and *Fuego*. He tells how

he always started with the former and had no luck getting buyers. One time he began with *Fuego*, and Columbia Pictures signed a contract. *Fuego* gave Sarli-Bó the leverage that they had not had before with Columbia, to distribute all those films he was to produce from that point onward. See Fernández and Nagy, *La gran Aventura*, 235–36.

57. On one of their US trips, Robert Aldrich had invited them to lunch at MGM. He offered Sarli a supporting role and all expenses paid with a four-year contract. Sarli was insulted and said she preferred to be the head of a mouse rather than the tail of a lion. See Fernández and Nagy, *La gran aventura*, 178.

58. By 1980 SIFA was not doing well. Sarli-Bó had sought support from the INC and had received funding for *Last Love in Tierra del Fuego*. The Censor Board had said they were eligible for a credit for the project of *A Madcap Widow*, but then the INC refused the credit, an estimated US $300,000. They justified their decisions based on the fact that the film "does not contribute to cinematography in cultural or artistic ways." See the *Una viuda descocada* file, ruling by Carlos Ezquiel Bellio in a letter dated 28 August 1980, Museo del Cine archives, Buenos Aires. In trying to stay within state requirements and self-censoring themselves, they filmed *A Madcap Widow* with no nude scenes and with very local references and humor. The incident caused the couple to leave Argentina for the United States to begin a new project called *Nueva York, Nueva York, te amo* (*New York, New York, I Love You*), to feature Latinos in the city. However, Bó's illness ended the shooting and brought them back to Argentina, where he died in 1981.

59. See Natalia Milanesio, *Destape: Sex, Democracy, and Freedom in Postdictatorial Argentina* (Pittsburgh: University of Pittsburgh Press, 2019). Milanesio describes the relationship between democracy and the freedom of sexuality that happened after 1983.

60. In many ways, Bó's cinema was pioneering in content. The intellectuals put him in a category of bad cinema that later became conflated with the sex comedies of the late 1960s and early 1970s. But his insistence on featuring sexuality from as early as 1956 was pioneering, not only in Argentina but throughout the world. As this book argues, Sarli and Bó's ability to push the limits on sexuality was not common in Latin America. They were bringing to the forefront questions about sexuality when the topic was ignored, particularly by the intellectuals, who treated it very differently.

61. Adelco Lanza, who started collaborating as a choreographer in *Heat*, appears for the first time in the role of a choreographer for a show in *Favela*. Later he is the "Magnolo," the help in the three comedies *The Shoemaker's Wife*, *La señora del intendente de Ombú Quemado* (*The Mayor's Wife*, 1967), and *A Madcap Widow*. He plays similar roles also in *Fever*, *Intimacies of a Prostitute*, *Una mariposa en la noche* (*A Butterfly in the Night*, 1977), and *Last Love in Tierra del Fuego*.

62. On the LGBT-friendly Here! Network on cable in 2006, John Waters introduced *Fuego* in a series titled "John Waters Presents Movies that Will Corrupt You." He explains how Isabel Sarli was the inspiration for Divine. See John Waters, "John Waters Presents Movies that Will Corrupt You," YouTube, 30 April 2010, www.youtube.com/watch?v=GAkMyj9_v2Q&t=7s.

63. Facundo Nazareno Saxe and Atilio Raúl Rubino, "Genealogiás disidentes de la teoría queer: Judith Butler/John Waters, *Gender Trouble/Female Trouble* y la torsión transnacional de Isabel Sarli," in *Fragmentos de lo queer: arte en América Latina e Iberoamérica*, ed. Lucas Martinelli (Buenos Aires: Editorial de la Facultad de Filosofía y Letras, 2016), 180.

64. Both films feature Sarli as a nymphomaniac who cannot be satisfied sexually in a monogamous relationship. She is married but never fulfilled, and she finds pleasure elsewhere with men and women. In the films she meets Armando Bó and he tries to change her because he is in love with her. While both films see Sarli's condition as an illness that must be cured, she speaks about being free and not changing her ways. However, the notable difference is in the endings. In the case of *Fuego*, Laura is in love with her husband, but she cannot change and thus commits suicide, as does her Carlos. In *Insatiable* she runs off with Alberto, but you suspect that there is no change to her "condition."

65. The discussions that take place about sexuality in *Insatiable* are much more open and contradictory to some of the ideals of a monogamous relationship. For instance, the husband, Luis, discusses his wife with Alberto and asks him: "What is a true expression of love? To let your loved one be free in love, or to kill for love?" The husband lives by this rule, and while it may hurt him, he allows Carmen to be free in her sexuality. In the end he loses her to Alberto. At one point, Carmen tells Alberto: "I am free to do as I please." Sexuality in both examples is excessive and includes moments of same-sex activity, such as her affair with her housemaid in *Fuego* and sexual encounters in bathrooms in *Insatiable*. However, neither Laura nor Carmen are ever "cured" of their illnesses. Laura's inability to conform to the mold of marriage leads her to suicide, while Carmen continues as she leaves the country to go to Chile to live with Alberto. The libertarian position in *Insatiable* may be a reflection of an international acceptance of female sexuality when the film was made. The comparison validates my argument that reading one film limits the way one can see sexuality in Sarli-Bó's work.

66. Eric Schaefer, "Dirty Little Secrets: Scholars, Archivists, and Dirty Movies," *The Moving Image* 5, no. 2 (Fall 2005): 79–105.

67. Kuhn speaks of an example of self-censorship through an anecdote about the final scene in *A Butterfly in the Night*, one of the most censored films. See Kuhn, *Armando Bó*, 23.

68. Romano, *Isabel Sarli al desnudo*, 133.

69. As a censor, Tato was overtly adversarial with their work and the work of others. However, as Fernando Martín Peña argues in the documentary *Un importante preestreno*, Ramiro de la Fuente was more dangerous as a censor because he created law 18.019, which would exist until the end of the dictatorship and prohibit entire films. See Santiago Calori, dir., *Un importante preestreno* (Buenos Aires: Tira Truenos, 2015), www.youtube.com/watch?v=y0FGH7qj-6Y.

70. Although Laura Podalsky explains that the retrospective in 1979 meant that censorship was easing (see *Specular City*, 204, 263), all the films that were made later still encountered problems. See note 26 for a discussion of *Last Love in Tierra del Fuego*. *Insatiable* was still prohibited until the end of the dictatorship and their final film *A Madcap Widow* was denied the funding.

71. There were many instances where filmmakers organized protests against censorship. In one such gathering that took place in August 1973, the intellectuals formed a panel and staged a protest. Over one hundred filmmakers were united to discuss censorship. However, Bó was never invited to the events. The couple was marginalized from the circles where such protests took place, although they did stage a hunger strike in the Plaza de Mayo when the INC denied them the box office money for *Fever*.

72. Romano reproduces the death threat that they received from the Triple A for their obscene and pro-Marxist behavior. The Triple A was a right-wing terrorist group made up of right-wing Peronist members. The note gives them seventy-two hours to leave the country. See Romano, *Isabel Sarli*, 130.

73. There are many terms used to describe the type of cinema that Sarli-Bó made. I have chosen to use the term *bad* to emphasize its class reference and its massive appeal. Instead of using a term like Jeffrey Sconce's *paracinema*, which really posits the contemporary reading protocol of a young male audience, *bad* does not limit the audience to a contentious one with the tools necessary to read the film properly, nor does it refer to only current fandom. See Jeffrey Sconce, "Trashing the Academy: Taste, Excess, and an Emerging Politics of Cinematic Style," *Screen* 36, no. 4 (Winter 1995): 371–93. Instead it encompasses the multiple possible audiences that have been able to appreciate the films at different historical moments for different reasons: identification, laughter, sexual gratification, beauty, or excess.

74. Francis Ferguson, "Pornography as a Utilitarian Social Structure: A Conversation," in *Porn Archives*, ed. Tim Dean, Steven Ruszczycky, and David Squires (Durham, NC: Duke University Press, 2014), 48.

75. Tim Dean, "Introduction: Pornography, Technology, Archive," in *Porn Archives*, 24.

76. Ferguson, "Pornography," 48.

CHAPTER 1. BODIES THROUGH TIME . . TIME THROUGH BODIES

1. Isabel Sarli, Placer Thibon, and Luis Gruss, "'Me acusaron de obscena y promarxista,'" *Cinemas d'Amerique Latine* 7 (1999): 55.

2. "Declárase 'Embajadora de la Cultura Popular Argentina,'" Decreto-Ley [proclamation] 1876, *Boletín Oficial de la República Argentina*, 12 October 2012, www.boletinoficial.gob.ar/detalleAviso/primera/77090/20121012.

3. Decreto-Ley 1876.

4. Perón recognized the importance of beauty pageants. A "Queen of Labor" was crowned each May Day. Even though the ritual began in 1890, it took on special meaning during Perón's administration from 1946 to 1955, when he owned the celebration of world Labor Day. For an analysis of the importance of beauty pageants during Perón's government, see Mirta Zaida Lobato, María Damilakou, and Litzel Tornay, "Working-Class Beauty Queens under Peronism," trans. Beatriz D. Gurwitz, in *The New Cultural History of Peronism: Power and Identity in Mid-Twentieth Century Argentina*, ed. Matthew B. Karush and Oscar Chamosa (Durham, NC: Duke University Press, 2010), 171–207.

5. Cited in Néstor Romano, *Isabel Sarli al Desnudo* (Buenos Aires: Ediciones de la Urraca, 1995), 31.

6. Diana Taylor, *The Archive and the Repertoire: Performing Cultural Memory in the Americas*, (Durham, NC: Duke University Press, 2003), 28–31.

7. Taylor, *Archive and the Repertoire*, 19–20.

8. Taylor, 21.

9. Matthew Karush argues that Perón's discourse is essentially melodramatic and draws on the culture of the tango. See Matthew Karush, "Populism, Melodrama, and the Market: The Mass Cultural Origins of Peronism," in Karush and Chamosa, *New Cultural History of Peronism*, 20–51.

10. An oral history to understand what Sarli and Bó's films meant for sexuality from 1960 to 1970 reveals some interesting results. The male interviewees identify the films as essential to their adolescent sexual coming of age, whereas the sole female interviewee admired Sarli but frames her within a maternal domestic space. See Ailin Basilio Fabris, "Las memorias del deseo: aproximaciones al consume cultural desde los públicos del cine erótico en Argentina (1960-1970)," *Question/Cuestión* (Universidad de la Plata) 1, no. 65 (April 2020), https://doi.org/10.24215/16696581e253.

11. As Sarlo explains, Kant defines the sublime as the object that resides beyond and in excess of form, in contrast to the beautiful, which resides in form. She also demonstrates that the sublime is the exaggeration of passions, an "affectionate dynamism of the imagination." Cited in Beatriz Sarlo, *La pasión y la excepción* (Buenos Aires: Siglo XXI Editores Argentina, 2003), 243–44.

12. Sarlo, *La pasión*, 71.

13. Sarlo, 83. Jamandreu's camp sensibility was also synonymous with the extravagant robes Sarli wore in her most famous films. He designed many of her costumes.

14. Sarlo, 96.

15. Taylor, *Archive and the Repertoire*, 6.

16. Taylor, 144.

17. Taylor, 144.

18. Melissa Gregg and Gregory J. Seigworth, "An Inventory of Shimmers," in *The Affect Theory Reader*, ed. Melissa Gregg and Gregory J. Seigworth (Durham, NC: Duke University Press, 2010), 3.

19. The principal question is how loyal the politician is to any party, as his switching of images changes with convenience. However, the changes are not based only on whims but can be explained historically. Frondizi made a pact with Perón in exile to govern with the general's support. The change from Mao to Perón marks another historical moment. Many on the ideological left believed that Perón was the only democratic choice in Argentina because the other leftist parties had very little chance of ever winning.

20. *The Mayor's Wife* begins with a disclaimer clarifying that references in the film are only imaginary, consciously distancing itself from the political context. The clear break with the social and political references that it makes is likely for the benefit of the censorship apparatus, which would not have allowed the film's release due to its politics.

21. Jill Hedges, *Argentina: A Modern History* (London: I.B. Tauris, 2011), 171.

22. Juan Perón fled to Paraguay and then Panama, where he stayed for nine months. He left Panama for Venezuela and then the Dominican Republic. In all of these countries dictators governed. He finally left for Spain in 1960, where he was received coldly by Francisco Franco, also a right-wing dictator, but allowed to stay with relative security.

23. David Rock, *Argentina 1516–1987: From Spanish Colonization to Alfonsín*, (Berkeley: University of California Press, 1985), 336.

24. Hedges, *Argentina*, 172.

25. By 1968 Perón published the book *La hora de los pueblos* (Madrid: Editorial Norte), which called for Latin American unity and announced the third position against imperialism, proposing a popular revolution. The reflection attracted the youth to the Peronist cause and laid the foundation for many of the revolutionary movements that developed in Argentina.

26. Rock, *Argentina 1516–1987*, 358.

27. Hedges, *Argentina*, 200.

28. Hedges, 201.

29. Jon Beasley-Murray, *Posthegemony: Political Theory and Latin America* (Minneapolis: University of Minnesota Press, 2010), 61.

30. Matthew Karush and Oscar Chimosa, introduction to *New Cultural History of Peronism*, 10–11.

31. Historian Mariano Plotkin contends that Perón tried to diversify his base by including sectors of society that were normally excluded from politics. He shows how the working class, the women, and the youth were incorporated into the party by Peronizing different aspects of everyday life and popular culture. See Mariano Ben Plotkin, *Mañana es San Perón: A Cultural History of Perón's Argentina*, trans. Keith Zahniser (Wilmington, DE: Scholarly Resources, 2003), 135. He argues that the ritualization of both May Day and October 17 helped working-class males to identify with Perón. For more information about how women and youth were swayed, see the chapter titled "The Peronization of Women and Youth."

32. Daniel James, *Resistance and Integration* (Cambridge: Cambridge University Press, 1988), 9.

33. Daniel James asserts that with the economic crisis real wages declined by the end of the regime, but the "shift of national income towards workers was unaffected." James, *Resistance and Integration*, 11.

34. James, 22.

35. Karush, "Populism," 25, 30.

36. Natalia Milanesio, "Peronists and *Cabecitas*: Stereotypes and Anxieties at the Peak of Social Change," in Karush and Chamosa, *New Cultural History of Peronism*, 64.

37. Milanesio, "Peronists and *Cabecitas*, 65.

38. Cited in Milanesio, 64.

39. James, *Resistance and Integration*, 23.

40. Arcángel Vardaro explains that Perón greeted Alberto Vaccarezza, who had recently been robbed on the streetcar with the following: "Hola Don Alberto, ¡así que lo afanaron en el bondi." [Hello Mr. Alberto, I heard they

swiped you on the bus]. The anecdote features many slang phrases. From that moment onward, everyone understood that censorship of *lunfardo* was abolished. See Arcángel Pascual Vardaro, *La censura radial del lunfardo 1943-1949* (Buenos Aires: Editorial Dunken, 2007), 62.

41. Milanesio, "Peronists and *Cabecitas*," 54, 73.
42. Milanesio, 59.
43. Milanesio, 54.
44. Milanesio, 55.
45. Milanesio, 70.
46. Milanesio, 77–78.
47. According to Milanesio, the Peronists demanded the importance of meeting basic needs, and the anti-Peronists criticized the dichotomy, claiming that it was an absurd negation of education. Milanesio, 63.
48. Ben Highmore, "Bitter after Taste: Affect, Food, and Social Aesthetics," in Gregg and Seigworth, *Affect Theory Reader*, 130.
49. David Wright, *Understanding Cultural Taste: Sensation, Skill and Sensibility* (New York: Palgrave MacMillan, 2015), 171.
50. Rodolfo Kuhn mentions the same scene to discuss Bó's disregard for the intelligentsia. He was never taken seriously by fellow directors and was mocked and laughed at for his work. Bó clearly differentiates himself from the art cinema that was being made in Buenos Aires. See Rodolfo Kuhn, *Armando Bó, el cine y la pornografía ingenua, y otras reflexiones* (Buenos Aires: Corregidor, 1984), 29.
51. Mario Casado was a supporting actor who generally played characters from the countryside, gauchos or *indios*. He was recognized for his roles in *El romance de un gaucho* (*The Romance of a Gaucho*, Rubén Cavallotti, Argentina, 1961) and *Martín Fierro* (Leopoldo Torre Nilsson, Argentina, 1968). In Bó-Sarli's cinema he plays secondary roles or is cast as an Indigenous man or a gaucho. As Marcos he represents someone from the city, but there is a clear class and even racial distinction about him. He is questioned before entering the country club, suggesting that he does not fit in the upper echelons of society.
52. Pierre Bourdieu, *Distinction: A Social Critique of the Judgment of Taste*, trans. Richard Nice (Cambridge, MA: Harvard University Press, 1984), 101.
53. Eric Schaefer, *"Bold! Daring! Shocking! True!" A History of Exploitation Films, 1919–1959* (Durham, NC: Duke University Press, 1999), 13.
54. Schaefer, *"Bold! Daring! Shocking! True!"*; Joan Hawkins, *Cutting Edge: Art-Horror and the Horrific Avant-garde* (Minneapolis: University of Minnesota Press, 2000); Jeffrey Sconce, "Trashing the Academy: Taste, Excess, and an Emerging Politics of Cinematic Style," *Screen* 36, no. 4 (Winter 1995): 371–93; Mark Jancovich, "Cult Fictions: Cult Movies, Subcultural Capital and the Production of Cultural Distinctions," *Cultural Studies* 16, no. 2 (2002): 306–22.
55. Sconce, "Trashing the Academy," 386.
56. Hawkins, *Cutting Edge*, 30.
57. Jancovich, "Cult Fictions," 307.
58. See Max Horkheimer and Theodor W. Adorno," The Culture Industry: Enlightenment as Mass Deception," *Dialectic of Enlightenment*, trans. John Cumming (New York: Continuum, 2001). The arguments made here are similar to the ones made by Adorno and Horkheimer's distinction between

intellectual culture and mass culture, which manipulates mass society into political passivity.

59. Jancovich, "Cult Fictions," 311.

60. For instance, Fernando Solanas and Octavio Getino critiqued the early phase of the Cinema Novo movement in Brazil for being a type of auteur cinema, what they called an example of Second Cinema. While unlike First Cinema, which was mainstream Hollywood, Second Cinema still did not challenge the political infrastructure of neocolonialism. See Fernando Solanas and Octavio Getino, "Towards a Third Cinema: Notes and Experiences for the Development of a Cinema of Liberation in the Third World," in *The New Latin American Cinema, vol. 1. Theory, Practices, and Transcontinental Articulations*, ed. Michael T. Martin (Detroit: Wayne State University Press, 1999), 33–58.

61. See Solanas and Getino, "Towards a Third Cinema"; Glauber Rocha, "An Esthetic of Hunger," in Martin, *New Latin American Cinema*, 1:59–61; Julio García Espinosa, "For an Imperfect Cinema," in Martin, *New Latin American Cinema*, 1:71–82.

62. Solanas and Getino, "Towards a Third Cinema."

63. Robert Stam, "Beyond Third Cinema: The Aesthetics of Hybridity." in *Rethinking Third Cinema*, ed. Anthony Guneratne and Wimal Dissanayake (New York: Routledge, 2003), 32.

64. Stam, "Beyond Third Cinema," 41.

65. Kenneth Harrow, *Trash: African Cinema from Below* (Bloomington: Indiana University Press, 2013), 23.

66. Dolores Tierney, "José Mojica Marins and the Cultural Politics of Marginality in 'Third World' Film Criticism," in *Latsploitation, Exploitation Cinemas, and Latin America*, ed. Victoria Ruétalo and Dolores Tierney (London: Routledge, 2009), 125.

67. Tierney, "José Mojica Marins," 125.

68. Wright, *Understanding Cultural Taste*, 14–15.

69. Wright, 11–12.

70. Highmore, "Bitter after Taste," 125.

71. Highmore, 128–29.

72. The critical reviews of their cinema as bad, the different court cases filed against their early films through penal code 128 for being obscene, and the difficult struggles presented by censorship as outlined in detail in chapter 3, all substantiate a reading of their work as pornographic based on class assumptions.

73. Mark Jancovich, "Naked Ambitions: Pornography, Taste, and the Problem of the Middlebrow," *Scope: An Online Journal of Film Studies* (June 2001): 2, www.nottingham.ac.uk/scope/documents/2001/june-2001/jancovich.pdf.

74. Valeria Manzano, "Juventud y modernización sociocultural en la Argentina de los sesenta," *Desarrollo Económico* 50, no. 199 (October-December 2010): 363.

75. Valeria Manzano, *The Age of Youth in Argentina: Culture, Politics, and Sexuality from Perón to Videla* (Chapel Hill: University of North Carolina Press, 2014), 8.

76. Manzano, *Age of Youth*, 13–14.

77. Manzano, "Juventud y modernización," 371.

78. Manzano, *Age of Youth*, 22.

79. Manzano, 31.
80. Isabella Cosse, "Una revolución discreta. El nuevo paradigma sexual en Buenos Aires (1960-1975)," *Secuencia* 77 (August 2010): 118.
81. Cosse, "Una revolución discreta," 119.
82. Cosse, 128.
83. Cosse, 128–29.
84. Manzano, *Age of Youth*, 119.
85. Maria Moreno and Marta Dillon, "The Children of Death," in *The Argentina Reader: History Culture, Politics*, ed. Gabriela Nouzeilles and Graciela Montaldo (Durham, NC: Duke University Press, 2002), 542.
86. It was not until well after the dictatorship that women's rights grew in importance with the creation of the Secretary of Women's Affairs in 1987 and Women's Council in 1991. Divorce, legal equality for children born in and out wedlock, and shared paternal rights were not won until then. See Marcela Nari, "Feminist Awakenings," in Nouzeilles and Montaldo, *Argentina Reader*, 533.
87. Nari, "Feminist Awakenings," 529.
88. Cosse, "Una revolución discreta," 125.
89. Cosse, 125.
90. Donna Guy, *Sex and Danger in Buenos Aires: Prostitution, Family, and Nation in Argentina* (Lincoln: University of Nebraska Press, 1991), 207.
91. Isabella Cosse, "Infidelities: Morality, Revolution, and Sexuality in Left-Wing Guerrilla Organizations in 1960s and 1970s Argentina," *Journal of the History of Sexuality* 23, no. 3 (September 2014): 417.
92. Cosse, "Infidelities," 425.
93. Cited in Cosse, "Infidelities," 436.
94. Cosse, 450.
95. Podalsky, *Specular City*, 22.
96. Ironically, *The Female* was the film that was most tampered with abroad, with the added sex scenes. The new additions question the claim that auteurs have complete control over their films. It was directed by the most important Argentine auteur, filmmaker Leopoldo Torre Nilsson, whose style and thematic concerns were greatly influenced by the European auteur movements of the 1960s, and who also led Argentine filmmaking and the Generation of 1960.
97. Alina Mazzaferro, "La 'Nuevaolera': Nuevos patrones de sexualidad y belleza en la television argentina (1962-69)," *Revista Latinoamericana de Estudios sobre Cuerpos, Emociones y Sociedad (RELACES)* 3, no. 6 (August-November 2011): 64.
98. Podalsky, *Specular City*, 193.
99. Bó-Sarli also dabbled in this genre of light sex comedies, such as the three related comedies made in small towns featuring Sarli as the bombshell flirtatious wife of older men who end up dying: *The Shoemaker's Wife*, *The Mayor's Wife*, and *A Madcap Widow*. All three were made with important comedian actors such as Pepe Arias and José Marrone. Curubeto's documentary shows the Argentine versions with Sarli in bathing suit or underwear and the foreign versions showing her nude body, but generally they featured very little sex. See Diego Curubeto, dir., *Carne sobre carne. Intimidades de Isabel Sarli* (Buenos Aires: Flesh & Fire, 2007), DVD, 95 min.
100. Podalsky, *Specular City*, 194.

101. Oscar Terán, "Cuando bajo los adoquines estaba la playa," in *Instituto Di Tella Experiencias '68*, ed. Patricia Rizzo (Buenos Aires: Fundación Proa, 1998), 18.

102. Patricia Rizzo, "Instituto Di Tella Experiencias '68," in *Instituto Di Tella Experiencias '68*, 30–31. Due to the many problems with the project, the institute never really became the center it was envisioned to become. The Di Tella was a center for the youth, which later became severely repressed due to its role in the vanguard of the city. See John King, *El Di Tella y el desarrollo cultural argentine en la década del sesenta* (Buenos Aires: Ediciones de Arte Gaglianone, 1985), 37–38.

103. The same foreign investment by the Ford Foundation and Rockefeller monies helped develop the Department of Sociology at the University of Buenos Aires and boost the Faculty of Philosophy and Letters and with it new degrees leading to the creation of programs such as CONICET, the foundation responsible for funding science research, including the social sciences and humanities.

104. Manzano, "Juventud y modernización," 371.

105. The first films (*Thunder among the Leaves*, *The Shad Fishermen*, *India*, *Heat*, *Favela*, *The Girl Ass-Keeper of Ypacaraí*, *Tropical Lust*, *The Impure Goddess*, and *The Lioness*) were all coproductions and represent different foreign settings. The duo made films in Argentina only to return to more foreign coproductions such as *Naked on the Sand* in Panama, and *Tropical Ecstasy* and *Bewitched* in Brazil.

106. Karush and Chamosa, introduction, 1, 9.

107. The comedian Jorge Porcel plays a very different role in *Naked on the Sand* than the roles the Argentine public were used to watching. The audience was accustomed to the adult-oriented comedies where Porcel is constantly making sexual advances to different women. In *Naked on the Sand*, he plays a prudish Mexican politician who is afraid of Alicia and terrified of having sex with a prostitute.

108. Federico Andahazi, *Pecadores y pecadoras: historia sexual de los argentinos III. Desde el golpe del 30 hasta Cristina Kirchner* (Buenos Aires: Planeta, 2010).

109. Natalia Milanesio, *Destape: Sex, Democracy, and Freedom in Postdictatorial Argentina* (Pittsburgh: University of Pittsburgh Press, 2019), 33.

110. Natalia Milanesio has written an excellent social history about the *destape* or unveiling of sex in Argentina, which she dates to 1983, the end of the dictatorship, where she argues a sexual unveiling occurs. See Milanesio, *Destape*.

111. The only one of the films to receive funding during the different dictatorial regimes is *Last Love in Tierra del Fuego*. There is an image with Sarli beside an Argentine flag, and many believe that the scene confirmed the complicity of Bó with the dictatorial regime.

CHAPTER 2. READING BAD CINEMA THROUGH "BAD ARCHIVES"

1. The official laws passed from 1963 to 1984 are a central part of the primary sources cited in the study of censorship to be presented in chapter 3.

Standards for film production were changing and becoming uniform through the implementation of legislation, particularly in 1963 and 1968, when crucial changes to the exhibition of films were legalized.

2. By 24 March 1976, when the military dictatorship came into power, new official guidelines for film production were released. The guidelines expanded laws 17.741/68 and 20.170/73 and gave details about producing films. They also inform as primary sources for this research.

3. For instance, the two-part article published by Maria Elena de las Carreras de Kuntz gives a very general sense of the context and some specific examples of the films censored. She presents a great overview, but the examples are not extensive. See María Elena de las Carreras de Kuntz, "El control del cine en la Argentina (primera parte: 1968-1984)," *Foro Político. Revista del Instituto de Ciencias Políticas* 19 (April 1997): 7–29. For more work by people who entered the archive see Andrés Avellaneda, *Censura, autoritarismo y cultura: Argentina 1960-1983*, vol. 1 (Buenos Aires: Centro Editor de América Latina, 1986); E. Susana Borgarello and Francisco Cipolla, *Regimen legal de calificación cinematográfica en la República Argentina: poder de policía jurisprudencia* (Córdoba: Editorial Advocatus, 2011); Octavio Getino, *Cine argentino entre lo possible y lo deseable* (Buenos Aires: Ediciones CICCUS, 1998).

4. Máharbiz was the director of Radio Nacional from 1989 to 1996, and the INCAA from 1995 to 1999. As a public servant appointed by Menem, Máharbiz followed the president's policy and footsteps. When Menem departed from his post as president, Mährbiz exited the INCAA, leaving the institution with a debt of US $20 million. As international relations specialist Francesca Lessa argues, during Menem's tenure there was a clear move toward impunity. See Francesca Lessa, *Memory and Transitional Justice in Argentina and Uruguay: Against Impunity* (New York: Palgrave Macmillan, 2013), 60. Menem worked to leave the past behind with a strategy to consign to oblivion, what has been referred to as "neoliberal techniques of forgetting." See Nelly Richard and Alberto Moreiras, eds., *Pensar en/la postdictadura* (Santiago, Chile: Editorial Cuarto Propio, 2001), 33.

5. Adrian Muoyo and Octavio Morelli gave a conference paper in 2009 where they explained what they have been able to uncover regarding the files. As a librarian at the Escuela Nacional de Experimentación y Realización Cinematográfica, Muoyo has been personally involved in trying to uncover the whereabouts of the files. The film files do exist, but they were in a precarious state. They have since been preserved in the correct conditions. Until now there has been no way for researchers to access the clips that the Classification Board kept in their deposit. See Adrián Muoyo and Octavio Morelli, "Reconstrucción de la Memoria Institucional: Ente de Calificación Cinematográfica," paper presented at the 3ra Jornada de Bibliotecas Gubernamentales conference, Buenos Aires, 21 April 2009, 5.

6. There are excellent efforts to document the human rights violations through collections such as *Museo de la Memoria*, mainly made up of documents donated by survivors or family members of the people who disappeared during the dictatorship. Official archives kept by the regime during the dictatorship do not exist. The only archives that have been found are those relating to

the connections that both the Vatican and the United States government had with the military regime. Due to the absence of documentation, the film censorship archive would have been arguably the most important internal source of information and would have helped to better understand the regimes' fears and strategies during different key moments of the era.

7. Antoinette Burton, *Archive Stories: Facts, Fiction and the Writing of History* (Durham, NC: Duke University Press, 2005), 14.

8. Freud's work shifted the perspective on sexuality in many fields and formed the foundation for French psychoanalyst Jacques Lacan, both of which inspired early film theory through thinking about the gaze, including the theories of feminist Laura Mulvey. See Laura Mulvey, "Visual Pleasure and Narrative Cinema," in *Narrative, Apparatus, Ideology. A Film Theory Reader*, ed. Philip Rosen (New York: Columbia University Press, 1986): 198–209. While some feminists were able to adapt psychoanalysis to their work (see Luce Irigaray, *Luce Irigaray: Key Writings* [London: Continuum, 2004]; Julia Kristeva and Toril Moi, *The Kristeva Reader* [New York: Columbia University Press, 1986]), it was severely criticized in Simone de Beauvoir's classic *The Second Sex*. See Simone de Beauvoir, *The Second Sex* (New York: Vintage Books, 1989). Ever since, feminists have had a problematic relationship with Freud's work.

9. Also, Nelly Richard, Alberto Moreiras, and Idelber Avelar have all published canonical studies on the effects of the dictatorship on culture in Argentina and Chile. All such studies rely on trauma theory through psychoanalysis to address issues surrounding memory and mourning from a societal point of view. Among film studies, see Laura Podalsky, *The Politics of Affect and Emotion in Contemporary Latin American Cinema* (New York: Palgrave, 2011); Dolores Tierney, *New Transnationalisms in Contemporary Latin American Cinemas* (Edinburgh: Edinburgh University Press, 2018).

10. Andreas Huyssen, *Twilight Memories: Marking Time in a Culture of Amnesia* (New York: Routledge, 1995), 3.

11. Huyssen, *Twilight Memories*, 5.

12. Nelly Richard, *Cultural Residues: Chile in Transition* (Minneapolis: University of Minnesota Press, 2004), 33.

13. Raúl Alfonsín, whose platform was based on persecuting the wrongs of the dictatorship, enacted the controversial Due Obedience Law (23.521) in 1987 after he was threatened with several uprisings from the military. Between 1989 and 1990, Carlos Menem unilaterally signed amnesty decrees that pardoned all those involved in the national conflict up until 1983. In 2003 the National Congress of Argentina denounced Law 23.521 as unconstitutional, and in 2006 the highest penal court declared the amnesty decrees also unconstitutional.

14. Huyssen, *Twilight Memories*, 3.

15. Susana Draper, *Afterlives of Confinement: Spatial Transitions in Postdictatorship Latin America* (Pittsburgh: University of Pittsburgh Press, 2012), 160.

16. Marlene Manoff, "Theories of the Archive from across the Disciplines," *Libraries and the Academy* 4, no. 1 (2004): 18.

17. Dominick LaCapra, *History and Criticism* (Ithaca, NY: Cornell University Press, 1985), 92.

18. LaCapra criticizes the type of historical research that only values discovering new facts in archives and not rereading already analyzed materials. Archives in such cases are seen as the real labor of the historian who is not afraid to "dirty his hands," whereas the intellectual historian is "a parasite who does little more than dilettantish" labor. LaCapra, *History and Criticism*, 93.

19. Manoff, "Theories of the Archive," 16.

20. Jacques Derrida, *Archive Fever: A Freudian Impression*, trans. Eric Prenowitz (Chicago: University of Chicago Press, 1996).

21. David Greetham, "Who's In, Who's Out: The Cultural Politics of Archival Exclusion," *Studies in the Literary Imagination* 32, no. 1 (Spring 1999): 9.

22. Ann Laura Stoler, *Along the Archival Grain: Epistemic Anxieties and Colonial Common Sense*, (Princeton, NJ: Princeton University Press, 2009), 41.

23. Tim Dean, "Introduction: Pornography, Technology, Archive," in *Porn Archives*, ed. Tim Dean, Steven Ruszczycky and David Squire (Durham, NC: Duke University Press, 2014): 14.

24. Burton, *Archive Stories*, 6.

25. Getino, *Cine argentino*, 88.

26. Derrida, *Archive Fever*, 36.

27. Derrida, 4.

28. Beatriz Sarli, "Postmodern Forgetfulness," in *The Argentina Reader: History, Culture, Politics*, ed. Gabriela Nouzeilles and Graciel Montaldo, trans. Patricia Owen Steiner (Durham, NC: Duke University Press, 2002), 556.

29. Anjali Arondekar, *For the Record: On Sexuality and the Colonial Archive in India* (Durham, NC: Duke University Press, 2009), 17.

30. Mary Ann Doane, *The Emergence of Cinematic Time: Modernity, Contingency, the Archive*, (Cambridge, MA: Harvard University Press, 2002), 222.

31. Doane, *Emergence of Cinematic Time*, 222.

32. The US Motion Picture Production Code (1930–68) made it clear that miscegenation could not be shown onscreen. While the code was very strict with standards surrounding sex onscreen, promiscuity was increasingly more prevalent when foreign films and exploitation began to flood the US market in the 1960s. However, when it came to miscegenation, the ramifications were strict before the arrival of the civil rights movement that eventually began to change the official race dynamics in the United States.

33. *Fuego*, released on VHS by the distribution company Something Weird Video in an English-language version, was in fact responsible for stimulating and creating the second wave of global fandom of their films in the 1990s.

34. Phillip Rosen, *Change Mummified: Cinema, Historicity, Theory* (Minneapolis: University of Minnesota Press, 2001), 351.

35. Rosen, *Change Mummified*, 354.

36. Rosen, 355.

37. Eric Schaefer is a film scholar who argues for the need to use and preserve archives in the study of adult film history. See Eric Schaefer, "Dirty Little Secrets: Scholars, Archivists, and Dirty Movies," *The Moving Image* 5, no. 2 (Fall 2005): 79–105.

38. One of Argentina's best directors, Leonard Favio, wanted to make a film about Isabel Sarli's persecution by the censors. Sarli was not ready for drudging

up the past. See Néstor Romano, *Isabel Sarli al desnudo* (Buenos Aires: Ediciones de la Urraca, 1995), 207.

39. Curubeto has authored many popular film books that can be classified as journalistic and from the perspective of a fan. He became most famous with *Babilonia gaucha: Hollywood en la Argentina, la Argentina en Hollywood* (1993) and then followed it with *Babilonia gaucha ataca de nuevo* (1998). He features the work of Sarli and Bó in *Cine bizarro: 100 años de peliculas de horror, sexo y violencia* (1996). In all of his books Curubeto is interested in popular but ignored films that were shot in Argentina or by Argentines.

40. See Gonzalo Aguilar, "Caso Cinemateca," in *¿Qué he hecho yo para merecer esto? Guía para el investigador de medios audiovisuales en la Argentina*, ed. Silvia Romano and Gonzalo Aguilar (Buenos Aires: ASAECA, 2010), 83–90.

41. Sarli donated the different screenplays of the scripts relating to Paraguay to Juan Carlos Maneglia, her greatest fan, who later went on to write and direct an important film in Paraguayan film history called *7 cajas* (*Seven Boxes*, 2012). I was lucky enough to consult all of the scripts during a trip to Paraguay. Maneglia was one of the many generous people on my journey to support my work.

42. Schaefer, "Dirty Little Secrets," 79–105.

43. Schaefer, 83–86.

44. Schaefer, 94.

45. Schaefer, 89.

46. Dean, introduction, 9.

47. Linda Williams, "Pornography, Porno, Porn: Thoughts on a Weedy Field," in Dean, Ruszczycky, and Squire, *Porn Archives*, 41.

48. See Romano and Aguilar, *¿Qué he hecho yo . . . ?*

49. Silvia Romano and Gonzalo Aguilar, "Diagnósticos sobre el estado de los archivos," in *¿Qué he hecho yo . . . ?*, 7.

50. Romano and Aguilar, "Diagnósticos," 9.

51. The Library of Congress believes that 70 percent of US silent feature films are lost. Yet, the 93 percent of Argentine silent films believed to have been lost is more astounding. Furthermore, to speak about 50 percent is to speak about half of the post-sound production. Luciano Delfabro, "Entrevista a Paula Félix-Didier, Museo del Cine," in *¿Qué he hecho yo . . . ?*, 70.

52. See Aguilar, "Caso Cinemateca."

53. Many of the Argentine films that were the lighter versions aired on TV.

54. In 1993 UNESCO convened a committee to look at the question of film preservation in the world. General Secretary Federico Mayor invited film personalities from across the world to sit on this committee and commit to the mission of film preservation. Solanas was chosen to be part of the task force and has thus worked to create CINAIN.

55. Aguilar, "Caso Cinemateca," 89.

56. For instance, from its inception CINAIN has begun to run courses and more recently a certificate in preservation and restoration. The increased emphasis on education, absent from Argentina historically, can only improve overall awareness and restoration efforts. In April 2018, CINAIN partnered

with Cinenacional.com and ENERC to add more documents and bolster the website with added information to make Argentine research more accessible online.

57. Gayatri Chakravorty Spivak, "The Rani of Sirmur: An Essay in Reading the Archive," *History and Theory* 24, no. 3 (October 1985): 250.

58. Spivak uses the example of the Rani of Sirmur, a widow who wanted to become a sati, the ritual of becoming cremated during her husband's funeral. The rani's (Hindu queen's) action provoked a crisis, because the colonial power wanted to use her as a native informant. Due to her act she disappears from history and we do not know whether she succumbs to the patriarchal traditions, which in her case can be construed as resistance to the colonial power, or whether she becomes the face of modernization for the colonial power. Arondekar, *For the Record*, 4.

59. Stoler, *Along the Archival Grain*, 20.

60. Stoler, 3.

61. Arondekar, *For the Record*, 1.

62. Eugenie Brinkema, "Rough Sex," in Dean, Ruszczycky, and Squire, *Porn Archives*, 281.

63. Karen Bishop, "Myth Turned Monument: Documenting the Historical Imaginary in Buenos Aires and Beyond," *Journal of Modern Literature* 30, no. 2 (2007): 155.

64. Draper, *Afterlives of Confinement*, 17.

CHAPTER 3. DISCIPLINING BODIES
THROUGH CENSORS' SHEARS

1. Latin America's other two big film industries, Brazil and Mexico, offer good points of comparison. Mexican censorship was less systemic and more based on tacit agreements with filmmakers. Misha MacLaird, *Aesthetics and Politics in the Mexican Film Industry* (New York: Palgrave Macmillan, 2013), 73. Dolores Tierney explains how alternative versions of films with explicit sexual content were disavowed, only allowed for export, and seen as problematic in Mexico. See Dolores Tiereney, "*El vampiro y el sexo* / The Vampire and Sex (René Cardona, 1969): El Santo, Sexploitation Films, and Politics in Mexico 1968," *Porn Studies* 6, no. 2 (Octobet 2019): 1–17, http://dx.doi.org/10.1080/23268743.2019.1627903.

Brazil's systematization preceded Argentina's and would follow a similar course, especially once the military dictatorship took over after 1964. Luis Nazario, "Censored Films in Brazil, 1908–1988," *Diario Cinematográfico* (blog), 31 July 2012, https://meucinediario.wordpress.com/2012/07/31/censored-films-in-brazil-1908-1988-2/#comments.

2. Ironically, while the films during the dictatorship were heavily censored, the Classification Board and the military saw the full versions with their friends in their own private microcinemas. As Sarli explains in an interview: "At that time, one lived with a mouth gag and a bandage over the eyes." See Isabel Sarli, Placer Thibon, and Luis Gruss, "'Me acusaron de obscena y promarxista,'" *Cinémas d'Amerique Latine* 7 (1999), 57.

3. The album, *Pequeñas anécdotas sobre las instituciones* (Short Anecdotes on Institutions) was released in 1974 and was also a victim of censorship. Its title was changed, two songs were eliminated, and many others modified, including the cutting of the final stanza from "The Incredible Adventures."

4. Clara Kriger, *Cine y Peronismo: el estado en escena* (Buenos Aires: Siglo Veintiuno Editores, 2009), 34.

5. Kriger, *Cine y Peronismo*, 37–38.

6. Kriger, 48.

7. See Ana López, "Crossing Nations and Genres: Traveling Filmmakers in Latin America," in *Visible Nations*, ed. Chon Noriega (Minneapolis: University of Minnesota Press, 2000): 33–50.

8. López, "Crossing Nations and Genres," 104.

9. See Diego P. Roldán, "Difusión, censura y control de las exhibiciones cinematográficas. La ciudad de Rosario (Argentina) durante el período de entreguerras," *Historia Crítica* 48 (2012), www.scielo.org.co/pdf/rhc/n48/n48a04.pdf.

10. Article 4 of the law asserts that freedom of expression as declared in the Argentine constitution shall be maintained unless it compromises minors, in which case they have to be protected. See "Boletín oficial de la República Argentina. Decreto-Ley 62," *Boletín Oficial de la República Argentina*, 9 January 1957, 1, https://www.boletinoficial.gob.ar/detalleAviso/primera/7030516/19570109.

11. See, for example: Andrés Avellaneda, *Censura, autoritarismo y cultura: Argentina 1960-1983*, vol. 1 (Buenos Aires: Centro Editor de América Latina, 1986). Susana E. Borgarello and Francisco Cipolla, *Regimen legal de calificación cinematográfica en la República Argentina: poder de policía jurisprudencia* (Córdoba: Editorial Advocatus, 2011). César Maranghello, "La pantalla y el estado," *Historia del cine argentino*, ed. Jorge Miguel Couselo (Buenos Aires: Centro Editor de América Latina, 1992), 89–108.

12. Tamara Leah Falicov, *The Cinematic Tango: Contemporary Argentine Film* (London: Wallflower Press, 2007), 35.

13. "Boletín oficial de la República Argentina. Ley 16.384," *Boletín Oficial de la República Argentina*, 18 December 1957, 1, www.boletinoficial.gob.ar/detalleAviso/primera/7030594/19571218.

14. "Boletín oficial de la República Argentina. Ley 8.205," *Boletín Oficial de la República Argentina*, 3 October 1963, 3, www.boletinoficial.gob.ar/detalleAviso/primera/10848732/19631003.

15. Law 8.205.

16. Law 8.205.

17. *Guía cinematográfica, 1954-1964*, 4th ed. (Buenos Aires: Accion Catolica ACA, 1965).

18. In a letter made public on 8 September 1957, Pope Pius XII claimed that while media springs from "ingenuity and human industry," it is nonetheless a gift from God. He claimed that the church could use media for their own spiritual quest and that governments and individuals could do the same as long as it was for intellectual and spiritual culture. But he warned against using avenues of communication "exclusively for the advancement and propagation of political measures or to achieve economic ends," or for anything "contrary

to sound morals" that would put souls in danger. Pope Pius XII, "Encíclica 'Miranda Prorsus," in *Guía cinematográfica*, 8–38.

19. *Guía cinematográfica*, 117.

20. *Guía cinematográfica*, 104, 143.

21. *Guía cinematográfica*, 212, 190, 227, 135, 146.

22. Octavio Getino, *Cine argentino entre lo possibly y lo deseable* (Buenos Aires: Ediciones CICCUS, 1998), 240.

23. Minister of the Interior Borda made his mark known in the legislation from 1967 to 1969. When law 17.741, an earlier form of 18.019, passed in 1968, he opened with a letter to the president. The same structure opens law 18.019 with a letter outlining the reasons why films need legislation. He justifies his position by referencing the protection of the youth and examples taken from different film industries and laws around the world.

24. "Boletín oficial de la República Argentina. Ley 16.955," *Boletín Oficial de la República Argentina*, 28 September 1966, 1, www.boletinoficial.gob.ar/detalleAviso/primera/7033948/19660928.

25. "Boletín oficial de la República Argentina. Ley 17.741," *Boletín Oficial de la República Argentina*, 30 May 1968, 2, www.boletinoficial.gob.ar/detalleAviso/primera/7034859/19680530.

26. "Boletín oficial de la República Argentina. Ley 18.019," *Boletín Oficial de la República Argentina*, 7 January 1969, 2, www.boletinoficial.gob.ar/detalleAviso/primera/7035141/19690107.

27. Laura Podalsky, *Specular City: Transforming Culture, Consumption, and Space in Buenos Aires, 1955-1972* (Philadelphia: Temple University Press, 2004), 199.

28. Miguel Grinberg, "Como nos llegan las películas," *Montaje* 1, no. 2 (April/May 1981): 38.

29. Grinberg, "Como nos llegan las películas," 39.

30. Grinberg, 38.

31. Avellaneda, *Censura, autoritarismo y cultura*, 120.

32. María Elena de las Carreras de Kuntz, "El control del cine en la Argentina (primera parte: 1968-1984)," *Foro Político. Revista del Instituto de Ciencias Políticas* 19 (April 1997): 13.

33. Elena Goity, "Armando Bó edifica a Isabel Sarli," in *Cine argentino: modernidad y vanguardias 1957-1983*. vol. 1 (Buenos Aires: Fondo Nacional de las Artes, 2004), 368.

34. Ministro de Justicia y Derechos Humanos, "Delitos contra la integridad sexual," *Codigo Penal de la Nación Argentina* (Buenos Aires, 1984), http://servicios.infoleg.gob.ar/infolegInternet/anexos/15000-19999/16546/texact.htm#17.

35. "Un proceso por obscenidad. ¿Puede desvestirse en la pantalla Isabel Sarli?" *Democracia* (Buenos Aires), 12 June 1960.

36. Néstor Romano, *Isabel Sarli al desnudo* (Buenos Aires: Ediciones de la Urraca, 1995), 40.

37. Romano, *Isabel Sarli al desnudo*, 59.

38. Goity, "Armando Bó edifica a Isabel Sarli," 369.

39. Goity, 369.

40. Jorge Abel Martín, "Un destape con un cuarto de siglo: *El trueno entre las hojas* del binomio Bo-Sarli cumple veinticinco años de polémica," in *Tiempo Argentino*, 20 September 1983, 3.

41. Avellaneda, *Censura, autoritarismo y cultura*, 54.

42. In 1961 the script of *The Girl Ass-Keeper of Ypacaraí* received a credit and later a prize: it placed fifteenth and won one million pesos from the INC. The prize was controversial as it beat out Fernando Birri's *Los inundados* (*Flooded Out*, Argentina, 1962). Two scenes in the film were contentious: a bath scene and a sex scene; but the film is perhaps the most romantic of all the Sarli-Bó productions. The current version in circulation does not show either controversial scene.

43. Jorge Abel Martín, *Los films de Armando Bó con Isabel Sarli* (Buenos Aires: Corregidor, 1981), 31.

44. *The Tigress* was a 1953 film directed by Torre Nilsson and produced by Bó. It had trouble with censorship and was never officially released. The film was accused of having questionable morals.

45. Leopoldo Torre Nilsson, "Catilinaria sobre la censura," *Heraldo del Cine*, 13 September 1979.

46. Nilsson, "Catilinaria."

47. *Tropical Lust* did not receive funding in 1964 but did win a prize for its color photography by Julio Lavera.

48. "Carta abierta. *La mujer del zapatero*: La ironía, la envidia, o el servilismo?" in *La mujer del zapatero* File, 1965, Museo del Cine Pablo Ducrós Hicken archives, Buenos Aires.

49. Avellaneda, *Censura, autoritarismo y cultura*, 74.

50. Fernando Martín Peña, "¿Qué pretende usted de mí?" *Página 12 Radar*, 30 June 2019, www.pagina12.com.ar/203278-que-pretende-usted-de-mi.

51. Peña, "¿Qué pretende usted de mí?"

52. "A gritos protestó Isabel 'Coca' Sarli," *Crónica* (Buenos Aires), 19 June 1971.

53. "A gritos."

54. César Maranghello, "La censura, con nuevo orden legal," in *Cine argentino: modernidad y vanguardias 1957-1983*, vol. 2 (Buenos Aires: Fondo Nacional de las Artes, 2005), 524.

55. De las Carreras de Kuntz, "El control del cine," 15.

56. *Fever* was made in 1970 and debuted in 1972. While the Classification Board allowed its release, it did receive a B category rating. Bó took them to court to appeal the decision, but it was upheld.

57. Maranghello, "La censura," 529.

58. Martín, *Los films*, 160.

59. Once Perón returned to Argentina, Hugo del Carril was asked to head the INC. At the time the classical actor and director had moved to work in Mexico. He accepted the offer and named Mario Soffici subdirector of the INC, to serve as interim director until del Carril's return. From this early announcement, del Carril explained that the INC was to take on a new direction—working toward abolishing law 18.019 and addressing other problems in the moribund Argentine industry. Del Carril never managed to take over the helm of the INC, a

decision he attributed to work obligations. Soffici, who had become official director on 4 January 1973, had a clear mission from the start, following del Carril's lead before Getino was named to head the Classification Board.

60. *Intimidades de una prostituta* File, in Octavio Getino Collection, Ente de Calificación Cinematográfica, File no. 504, 1972–74, ENERC, Buenos Aires.

61. *Intimidades de una prostituta* File.

62. *Intimidades de una prostituta* File.

63. Like the files, the film fragments deposited with the Classification Board were kept. In the case of Bó, he kept some of the cuts he made to his own films, and these were donated to Diego Curubeto, who used them to make his documentary *Meat on Meat*. The cuts kept by the Classification Board in deposit have not been accessible to researchers.

64. "Boletín Oficial de la República Argentina. Ley 18.019," 2.

65. *Intimidades de una prostituta* File.

66. Getino had had his own struggles with the censorship apparatus. The film he had directed with Solanas, *The Hour of the Furnaces*, which would influence filmmakers worldwide with its praxis of their Third Cinema manifesto, would not be officially released in Argentina until he became comptroller in 1973.

67. Getino gives a testimony of the work he did: "When I took on the directorship of the Classification Board . . . we had to end with the habit of cutting and banning. Within these criteria we began to release, little by little, the films that were stalled. . . . If the final decision had always been mine, I relied on the wise counsel of a group of men of culture. There were directors like Rodolfo Kuhn and Rene Mujica, critics like Agustín Mahieu and Edmundo Eichelbaum, sociologists, educators, priests, representatives of different official groups." Avellaneda, *Censura, autoritarismo y cultura*, 115.

68. César Maranghello, "La censura afloja sus cuerdas: Octavio Getino libera films prohibidos, se respira libertad cultural," *Cine argentino: modernidad y vanguardias 1957-1983*, vol. 2 (Buenos Aires: Fondo Nacional de las Artes, 2005), 652.

69. Maranghello, "La censura afloja sus cuerdas," 654.

70. After a failed kidnapping attempt on him, Getino left Buenos Aires for Lima, Peru. The military government filed an extradition order in 1978 charging him with the release of *Last Tango in Paris* during his time as comptroller. The order called for his return to Argentina to answer to crimes committed with the release of the film, but the Peruvian government denied his extradition. See Nicolás Mazzeo, "Entre lo posible y lo deseable: Octavio Getino frente a la gestión pública en 1973," *Cine documental* 7 (2013), http://revista.cinedocumental.com.ar/entre-lo-posible-y-lo-deseable-octavio-getino-frente-a-la-gestion-publica-en-1973.

71. *Intimidades de una prostituta* File.

72. "No tanto erotismo, advirtió Getino," *Gacetas de los Espectáculos* 7, no. 368 (11 September 1973), 289.

73. "No tanto erotismo," 289.

74. *Pautas* File, 1976, ENERC, Buenos Aires.

75. *Pautas* File.

76. *Pautas* File.
77. Maranghello, "La censura afloja sus cuerdas," 658.
78. Falicov, *Cinematic Tango*, 44.
79. "Tough (Also 'Inconsistent') Sums Up Censorship Style," *Variety*, 19 March 1980, 62.
80. *Una Viuda Descocada* File, ruling by Carlos Exequiel Bellio in a letter dated 28 August 1980, Museo del Cine archives, Buenos Aires.
81. "Boletín oficial de la República Argentina. Ley 23.052," *Boletín Oficial de la República Argentina*, 16 March 1984, www.boletinoficial.gob.ar/detalleAviso/primera/7091707/19840321.
82. Ben Anderson, "Modulating the Excess of Affect: Morale in a State of 'Total War,'" in *The Affect Theory Reader*, ed. Melissa Gregg and Gregory J. Seigworth (Durham, NC: Duke University Press, 2010), 162.

CHAPTER 4. COLLECTIVE WORKING-CLASS MALE BODIES

1. Ana M. López, "Our Welcomed Guests: Television in Latin America," in *To Be Continued . . . Soap Operas around the World*, edited by Robert C. Allen (London: Routledge, 2002), 260.
2. Peter Brooks, "The Melodramatic Imagination," in *Imitations of Life. A Reader on Film and Television Melodrama*, ed. Marcia Landy (Detroit: Wayne State University Press, 1991), 64.
3. Thomas Elsaesser, "Tales of Sound and Fury: Observations on the Family Melodrama," in Landy, *Imitations of Life*, 70–72.
4. Elsaesser, "Tales of Sound," 75–76.
5. Ana M. López, "Tears and Desire: Women and Melodrama in the 'Old' Mexican Cinema," in *Mediating Two Worlds: Cinematic Encounters in the Americas*, ed. John King, Ana M. López, and Manuel Alvarado (London: BFI Publishing, 1993), 149.
6. López, "Tears and Desire," 147–63.
7. López, 152–53.
8. Matthew Karush, *The Culture of Class: Radio and Cinema in the Making of a Divided Argentina, 1920-1946* (Durham, NC: Duke University Press, 2012), 41.
9. Karush, *Culture of Class*, 216.
10. Matthew Karush, "Populism, Melodrama, and the Market: The Mass Cultural Origins of Peronism," in *The New Cultural History of Peronism: Power and Identity in Mid-Twentieth Century Argentina*, ed. Mathew B. Karush and Oscar Chamosa (Durham, NC: Duke University Press, 2010), 47.
11. Tamara Leah Falicov, *The Cinematic Tango: Contemporary Argentine Film* (London: Wallflower Press, 2007), 67. For a discussion about class politics in *La historia oficial*, an internationally marketed melodrama meant for a European spectatorship, see Falicov's second chapter, "The 1980s: Cinema, Democracy, and Film Policy with Views towards Europe."
12. Octavio Getino, *Cine argentino entre lo possible y lo deseable* (Buenos Aires: Ediciones Ciccus, 1998), 31–32.

13. It can be argued that the *mensúes* replicated what happened in the missions. Structurally, like the missions and yerba maté plantations, they are considered the first expressions of capitalist exploitation in Latin America, similar to industrial capitalism. This entailed the exploitation of national resources by foreign owners. The *mensúes* were slaves just like the inhabitants of the missions, owned by foreigner exploiters for the purpose of producing capital for a select few.

14. Famed Mexican cinematographer Gabriel Figueroa created a mood through a symbolic cinematography, where hopeful clouds were his trademark. In Argentina's classical period, American John Alton influenced cinematography in the studio system during the 1930s and inspired others to create a similar metaphorical visual aesthetic.

15. Clara Kriger, *Cine y peronismo: El estado en escena* (Buenos Aires: Siglo Veintiuno Editores, 2009), 191.

16. Ana Laura Lusnich, "*Las aguas bajan turbias*, un modelo de transición," in *Ciudad/Campo en las artes en Argentina y Latinoamérica*, vol. 3 (1991): 184.

17. Lusnich, "*Las aguas bajan turbias*," 185.

18. See Kriger, *Cine y peronismo*, 136–55; and Karush, *Culture of Class*, 190–91.

19. As Marcos Zangrandi explains, Bó had gone to Paraguay to promote *Honrarás a tu madre* (*Honor Thy Mother*, Argentina, Alberto D'Aversa, 1951) when he met Nicolás Bó, unrelated to Armando, who approached him with a proposal to make a movie about Paraguay. He then convinced the up-and-coming author Roa Bastos to write the script after he had read his short stories. Roa Bastos also cowrote the script with Bó for the second feature, *The Shad Fishermen*. Zangrandi argues that the collaboration between the two was strained and the leftist work of the author was at odds with the B films shot by Bó. See Marcos Zangrandi, "Una mujer desnuda en la selva. Bó, Roa Bastos y *El trueno entre las hojas*," *Imagofagia: Revista de la Asociacion Argentina de Estudios de Cine y Audiovisual* 14 (2016): 12, www.asaeca.org/imagofagia/index.php/imagofagia/article/view/1159.

20. Zangrandi, "Una mujer desnuda en la selva," 3.

21. *Thunder among the Leaves* was the first script written by Roa Bastos. He confesses to having worked on twenty or thirty scripts, all B or even C movies, although he was credited for only fifteen between 1956 and 1974, some of which were in collaboration. A dozen or so were never filmed and have since been lost. As Zangrandi explains, Roa Bastos saw scriptwriting as a way of earning a living. His militant politics would not allow him to include a serious message in popular film. See Zangrandi, "Una mujer desnuda en la selva," 4–5.

22. Nicolás Bó was interested in producing a film that highlighted Paraguay as a nation, since it had no industry and few films were made in the country. On many levels *Thunder among the Leaves* featured Paraguay, which explains why Bó and Sarli became an important part of the national film imaginary.

23. Sarli's debut onscreen took place with another's voice. Eva Donge dubbed her voice in the only film where Sarli does not voice her own scenes.

24. Elsaesser, "Tales of Sound."

25. Getino, *Cine argentino*, 31–33.

26. Laura Podalsky, *The Politics of Affect and Emotion in Contemporary Latin American Cinema: Argentina, Brazil, Cuba, and Mexico* (New York: Palgrave Macmillan, 2011), 33.

27. Podalsky, *Politics of Affect*, 33.

28. See Doris Sommer, *Foundational Fictions: The National Romances of Latin America* (Berkeley: University of California Press, 1991).

29. Sommer, *Foundational Fictions*, 43.

30. Sommer, 46.

31. Elena del Río, *Deleuze and the Cinemas of Performance: Powers of Affection* (Edinburgh: Edinburgh University Press, 2012), 14.

32. Linda Williams, "Film Bodies: Gender, Genre, and Excess," *Film Quarterly* 44, no. 4 (Summer 1991): 3.

33. Williams, "Film Bodies," 4.

34. Del Río, *Deleuze*, 15.

35. Del Río, 16.

36. The script that I saw is missing its first pages, but on pages 65 and 66 Roa Bastos describes the opening scenes that form part of the narrative when Guillén discovers "the woodcutter" who dies in his arms. The script says, "This scene belongs to the first shot of the film." The script describes the scene in the following way: "The woodcutter gives repetitive blows with his axe. It's clear that he has reached the limits of his strength. His blows become weaker." From the description, the woodcutter is very exhausted and yet nobly continues his work. Augusto Roa Bastos and Armando Bó, *El trueno entre las hojas*, film script, 1956, 65–66.

37. Bó also directed *Sin familia* (*Without a Family*, 1954) and *Adiós muchachos* (*Goodbye Lads*, 1955).

38. Roa Bastos and Bó, *El trueno entre las hojas*, 151. All of the other quotations in this paragraph come from the same page of the script.

39. See Victoria Ruétalo, "Temptations: Isabel Sarli Exposed," *Journal of Latin American Cultural Studies* 13, no. 1 (2004): 84.

40. From the early psychoanalytical readings, voyeurism developed as a concept in film theory, where the screen was seen as a mirror. See Christian Metz, *The Imaginary Signifier: Psychoanalysis and the Cinema* (Bloomington: Indiana University Press, 1982); Jean-Louis Baudry, "Ideological Effects of the Basic Cinematographic Apparatus," *Film Quarterly* 28, no. 2 (Winter 1974–75): 39–47. In early film theory, the apparatus was responsible for positioning the spectator as an illicit onlooker. Feminist theorists then questioned such spectator power to instead define the position of women both on the screen and outside of it. Laura Mulvey's classic essay defined the concept of scopophilia and elaborated the voyeuristic position of the spectator while exposing the fetishistic position of the onscreen woman. See Laura Mulvey, "Visual Pleasure and Narrative Cinema," in *Visual and Other Pleasures*, 2nd ed. (Basingstoke, UK: Palgrave Macmillan, 2009), 14–27. The feminists of the 1980s widened the scope of the spectator, shifting perspectives from the position of subject of the apparatus of film to one of power. The notion of empowering the spectator materializes in the work of Bó-Sarli when one thinks of the censors, who as spectators had the power to cut the images of the female body and impose a certain regime of looking.

41. David Andrews, *Soft in the Middle: The Contemporary Softcore Feature in its Contexts* (Columbus: The Ohio State University Press, 2006), 53–54.

42. Elena Gorfinkel, *Lewd Looks: American Sexploitation Cinema in the 1960s* (Minneapolis: University of Minnesota Press, 2018), 102.

43. Here Isabel Sarli recalls Armando Bó's words. Isabel Sarli, Placer Thibon, and Luis Gruss, "'Me acusaron de obscena y promarxista,'" *Cinemas d'Amerique Latine* 7 (1999), 56.

44. I argue elsewhere that *Thunder among the Leaves* is a model for Sarli-Bó productions in regard to its details. See Victoria Ruétalo, "Armando Bó and Isabel Sarli beyond the Nation: Co-productions with Paraguay," *Estudios Interdisciplinarios de América Latina y el Caribe* 24, no. 1 (Jan.-June 2013): 83–98. The film offers an example of the role of popular cinema in constructing national cinemas beyond the nation. This 1958 film not only begins the phenomenon of Sarli as a sex goddess but also ingrains itself in the Paraguayan imagination by offering a national identity on celluloid, one that remains present today in the room dedicated to film in the Centro Cultural de la República in Asunción's Cabildo and as an influence to filmmakers like Juan Carlos Maneglia, the duo's biggest fan, who went on to make an award-winning film with Tana Schémbori, *7 cajas* (*7 Boxes*, Paraguay/Spain, 2012).

45. The *patrón* or demanding boss makes a clear appearance throughout Bó-Sarli's film trajectory. In *The Lioness*, *The Hot Days*, *Meat*, *Bewitched*, *Fever*, and *Ardent Summer*, the boss has a similar role and thus exploits the common workers. Sarli is either a victim to or is married to the authoritarian characters. In the cases where she is married to a controlling husband, she often connects to a lover from the working class—in *Thunder among the Leaves*, *The Lioness*, *Bewitched*, *Fever*, and *Ardent Summer*.

46. Matt Losada, *The Projected Nation: Argentine Cinema and the Social Margins* (Albany: State University of New York Press, 2018), 117–22.

47. The film references England's accusation that Argentine meat was contaminated with hoof-and-mouth disease. Yet it argues that it is a fallacy, since both beef and Sarli are indeed consumable and delicious or a delicacy, as the main character's name indicates.

48. Gorfinkel, *Lewd Looks*, 130.

49. Gorfinkel, 130.

50. Rodolfo Kuhn, *Armando Bó, el cine, la pornografía ingenua y otras reflexiones* (Buenos Aires: Corregidor, 1984), 52.

51. Estéban Echeverría, *"El matadero"/"La cautiva,"* 6th ed., ed. Leonor Fleming (Madrid: Catedra, 1999).

52. See David T. Haberly, "Male Anxiety and Sacrificial Masculinity: The Case of Echeverría," in *Hispanic Review* 73, no. 3 (Summer 2005): 291–307. Irene S. Coromina, "La mujer en los escritos antirrosistas de Echeverría, Sarmiento y Mármol," in *Hispania* 89, no. 1 (2006): 13–19. Jennifer Linda Monti, "La visión del 'otro': racismo y ostracismo en 'El Matadero' y *Facundo*," *Catedral Tomada: Journal of Latin American Criticism* 1, no. 1 (2013): 32–53. Jeffrey M. Shumway, "'The Purity of My Blood Cannot Put Food on My Table': Changing Attitudes towards Interracial Marriage in Nineteenth-Century Buenos Aires," *The Americas* 58, no. 2 (2001): 201–20.

53. Natalia Milanesio, "Food Politics and Consumption in Peronist Argentina," *Hispanic American Historical Review* 90, no. 1 (2010): 87.
54. Milanesio, "Food Politics," 79.
55. Milanesio, 81.
56. Milanesio, 80.
57. Milanesio, 84.
58. Mirta Zaida Lobato, *La vida en las fabricas. Trabajo, protesta y politica en una comunidad obrera, Berisso (1904-1970)* (Buenos Aires: Prometeo Libros, 2001), 286.
59. Lobato, *La vida en las fabricas*, 315.
60. Isabel Sarli's body is still being used to advertise the industry with a medium shot from the film. An ad with a background of the sun reproduced on the truck of Frigorífico Fura, a meatpacking company fully owned by Argentine capital, explains that they sell 100 percent "Argentine meat."
61. Tamara Drajner Barredo, "¿Cosificación o uso político? *Carne* de Armando Bo–Isabel Sarli," in *Imagofagia: Revista de la Asociación Argentina de Estudios de Cine y Audiovisual* 14 (2016): 21, www.asaeca.org/imagofagia/index.php/imagofagia/article/view/1105.
62. Barredo, "¿Cosificación o uso político?" 25.
63. In many of the films, Sarli plays the wife of a wealthy owner who falls in love with one of the workers, such as in *Thunder among the Leaves, Bewitched,* and *Fever*. In all of them, love is frustrated due to some other circumstance, such as the lover's death (*Fever, Bewitched*), or the wife's own death (*Thunder among the Leaves*). In *Favela* she manages to leave the shantytown behind and become a star despite her lover, who lives in the favela and is content with his social status. Other examples of social ascendance are found in *A Madcap Widow*, when the kiosk owner wins the lottery, or in *The Mayor's Wife*, when Flor Tetis marries Dr. Gambetta to become his political supporter. The love stories outdo class divides, where one character is willing to share or lose class privilege for love. Love across class lines is always at play. In all films, mobility is fluid. For instance, in *Bewitched*, Ansisé, the mixed-blood protagonist of *India*, has married a Caucasian landowner who mistreated his workers and thus deserves her treason with other men who work for him.
64. Many identify the protest in New York against the film *Snuff* (Michael Findlay and Roberta Findlay, USA/Canada/Argentina, 1976), which was filmed in Argentina, as the beginning of the anti-porn movement. For a discussion about the film and its political and North-South context see Glen Ward, "Made in South America, Locating Snuff," in *Latsploitation, Exploitation Cinemas, and Latin America*, ed. Victoria Ruétalo and Dolores Tierney (London: Routledge, 2009). The anti-pornography side of the debate was headed by Andrea Dworkin and Catherine MacKinnon. They argue that pornography encourages violence against women. See Andrea Dworkin, *Pornography: Men Possessing Women* (New York: Perigee Books, 1981). The other side, known as sex-positive feminists, embraced the entire range of sexualities. See Gayle S. Rubin, "Thinking Sex: Notes for a Radical Theory of the Politics of Sexuality," in *Pleasure and Danger: Exploring Female Sexuality*, ed. Carol Vance (Boston: Routledge & Kegan Paul, 1984), 267–93.

65. Donna Guy, *Sex and Danger in Buenos Aires: Prostitution, Family, and Nation in Argentina* (Lincoln: University of Nebraska Press, 1991), 182.

66. Cristiana Schettini, "A Social History of Prostitution in Buenos Aires," in *Selling Sex in the City: A Global History of Prostitution, 1600s-2000s*, ed. Magaly Rodríguez García, Lex Heerma van Voss, and Elise van Nederveen Meerkerk (Leiden, The Netherlands: Brill Books, 2017), 360.

67. Guy, *Sex and Danger in Buenos Aires*, 209.

68. In an anecdote Kuhn tells, the film was to end with a speech by Yvonne. The scene was shot to be blurry, allowing Sarli to improvise the speech afterward so that rules of synchronization need not be followed. According to Kuhn, she ended her speech with the proclamation: "Y al que no le gustan las putas, que se vaya a la puta m . . . que lo parió." See Kuhn, *Armando Bó*, 23. The sentence does not translate well into English because of its double use of the word *puta*, meaning "slut" but also used in the saying "fuck off," literally "the slut who bore him." However, the gist of the sentence is "whoever doesn't like sluts, can go fuck off." Kuhn encouraged Bó to leave the ending, because he said it was the best ending possible for a film in the history of filmmaking. The phrase disappeared in an episode of self-censorship before it was severely censored by the authorities.

69. Elena Gorfinkel, "The Body's Failed Labor: Performance Work in Sexploitation Cinema," *Framework* 53, no. 1 (Spring 2012): 81.

CHAPTER 5. AFFECTIVE INTIMATE INTERLUDES

1. César Seveso, "Political Emotions and the Origins of the Peronist Resistance," in *The New Cultural History of Peronism: Power and Identity in Mid-Twentieth Century Argentina*, ed. Matthew B. Karush and Oscar Chamosa (Durham, NC: Duke University Press, 2010), 254–55.

2. Seveso, "Political Emotions," 255. "Descamisados" (shirtless ones) was the derogatory name given to Perón's followers, mainly working-class men, referencing their impoverished and underprivileged status.

3. *Descamisada* with an *a* is the regendered feminine version of *descamisado*.

4. Linda Williams, "Film Bodies: Gender, Genre, and Excess," *Film Quarterly* 44, no. 4 (Summer 1991): 2–13.

5. Williams, "Film Bodies," 11.

6. Elena Gorfinkel, "The Body's Failed Labor: Performance Work in Sexploitation Cinema," *Framework* 53, no. 1 (Spring 2012): 81.

7. See Gilles Deleuze, *Cinema 1: The Movement-Image*, trans. Hugh Tomlinson and Barbara Habberjam (Minneapolis: University of Minnesota Press, 1986).

8. See Gilles Deleuze, *Cinema 2: The Time-Image*, trans. Hugh Tomlinson and Robert Galeta (Minneapolis: University of Minnesota Press, 1989).

9. Linda Williams, *Hardcore: Power, Pleasure, and the "Frenzy of the Visible,"* 2nd ed. (1989; Berkeley: University of California Press, 1999), 130–34.

10. Andrew Syder and Dolores Tierney probe the nuances of the role of the wrestling interludes that appear in the *lucha libre* horror films of Santo Neutron, Blue Demon, Mil Máscaras, and Santo. They argue that the spectacles bridge the fictional and real worlds for the local audience by including actual

footage of real fights not integrated into the narrative. These scenes suspend the narrative plot in many ways but mainly through the length of the sequence. In sum, Syder and Tierney explain that the films offered different pleasures to diverse audiences. Andrew Syder and Dolores Tierney, "Importation/Mexploitation, or, How a Crime-Fighting, Vampire-Slaying Mexican Wrestler Almost Found Himself in an Italian Sword-and-Sandals Epic," in *Horror International*, ed. Jay Schneider and Tony Williams (Detroit: Wayne State University Press, 2005), 40–41.

11. Victoria Ruétalo, "Temptations: Isabel Sarli Exposed," *Journal of Latin American Cultural Studies* 13, no. 1 (2004): 79–95.

12. Laura Mulvey, "Visual Pleasure and Narrative Cinema," in *Visual and Other Pleasures*, 2nd ed. (Basingstoke, UK: Palgrave Macmillan, 2009), 14–27.

13. Mulvey, "Visual Pleasure," 16.

14. Mulvey, 19.

15. See Rodolfo Kuhn, *Armando Bó, el cine, la pornografía ingenua y otras reflexiones* (Buenos Aires: Corregidor, 1984), 38–42; Eliana Braslavsky, Tamara Drajner Barredo, and Barbara Pereyra, "*Insaciable* (Armando Bo, 1984), entre la liberación sexual y el castigo moralizante," *Imagofagia: Revista Argentina de Estudios de Cine y Audiovisual* 8 (2013), www.asaeca.org/imagofagia/index.php/imagofagia/article/view/415. Braslavsky, Drajner Barredo, and Pereyra define Sarli in *Insatiable* as a sexual object rather than a subject.

16. Paco Jamandreu met Sarli in 1955, when she became Miss Argentina. They became friends and he designed many of her onscreen costumes. He was also First Lady Evita Duarte Perón's favorite Argentine designer. Jamandreu worked in the studios and designed for many other female stars, such as Fanny Navarro and Zully Moreno. See Horace Lannes, *Moda y vestuario en el cine argentino* (Buenos Aires: Instituto de Cine y Artes Audiovisuales, 2010), 31.

17. Rodolfo Kuhn calls Jamandreu's costumes "surrealist." Kuhn, *Armando Bó*, 42.

18. Kuhn argues that Argentina holds stars to a higher standard, expecting them to live according to a higher moral ethic. Nonetheless, Sarli embraces her contradictions by playing very unconventional characters on the screen while leading a very mundane everyday existence that the press would feature often. She lived with her mother and animals in her suburban home in Martínez. She was a homebody who did not enjoy public appearances. Kuhn, *Armando Bó*, 42–45.

19. Leon Hunt, *British Low Culture: From Safari Suits to Sexploitation* (London: Routledge, 1998).

20. Tom Gunning, "The Cinema of Attractions: Early Film, its Spectator, and the Avant-Garde," in *The Cinema of Attractions Reloaded*, ed. Wanda Strauven (Amsterdam: Amsterdam University Press, 2006), 382.

21. Gunning, "Cinema of Attractions," 384.

22. See Eric Schaefer, *"Bold! Daring! Shocking! True!" A History of Exploitation Films, 1919-1959* (Durham, NC: Duke University Press, 1999); Hunt, *British Low Culture*.

23. Schaefer, *"Bold! Daring!,"* 385.

24. Hunt, *British Low Culture*, 93.

25. Gunning, "Cinema of Attractions," 383.
26. "The Wild Belle of the Pampas," *Playboy*, April 1960, 64–67.
27. Ruétalo, "Temptations," 79–95.
28. Bill Osgerby, *Playboys in Paradise: Masculinity, Youth and Leisure-Style in Modern America* (Oxford: Berg, 2001), 125–26.
29. The pose may have been one reason why Roger Ebert has identified Sarli's narcissism. See Roger Ebert's *Movie Yearbook 2009* (Kansas City, MO: Andrews McMeel Publishing, 2008), 383–84. Rodolfo Kuhn sees her as a passive star with a monochord voice, whereby the pose could be seen to emphasize her passivity. See Kuhn, *Armando Bó*, 39.
30. See Ana López, "Tears and Desire: Women and Melodrama in the Old Mexican Cinema," in *Mediating Two Worlds: Cinematic Encounters in the Americas*, ed. John King, Ana M. López, and Manuel Alvarado (London: BFI Publishing, 1993), 147–63, for a summary of the *cabaretera* and the contradictory role of its female stars in Mexican cinema.
31. Schaefer, *"Bold! Daring!,"* 311–12.
32. Schaefer, 311.
33. Schaefer, 312.
34. López, "Tears and Desire," 158.
35. According to Rodrigo Fernández and Denise Nagy, the dancing in the cabaret "Le chat noir" replicates the striptease scene in *Gilda* (Charles Vidor, 1946), a film that is located and partly filmed in Buenos Aires. In the scene in question, Gilda dances and sings in a cabaret to "Put the Blame on Mame." She only takes off her gloves and her necklace but encourages someone to help her take off the rest. She is interrupted. In *Heat*, Marcos tries to take off Magda's dress but is stopped by another member of the audience. See Rodrigo Fernández and Denise Nagy, *La gran aventura de Armando Bó: biografía total* (Buenos Aires: Libros Perfil, 1999), 156.
36. Adelco Lanza began his work as Sarli's choreographer for the scene described here. He taught her how to dance because she always had problems with the dancing. See Néstor Romano, *Isabel Sarli al desnudo* (Buenos Aires: Ediciones de la Urraca, 1995), 69.
37. Similarly, Concepción in *Favela* dances on the street of the shantytown among Afro-Brazilian actors. Her skin color contrasts with that of her neighbors. She is the center of the narrative, but even the children dancing show more authentic movements to the rhythmic drumming. Concepción's moves are rather exaggerated and unnatural. Nonetheless, scouts single her out and comment: "This woman will triumph in the theater one day." While she lives in the favela, the only things that differentiates her during the festivities are her white skin and inept dancing.
38. Linda Williams, *Screening Sex* (Durham, NC: Duke University Press, 2008), 7.
39. See Diego Curubeto, dir., *Carne sobre carne. Intimidades de Isabel Sarli* (Buenos Aires: Fire and Flesh, 2007), DVD, 95 min. The film mentions that the music in *India* is played backward to create unique and whimsical sounds, highlighting the unnatural concentric circles that were imposed on the scene to keep it in the film.

40. The Pombéro is a legendary humanoid figure of small stature that comes from Guaraní mythology. It is popular in northeast Argentina, all of Paraguay, and southern Brazil. The legend states that the Pombéro captures ungrateful girls and forces them to kiss him and have sexual intercourse with him.

41. In *India* the five-minute waterfall scene was shot on Agfacolor stock in 1959, whereas *Bewitched* was shot on Eastmancolor exactly a decade later.

42. After meeting *Deep Throat* director Gerard Damiano in 1975 and becoming his mistress, Annie Sprinkle went to New York, where she began to make pornographic films. She starred in many films, including some of Doris Wishman's movies (*Satan Was a Lady*, USA, 1975; *Come with Me, My Love*, USA, 1976) and, with sexploitation veteran Joseph W. Sarno, coproduced *Deep Inside Annie Sprinkle* (USA). The film was the second highest grossing porn film in 1981. She worked as a sex worker, feminist stripper, and sex educator. She received her PhD in human sexuality and became a well-known performance artist and activist, which continues in her current work with wife Beth Stephens. Beth Stephens is an artist, sculptor, filmmaker, photographer, and academic who currently is a professor and chair in the Art Department at the University of California, Santa Cruz.

43. Fernández and Nagy explain that the Bó-Sarli films saw women as natural ecological beings that allegorized the conflict between men, literally represented by the males in the stories, versus nature, represented by Sarli's characters. See Fernández and Nagy, *La gran aventura*, 154.

44. The films post *Fuego* all feature more explicit sexuality in the scenes or in the plots, unlike the ones that came before. Until the end of their film trajectory, excluding the last two films that were produced under heavy scrutiny, the others all feature explicit sexuality. This was the height of the soft-core era, and the Sarli-Bó films fit into the international shift toward more explicit sex onscreen.

45. Leo Bersani, *The Freudian Body: Psychoanalysis and Art* (New York: Columbia University Press, 1986), 34.

46. Bersani, *Freudian Body*, 34.

47. Roger Ebert, "Guilty Pleasures," *Film Comment* 14, no. 4 (July/August 1978): 49–51, 80.

48. Schaefer, "Bold! Daring!," 34–35.

49. Schaefer, 35.

50. Schaefer, 201.

51. David Andrews, *Soft in the Middle: The Contemporary Softcore Feature in its Contexts*, (Columbus: The Ohio State University Press, 2006), 53.

52. Andrews, *Soft in the Middle*, 53.

53. Elena Gorfinkel, *Lewd Looks: American Sexploitation Cinema in the 1960s* (Minneapolis: University of Minnesota Press, 2017), 117.

54. Andrews, *Soft in the Middle*, 54.

55. As Dave Andrews argues, the soft-core period highlighted the face as the most crucial and performative part of the spectacle, a legacy left by classical sexploitation. See Andrews, *Soft in the Middle*, 14.

56. Williams, *Screening Sex*, 168–70.

57. Williams, *Hardcore*, 240.

58. Jon Cairns, "Critical Closeness, Intimate Distance: Encounters in the Love Art Laboratory," *Journal of Visual Art Practice* 16, no. 3 (2017): 255.

CONCLUSION

1. See "BAFICI 2018 encuentro entre John Waters y la Coca Sarli," YouTube, 16 April 2018, www.youtube.com/watch?v=5e3eaoqzLiw.

2. Milanesio argues that after the dictatorship ended, in the 1980s there was a profound transformation in how Argentines talked about, understood, and experienced sexuality. See Natalia Milanesio, *Destape: Sex, Democracy, and Freedom in Postdictatorial Argentina* (Pittsburgh: University of Pittsburgh Press, 2019): 51.

3. In 1987 when Pedro Almodóvar's films were first screened in Buenos Aires, people compared his work to Bó's. The same thing happened when *Meat* was finally screened in Barcelona years later. The height of the Sarli-Bó period was during Francisco Franco's dictatorship in Spain, and thus their films were not seen in the country until decades later. See "La Coca en lo de Almodóvar," 1991, MS 88987, Armando Bó Folder, Museo del Cine archives, Buenos Aires. Richard Corliss, "Isabel Sarli: A Sex Bomb at Lincoln Center," *Time*, 7 August 2010.

4. Federico Rivas Molina, "Muere Isabel Sarli, ícono del cine erótico argentino," *El País*, 25 June 2019, https://elpais.com/cultura/2019/06/25/actualidad/1561487472_035311.html; Daniel Politi, "Isabel Sarli, Popular Star of Racy Argentine Films, Dies at 89," *The New York Times*, 28 June 2019, www.nytimes.com/2019/06/28/movies/isabel-sarli-dead.html; "Addio all'attrice Isabel Sarli," *Il Centro*, 26 June 2019, www.ilcentro.it/cultura-e-spettacoli/addio-all-attrice-isabel-sarli-1.2249221; Veronica Smink, "Muere la actriz argentina Isabel 'la Coca' Sarli, famosa por sus films eróticos," *BBC News*, 25 June 2019, www.bbc.com/mundo/noticias-48763360.

5. See Jorge Abel Martín, *Los films de Armando Bó con Isabel Sarli* (Buenos Aires: Corregidor, 1981). Martín's book showcases posters from film premieres in New York, the Philippines, Australia, Brazil, and Buenos Aires.

6. See Rodolfo Kuhn, *Armando Bó, el cine y la pornografía ingenua, y otras reflexiones* (Buenos Aires: Corregidor, 1984), 9.

Selected Filmography

All of the following films were directed by Armando Bó. Included are the original title, the English titles, scriptwriter, starring actors, production companies, distribution companies, countries of origin, year of release, and running time at release.

El trueno entre las hojas (*Thunder among the Leaves*). 1958. Script by Augusto Roa Bastos, starring Isabel Sarli and Armando Bó. Prod. Sociedad Independiente Filmadora Argentina/ Film AM. Dist. Film AM. Argentina/Paraguay. 99 min.

Sabaleros (*The Shad Fishermen*, *Put Up or Shut Up*, *Positions of Love*). 1959. Script by Armando Bó and Augusto Roa Bastos, starring Isabel Sarli and Armando Bó. Prod. Sociedad Independiente Filmadora Argentina/Araucania Films. Dist. Araucania Films. Argentina. 93 min.

India. 1960. Script by Sergio Leonardo, starring Isabel Sarli and Guillermo Murray. Prod. Sociedad Independiente Filmadora Argentina. Dist. SIFA. Argentina. 90 min.

. . . Y el demonio creó a los hombres (*Heat*). 1960. Script by Armando Bó, starring Isabel Sarli and Armando Bó. Prod. Sociedad Independiente Filmadora Argentina/Punta del Este Film. Dist. Araucania Film. Argentina/Uruguay. 98 min.

Favela. 1961. Script by Armando Bó with argument by Hugo Mac Dougall, starring Isabel Sarli and José Veladao. Prod. Antonio Motti/ Geralartis. Dist. Araucania Films. Argentina/Brazil. 85 min.

La burrerita de Ypacaraí (*The Girl Ass-Keeper of Ypacaraí*). 1962. Script by Armando Bó, starring Isabel Sarli and Armando Bó. Prod. Sociedad Independiente Filmadora Argentina/Asunción Film. Dist. Araucania Films. Argentina/Paraguay. 93 min.

Lujuria tropical (*Tropical Lust, Tropical Sun*). 1964. Script by Armando Bó, starring Isabel Sarli and Luis Salazar. Prod. Sociedad Independiente Filmadora Argentina/Tropical Films. Dist. DASA. Argentina/Venezuela. 95 min.

La diosa impura (*The Impure Goddess*). 1964. Script by Alfredo Ruanova and Armando Bó, starring Isabel Sarli and Julio Alemán. Prod. Filmex Argentina/Filmex Mexicana. Dist. Pel-Mex. Argentina/Mexico. 105 min.

La leona (*The Lioness*). 1964. Script by Armando Bó, starring Isabel Sarli and Armando Bó. Prod. Sociedad Independiente Filmadora Argentina. Dist. Columbia Pictures. Argentina. 93 min.

La mujer del zapatero (*The Shoemaker's Wife*). 1965. Script by Armando Bó, starring Isabel Sarli and Pepe Arias. Prod. Sociedad Independiente Filmadora Argentina/Filmadora de Plata. Dist. Buenos Aires Films. Argentina. 62 min.

Los días calientes (*The Hot Days*). 1965. Script by Armando Bó, starring Isabel Sarli and Mario Passano. Prod. Sociedad Independiente Filmadora Argentina. Dist. Pel-Mex. Argentina. 95 min.

La tentación desnuda (*Naked Temptation, Woman and Temptation*). 1966. Script by Armando Bó, starring Isabel Sarli and Armando Bó. Prod. Sociedad Independiente Filmadora Argentina. Dist. Pel-Mex. Argentina. 102 min.

La señora del intendente de Ombú Quemado (*The Mayor's Wife*). 1967. Script by Armando Bó, starring Isabel Sarli and Pepe Arias. Prod. Sociedad Independiente Filmadora Argentina. Dist. Pel-Mex. Argentina. 90 min.

La mujer de mi padre (*My Father's Wife, Muhair*). 1968. Script by Armando Bó, starring Isabel Sarli and Armando Bó. Prod. Sociedad Independiente Filmadora Argentina. Dist. Cinematográfica Landini. Argentina. 90 min.

Carne (*Meat, Flesh*). 1968. Script by Armando Bó, starring Isabel Sarli and Victor Bó. Prod. Sociedad Independiente Filmadora Argentina. Dist. SIFA. Argentina. 90 min.

Desnuda en la arena (*Naked on the Sand*). 1969. Script by Armando Bó, starring Isabel Sarli and Victor Bó. Prod. Sociedad Independiente Filmadora Argentina. Dist. Unifilm. Argentina. 87 min.

Fuego. 1969. Script by Armando Bó, starring Isabel Sarli and Armando Bó. Prod. Sociedad Independiente Filmadora Argentina. Dist. Columbia Pictures. Argentina. 81 min.

Fiebre (*Fever, Heat*). 1972. Script by Armando Bó, starring Isabel Sarli and Armando Bó. Prod. Sociedad Independiente Filmadora Argentina. Dist. Columbia-Warner. Argentina. 90 min.

Furia infernal (*Ardent Summer, Fury Femina, The Hot Days*). 1973. Script by Armando Bó, starring Isabel Sarli and Juan José Miguez. Prod. Sociedad Independiente Filmadora Argentina. Dist. Columbia-Warner. Argentina. 100 min.

El sexo y el amor (*Sex and Love*). 1974. Script by Armando Bó, starring Isabel Sarli and Armando Bó. Prod. Sociedad Independiente Filmadora Argentina. Dist. Columbia-Warner. Argentina. 85 min.

Intimidades de una cualquiera (*Intimacies of a Prostitute, Sex is the Name of the Game, Indiscretions of a Prostitute*). 1974. Script by Armando Bó, starring Isabel Sarli and Armando Bó. Prod. Sociedad Independiente Filmadora Argentina. Dist. Columbia-Warner. Argentina. 95 min.

Embrujada (*Bewitched, Mulher pecado*). 1976. Script by Armando Bó and Gilberto Sierra, starring Isabel Sarli and Daniel de Alvarado. Prod. Uranio Limitada. Dist. Columbia-Warner. Brazil. 70 min.

Una mariposa en la noche (*A Butterfly in the Night, Like a Bitch in Heat, Like a Dog in Heat*). 1977. Script by Armando Bó, starring Isabel Sarli and Armando Bó. Prod. Sociedad Independiente Filmadora Argentina. Dist. Distrifilms. Argentina. 95 min.

Extasis tropical (*Tropical Ecstasy*). 1978. Script by Armando Bó with argument by José Da Costa Cordeiro, starring Isabel Sarli and Armando Bó. Prod. Uranio Limitada. Dist. Columbia-Warner. Brazil. 78 min.

El último amor en Tierra del Fuego (*Last Love in Tierra del Fuego*). 1979. Script by Armando Bó, starring Isabel Sarli and Armando Bó. Prod. Sociedad Independiente Filmadora Argentina. Dist. Columbia-Fox. Argentina. 110 min.

Una viuda descocada (*A Madcap Widow*). 1980. Script by Armando Bó, starring Isabel Sarli and José Marrone. Prod. Sociedad Independiente Filmadora Argentina. Dist. Trasmundo. Argentina. 95 min.

Insaciable (*Insatiable, The Insatiable Widow*). 1984. Script by Armando Bó, starring Isabel Sarli and Armando Bó. Prod. Sociedad Independiente Filmadora Argentina. Dist Lucian Films SA. Argentina. 86 min.

Index

affect, 15, 28, 70, 72; and censorship, 86, 117–18; female body, 23, 84, 134, 142, 159–62, 181–86, 189–91; and immaterial, 151–52; labor as, 119, 121, 130–34, 138–40; and Peronism, 13, 22, 29, 30–32, 37, 39–41, 47, 57, 193; and taste, 45–47, 164; theory, 22–23, 28, 76, 78, 128–30, 157–58, 205n18; and time, 164, 172–79
Las aguas bajan turbias (*Dark River*, 1952), 94, 120–21, 124–28, 132, 138
Alfonsín, Raúl, 116, 212n13
Almodóvar, Pedro, 56, 193, 229n3
Andahazi, Federico, 56
Andrews, Dave, 184, 228n55
Apold, Raúl Alejandro, 87
Aramburu, Pedro Eugenio, 31, 34, 87
archives, 20, 28–29, 57; of adult film, 71–72, 213n37; in Argentina, 72–74; disappeared archive, 20, 59–61, 69, 70, 74–79, 107; exclusion in, 63–64, 74; film as, 68–70; forgetting in, 58, 62–64, 68, 211n4; for the future, 61–64, 67–69, 71, 75, 79; memory and, 28, 58, 62–65, 67, 72–79, 211n6; private ownership of, 14, 70–71, 73
Ardent Summer, 9, 55, 176; and labor, 121, 132, 141, 223n45; and sexuality, 136, 167, 171, 176, 181, 185, 186*fig*.

Arias, Pepe, 6, 209n99
Aries Cinematografía Argentina, 54, 66, 113
Arondekar, Anjali, 68, 76

Baéz, Ernesto, 6
Barbarella (1968), 184–85
Barreiro, Jorge, 6
Beasley Murray, Jon, 35
Behind the Green Door (1972), 184
Belle de Jour (1967), 152, 184
Benjamin, Walter, 31, 68–69
Bermúdez-Barrios, Nayibe, 17–18, 21
Bewitched, 11, 100, 101, 113, 210n105, 228n41; and labor, 132, 141, 152, 223n45, 224n63; and female body, 175, 177–79, 177*fig*., 178*fig*., 181
Birri, Fernando, 128, 218n42
Bó, Armando: as auteur, 3–12; as Ayala Morín, Eligio, 6; cheap mode of production, 7–8, 55, 106, 120, 162, 169; death of, 3, 114, 115*fig*.; as independent producer, 3–5, 10–11, 21, 54, 87–88, 93, 199n35; in international markets, 10–12, 14–15, 66, 98–99, 100, 166, 172, 180, 200n38, 228n44; practicing self-censorship, 21, 163, 181, 203n66, 225n68; as Sarli-Bó trademark, 6, 23, 98, 132

235

236 | Index

Bó, Nicolás, 198n15, 221nn19,22
Bó, Victor, 52, 198n24
Borcosque, Carlos, 3
Borges, Jorge Luis, 4, 31, 166
Bourdieu, Pierre, 28, 41–43, 45
Brinkema, Eugenie, 77
Brooks, Peter, 122
Bruno, Jorge, 7
Buenos Aires, 18, 30, 37, 39, 49, 200n45, 207n50; as culture, 40, 53–55, 143; displacement of in Bó-Sarli, 55, 69; foreign films in, 94; province of, 11, 147
La burrerita de Ypacaraí. See *The Girl Ass-Keeper of Ypacaraí*
A Butterfly in the Night, 55, 154, 202n61; and censorship, 56, 114, 203n67; and prostitution, 152, 154; spectators in 136, 137fig.

La cabalgata del circo (*Circus Cavalcade*, 1944), 3, 31
Campora, Héctor, 29, 35, 50, 107
Carne. See *Meat*
Carne sobre carne. Intimidades de Isabel Sarli (*Meat on Meat: Intimacies of Isabel Sarli*, 2007), 70, 77–78, 107, 209n99, 219n63, 227n39
Casado, Mario, 6, 207n51
Casán, Moria, 55, 113
Caterbetti, Rosalino, 7–8
Catholic Church, 86, 90–92; Catholic audience, 90, 142; influence in Argentina, 18, 91, 142; norms, 57, 106; under Onganía, 92
censorship: in Brazil, 215n1; documentary about 203n69; financial reasons for, 93; in Mexico, 215n1; moral reasons for, 88–92, 101, 104, 107–9, 112, 114, 117; political reasons for, 85–89, 91, 94, 108; in Production Code, 69, 213n32; role of civil leagues, 89, 99, 108, 113, 114; and taste, 86–89, 94, 97, 112, 116. See also Catholic Church
Christensen, Carlos Hugo, 87
Cinematheque and Archive of National Images (CINAIN), 73, 214nn54,56
class, 22, 42, 50, 66, 75, 148–49, 193–94; and labor, 119–32, 144–46, 152, 155, 156; and Peronism, 23, 29–30, 36, 38–40, 132, 138, 206n31; and taste, 41–47, 53–54, 204n73, 208n72. See also Peronism
classical filmmaking, 3, 5, 66; directors, 4, 108, 198n17; genre, 10, 119–20, 122–23, 160, 162; style, 8, 124, 221n14

El club del clan ("The Gang's Club," 1962–1964), 53–54, 56
Columbia Pictures, 11, 12, 18, 66, 109, 198nn14,16; and *Fuego*, 12, 17, 200n38, 202n56; and *The Virgin Goddess*, 18, 198n16
coproductions, 11, 66, 88, 98, 199n35, 210n105; with Mexico, 11, 198n18; with Panama, 11, 180, 210n105; with Paraguay, 11, 98; with Venezuela, 11, 12
Cosse, Isabella, 47, 50–51
Curubeto, Diego, 70–71, 77–78, 107, 209n99, 214n39, 219n63, 227n39

La dama regresa (*The Lady is Back*, 1996), 162
Dean, Tim, 71
Deep Throat (1972), 20, 182, 186, 228n42
de la Fuente, Ramiro, 99, 101, 103, 203n69
de las Carreras de Kuntz, María Elena, 211n3
del Carril, Hugo, 66, 94, 121, 124–26, 134; and Peronism, 87, 107, 124, 218n59. See also *Las aguas bajan turbias* (*Dark River*, 1952)
Deleuze, Gilles, 159–60, 172
del Paraná, Luis Alberto, 7
del Río, Elena, 129
de Rosas, Juan Manuel, 39, 143
Derrida, Jacques, 64, 67
desaparecidos, 61, 110
Desnuda en la arena. See *Naked on the Sand*
destape, 50, 56, 192, 210n110
de Villiers, Dirk, 7, 198n16
Los días calientes. See *The Hot Days*
La diosa impure. See *The Impure Goddess*
Doane, Mary Ann, 68–69, 71
documentary: about Bó and Sarli, 70, 77, 78, 107, 209n99, 219n63; in Bó and Sarli, 8, 131–32, 133fig., 143, 171; in the New Latin American Cinema, 65, 128, 145, 148
Draper, Susana, 62, 79

Ebert, Roger, 14–15, 182, 200n47, 227n29
Echeverría, Ernesto, 40, 143–45
Elsaesser, Thomas, 122
Embrujada. See *Bewitched*
Ente de Calificación Cinematográfica (Film Classification Board), 116, 215n2, 218n56; archive, 20–21, 58–61, 65–67, 70, 78, 211n5, 219n63; history of, 83, 85–86, 88, 92–93, 219nn59,67; *Intimacies* case, 103–10, 113

Escuela Nacional de Experimentación y Realización Cinematográfica (ENERC), 65, 78–79, 85, 112, 215n56
Extasis tropical. See *Tropical Ecstasy*

Falicov, Tamara Leah, 220n11
Favela, 6, 9, 10, 11, 202n61, 210n105; and censorship, 90, 97, 98; dancing in, 168, 169*fig.*, 227n37; and labor, 121, 132, 141, 224n63
feminism, 46, 49–50, 70, 152–53, 162, 181, 194–95; ecofeminism, 180, 189; film theory, 162, 212n8, 222n40; #MeToo, 195; #NiUnaMenos, 195; pornography debates, 224n64
Ferguson, Francis, 22, 64
Fernández, Rodrigo, 8, 227n35, 228n43. *See also* Nagy, Denise
Fernández de Kirchner, Cristina, 27, 73
Fever, 12, 55, 132, 141, 204n71; and censorship, 100, 101, 218n56; and labor, 132, 141, 223n45, 224n63; and masturbation, 7, 136, 186–89, 187*fig.*, 188*fig.*; and sexuality, 9, 181, 202n61
Fiebre. See *Fever*
film distribution, 12, 17, 68, 85, 87, 199n35; Something Weird Video, 14, 213n33
film industry: in Argentina, 4, 10, 14, 87–88, 92, 120, 198n9; in Brazil, 215n1; in Mexico, 215n1
film preservation. *See* archives
First Cinema, 44, 208n60
Flesh. See *Meat*
Franco, Francisco, 56, 91, 206n22, 229n3
French New Wave, 8
Freud, Sigmund, 58, 61–62, 64, 212n8,
Frondizi, Arturo, 5, 29, 33, 48, 54, 205n19
Fuego, 55, 137, 192, 202n62; and censorship, 100, 101, 109, 228n44; and lesbian desire, 15–21, 16*fig.*; release of, 12, 14, 213n33; reviews of, 197n7, 201nn51,52,53; and sexuality, 175, 176, 181, 185, 203nn64,65, 228n44; success of, 200n38, 201nn49,56
Furia infernal. See *Ardent Summer*
Fury Femina. See *Ardent Summer*

García Espinosa, Julio, 44
gender, 19–20, 119, 152–53, 159, 184, 194–95, 225n3; intersectionality, 17, 22–23, 46–47, 121, 142, 144–49, 156–57; and youth, 49–52, 53, 56. *See also* masculinity
genre, 42, 106, 119, 120, 127–29, 159; adult film, 20, 56, 69, 71, 194, 213n37;

body genres, 129, 159; burlesque, 167–68, 171, 184; cabareteras, 167–68, 227n30; ficheras, 167; lucha libre films, 160, 225n10; melodrama, 10, 30, 31, 103, 120–30, 134, 138–40, 159, 167, 220n11; pornography, 22, 43, 46, 64, 71–72, 109, 129, 152, 159–61, 184–85, 224n64
Germani, Gino, 49, 54
Getino, Octavio: as author, 65–67, 75, 78, 85, 123; as comptroller, 19, 65, 91, 103–4, 108–9, 219nn59,67,70; as director, 44, 54, 65, 66, 144–45, 208n60, 219n66. *See also La hora de los hornos*; Third Cinema
Giberti, Eva, 48, 54
Giménez, Susana, 55, 113
The Girl Ass-Keeper of Ypacaraí, 11–12, 162, 210n105; and censorship, 97, 218n42; and labor, 121, 132, 141
Godard, Jean Luc, 8, 54
Gómez Cou, Santiago, 6
Gorfinkel, Elena, 136, 155, 159–60, 184
guerrilla movements, 34–35, 50–52, 55; Montoneros Peronist Movement, 35, 48, 50–52; People's Revolutionary Party, 48
Guía cinematográfica, 90–91, 217n18
Gunning, Tom, 162–64
Guy, Donna, 50, 153

Harrow, Kenneth, 44–45
Hawkins, Joan, 43–44
Heat, 6, 9, 11, 41–42, 53, 202n61, 210n105; and censorship, 90, 97; dancing in, 168, 169–70, 227n35; and labor, 132, 141
Heat (for *Fiebre*). See *Fever*
Highmore, Ben, 41, 46
HIJOS (Children for Identity and Justice against Forgetfulness and Silence), 49, 76
homosexuality, 9, 15, 50–51, 151, 153, 193, 203n65; gay sexuality, 19, 50, 150, 193; lesbian sexuality, 4, 16*fig.*, 17–19, 101, 104–9
La hora de los hornos (*The Hour of the Furnaces*, 1968), 44, 54, 65–66, 128, 143–48, 151, 219n66
Hoss, Américo, 6
The Hot Days, 9, 12, 55, 132, 141, 223n45
The Hot Days (for *Furia infernal*). See *Ardent Summer*
Hunt, Leon, 162–64
Huyssen, Andreas, 62, 67

238 | Index

The Immoral Mr. Teas (1959), 136, 184
The Impure Goddess, 11, 90, 98, 168, 198n18, 210n105
India, 6, 11, 69, 210n105, 227n39; and censorship, 90, 95-97, 96*fig.*, 98; dancing in, 168, 170-71, 170*fig.*; and labor, 121, 141, 224n63; and water, 175-79, 177*fig.*, 178*fig.*, 228n41
Indiscretions of a Prostitute. See *Intimacies of a Prostitute*
Insaciable. See *Insatiable*
Insatiable, 136; and censorship, 56-57, 69, 101, 114, 115*fig.*, 117, 203n70; release of, 2, 19; sexuality in, 164, 165, 203nn64,65, 226n15
The Insatiable Widow. See *Insatiable*
Instituto Di Tella, 54, 210n102
Instituto Nacional de Cine (INC), 4-5, 60, 65, 91, 218nn42,59; and censorship, 86-90, 92-95, 97, 100-101, 103, 107-10, 114, 116; funding, 18, 87-88, 91, 101, 112, 115, 202n58, 204n71
Instituto Nacional de Cine y Artes Audiovisuales (INCAA), 59, 65, 70, 73, 211n4
Intimacies of a Prostitute, 6, 12, 19, 55, 181, 202n61; censorship file, 21, 65, 78, 85-86, 103-7, 108-11, 111*fig.*, 116-17; dancing in, 167, 171; prostitution and, 152, 154
Intimidades de una cualquiera. See *Intimacies of a Prostitute*
Los Iracundos, 7

Jamandreu, Paco, 7, 31, 162, 199n23, 205n13, 226nn16,17
James, Daniel, 38, 206n33
Jancovich, Mark, 43, 45-46
Justicialismo. *See* Peronism

Karush, Matthew, 122-24, 134, 205n9
Kinsey Report, 49, 183
Kriger, Clara, 87, 124
Kuhn, Rodolfo, 14, 197n7, 203n67, 219n67, 225n68, 226n17; Bó as moralistic, 10, 22, 142, 200n45; on Bo's style, 8, 199n21, 207n50; on Sarli, 162, 226n18, 227n29

LaCapra, Dominick, 64, 213n18
Lanusse, Alejandro Agustín, 29, 34, 91
Last Love in Tierra del Fuego, 55, 121, 197n2, 202n61; and censorship, 56, 114-15, 117*fig.*, 199n26, 202n58, 203n70, 210n111; posing in, 166-67, 200n45

Lavera, Julio, 6, 97, 218n47
law/decree 62/57, 10, 87-89, 91-92, 94-95
law/decree 8.205, 89, 98-99
law/decree 18.019, 10, 18, 91-93, 100, 116, 203n69, 217n23; articles in, 92, 106, 108; cuts, 59, 92; end of, 103, 116, 218n59; and *Pautas*, 111
Leblanc, Libertad, 66
La Leona. See *The Lioness*
Like a Bitch in Heat. See *A Butterfly in the Night*
Like a Dog in Heat. See *A Butterfly in the Night*
The Lioness, 11, 90, 98, 121, 141, 210n105, 223n45; interracial kiss, 10, 68-69
Lobato, Mirta Zaida, 147-48
López, Ana, 122, 168
López Rega, José, 35
Losada, Matt, 141, 197n6
Lujuria tropical. See *Tropical Lust*
lunfardo, 39, 207n40
Lusnich, Ana Laura, 125

Macri, Mauricio, 73
A Madcap Widow, 52, 55, 132, 141, 202n61, 224n63; and censorship, 56, 114-16, 132, 141, 209n99; funding, 18, 202n58, 203n70; spectator in, 136, 137*fig.*
Madedo, Fernando, 73
Máharbiz, Julio, 60, 73, 211n4
Maká, 95, 96*fig.*, 127
Maneglia, Juan Carlos, 78, 214n41, 223n44
Manzano, Valeria, 47-48
Una mariposa en la noche. See *A Butterfly in the Night*
Marrone, José, 6, 209n99
Martín, Jorge Abel, 14, 229n5
Martínez, José, 6
masculinity, 121-22, 140-41, 146-47, 149-51, 155, 189. *See also* gender
masturbation, 7, 49, 161, 181-89, 182*fig.*, 183*fig.*, 186*fig.*
"El matadero." *See* "The Slaughter Yard"
The Mayor's Wife, 52, 55, 100, 202n61, 209n99; and labor, 132, 141, 224n63; and Peronism, 33-34, 37, 205n20
Mazzaferro, Alina, 53
Meat, 2, 9, 10, 52; and censorship, 100-101, 102*fig.*; and labor, 120, 121, 134, 141-51, 146*fig.*, 152, 223nn45,47, 224n60; and posing, 165, 165*fig.*
memory, 28, 34, 58, 79; and bodies, 32, 161, 172, 179, 187, 188; film

preservation, 41, 65, 72–73; movements, 49, 76–77; of the past, 62–65, 67, 72, 75. *See also* archives
Menem, Carlos, 60, 62, 79, 211n4, 212n13
mensúes, 124–25, 127, 221n13
Meyer, Russ, 15, 136, 184
Milanesio, Natalia, 40, 56, 147, 193, 202n59, 207n47, 210n110, 229n2
Mirada, Francisco, 6–7
Morera, Eduardo, 3
Mothers of the Plaza de Mayo, 76
Muhair. See *My Father's Wife*
La mujer de mi padre. See *My Father's Wife*
La mujer del zapatero. See *The Shoemaker's Wife*
Mujica, Alba, 6–8, 201n49
Mulher pecado. See *Bewitched*
Mulvey, Laura, 161–63, 212n8, 222n40
Museo del Cine Pablo Ducrós Hicken, 1, 69–70, 79
My Father's Wife, 9, 10, 17, 52, 141, 152, 175, 201n56; and censorship, 100–101; dancing in, 162, 163*fig.*, 167; location of, 11, 55

Nagy, Denise, 8, 227n35, 228n43. *See also* Fernández, Rodrigo
Naked on the Sand, 11, 100, 121, 141, 152, 210nn105,107; dancing in, 167–68; and masturbation, 180–83, 182*fig.*, 183*fig.*, 185
Naked Temptation, 6, 9, 12, 55, 100; and labor, 132, 133*fig.*, 141; and posing, 165, 166*fig.*; and water, 175–76
National Classification Honorary Council, 89, 91, 99
Navarro, Fanny, 6, 87, 226n16
New Latin American cinema, 44–45, 128
New York, 14, 224n64, 228n42; as location, 16, 18, 33, 202n58; screenings in, 2, 11–12, 101, 192–93, 19, 201n56, 229n5
nymphomania, 9, 16, 69, 114, 165, 203n64

Olmedo, Alberto, 55, 66, 113
Olmos, Miguel Ángel, 6
One Summer of Happiness (1951), 94
Onganía, Juan Carlos, 18, 33, 47, 91–92
orgasm, 129, 184–85, 189

Panama, 11, 55, 180, 200n45, 206n22, 210n105
Paraguay, 2, 7, 79, 166, 206n22, 214n41, 223n44, 228n40; Nicolás Bó, 198n15;

221nn19,22; as location, 9, 11, 55, 98, 126–27, 131, 139, 180; Augusto Roa Bastos, 6, 126, 134, 140. *See also* Roa Bastos, Augusto
Pautas, 111–16
Pel-Mex, 66, 98, 199n35
Pelota de cuero (Leather Ball, 1962), 98, 198n16
Pelota de trapo (Ragged Football, 1948), 4
Penal Code 128, 94–95, 97, 109, 208n72
Peronism: affective mode, 13, 22, 30, 36–41; Eva Perón's body, 13, 29, 30–33, 57, 162; supporters of, 30, 36–41, 48, 120
Playboy, 165–66
Plaza de Mayo, 39, 76, 101, 204n71
Podalsky, Laura, 4–5, 14, 54, 92, 128–29, 203n70, 212n9
populism, 13, 15, 35, 201n50
Porcel, Jorge, 6, 55, 66, 113, 210n107
pornography. See genre
Prisioneros de la tierra (Prisoners of the Earth, 1939), 120, 123–27, 139
prostitution. See sex work
psychoanalysis, 49, 58, 62, 108, 162, 212nn8,9, 222n40
Put Up or Shut Up, Positions of Love. See *The Shad Fishermen*

race, 207n51, 213n32; in *Bewitched*, 100; in *Favela*, 227n37; in *India*, 95, 96*fig.*, 170, 170*fig.*, 175; and intersectionality, 23, 47, 144, 146; and Peronism, 46, 39–40, 46; in *Thunder among the Leaves*, 138–39, 141, 175, 197n6
realism, 5, 7–8, 108, 120, 128–30, 158, 193; neorealism, 10, 120, 124, 126, 128, 130, 158
repertoire, 28, 76–78, 165, 182
Rialto Theatre, 12
Richard, Nelly, 62, 212n9
Roa Bastos, Augusto, 198n17; influence on, 132, 140–41; as scriptwriter, 6, 126–27, 134, 136, 221nn19,21, 222n36
Rocha, Glauber, 44
Romano, Néstor, 13, 204n72
Romero, Manuel, 121, 123, 124
Rosen, Phillip, 69, 71

Sabaleros. See *The Shad Fishermen*
Sarli, Isabel, as "Coca," 2, 193; death, 193; performance, 167–72, 169*fig.*, 170*fig.*; in water, 173–79, 173*fig.*, 177*fig.*, 178*fig.*; posing, 161–67, 163*fig.*, 165*fig.*,

240 | Index

Sarli, Isabel (*continued*)
 166*fig.*; stardom, 1–2, 127, 130, 134, 136, 160, 181
Sarlo, Beatriz, 30–32, 68, 205n11
Sartre, Jean Paul, 40, 53
scenarios, 13, 28–29, 36, 57
Schaefer, Eric, 20, 43, 71–72, 163, 167–68, 213n37
Schettini, Cristiana, 153
Sconce, Jeffrey, 43–44, 71, 204n73
scopophilia, 162, 222n40. *See also* to-be-looked-at-ness
Second Cinema, 44, 66, 194, 208n60
La señora del intendente de Ombú Quemado. See *The Mayor's Wife*
Sesenta veces siete (The Female: Seventy Times Seven, 1962), 53, 97, 198n16, 209n96
Sex and Love, 9, 68, 141, 181
Sex is the Name of the Game. See *Intimacies of a Prostitute*
sexploitation, 17, 20, 158–59, 162, 179, 187, 190, 228nn42,55; markets, 3, 12, 100, 180, 189, 194; nudie cuties, 10, 142, 180, 181, 184; roughies, 10, 137, 142; sex comedies, 52, 54–56, 113, 132, 202nn60,61, 209n99, 210n10; style, 9, 15, 100, 164; women in prison films, 106
sexuality, 20, 61–63, 72, 78, 89, 194, 205n10, 212n8; and archives, 3, 22, 70, 76; control of, 22, 85, 90, 153–54; gendered, 112, 136–37, 139, 142, 148–49, 156–58, 162, 179, 182, 190, 193–95; nonnormative, 9–10, 15, 18, 109, 151, 153, 188, 193; onscreen, 29, 53, 57, 86, 94, 105, 134, 140, 193, 202n60, 228n44; Sarli's body, 9, 11, 19, 95, 182, 185; sexual freedom, 19, 20, 136, 157–58, 186, 202n59, 203n65; sexual norms, 3, 20, 42, 94, 112, 229n2; youth, 47–52, 157. *See also* censorship; homosexuality; masturbation; nymphomania; orgasm; sex work
sex wars, 152, 224n64
sex work, 103–7, 110, 121, 149, 151–55, 162
The Shad Fishermen, 7–8, 9, 11, 165, 198n17, 210n105, 221n19; and censorship, 90, 95, 97, 98; and labor, 121, 126, 132, 133*fig.*, 140, 146
The Shoemaker's Wife, 12, 52, 55, 99, 202n61, 209n99; and labor, 132, 141
"The Slaughter Yard," 143–46, 148–49

Sociedad Independiente Filmadora Argentina (SIFA), 4–5, 18, 202n58
Soffici, Mario, 3, 31, 66, 108, 110, 218n59
Solanas, Fernando: and Third Cinema, 44, 54, 65–66, 144–45, 208n60, 219n66; and CINAIN, 73, 214n54. *See also La hora de los hornos;* Third Cinema
Something Weird Video, 14, 213n33
Sommer, Doris, 128
spectator, 13, 30, 37, 77, 144, 220n11, 222n40; and affect, 121, 129–30, 158, 159, 161–62, 179, 185; and censorship, 90, 222n40; as female, 22, 185, 190, 193; as male worker, 22, 52, 120–21, 134–38, 135*fig.*, 137*fig.*, 173–74; and sexploitation, 162–64, 168, 169, 172–74, 176, 190. *See also* voyeur
Spivak, Gayatri Chakravorty, 74–75, 215n58
Sprinkle, Annie, 19, 179–81, 189, 228n42
Stam, Robert, 44
Stephens, Beth, 179–81, 189, 228n42
Stoler, Ann Laura, 75
Sui Generis, 83–85, 110, 216n3
Summer with Monika (1953), 94

taste, 143, 168, 201n51; in archiving and preservation, 64, 66–67, 77; in bad cinema, 22–23, 41, 43, 45, 47, 99, 192–93, 202n60; and the body, 28–30, 54, 57, 97; and censorship, 86–91, 112, 116, 168, 192–93, 208n72; in film studies, 43–46, 204n73; and Peronism, 13, 28–30, 46; and pornography, 22–24, 46–47; and race, 40–41; and working class, 4, 15, 41–42
Tato, Miguel Paulino, 83, 85, 93, 103, 108, 110, 203n69; retirement of, 21, 113, 167, 199n26
Taylor, Diana, 13, 28, 31, 76, 77
La tentación desnuda. See *Naked Temptation*
Third Cinema, 147, 194; *La hora de los hornos,* 65–66, 128, 144–45, 219n66; manifesto, 44, 66, 208n60. *See also La hora de los hornos;* Getino, Octavio; Solanas, Fernando
Thunder among the Leaves, 11, 210n105, 223n45, 224n63; as affective belonging, 138–43, 146, 151; and censorship, 90, 94, 97, 117; in comparison to classic films, 126–27; and labor, 22, 119–20, 130–34, 131*fig.*; features of, 2, 5, 9, 11, 223n45; nudity in the water, 94,

161, 172–77, 173*fig.*, 180, 197n6; and Paraguay, 11, 198n15, 221n22, 223n44; script of, 66, 198n17, 221n21; spectator in 134–35, 135*fig.*

Tierney, Dolores, 20, 45, 215n1, 225n10

La tigra (*The Tigress*, 1953), 4, 19, 98, 218n44

Tiré Dié (*Toss Me a Dime*, 1958), 128–29

to-be-looked-at-ness, 162, 189. *See also* scopophilia

Torre Nilsson, Leopoldo, 128, 207n51; and censorship, 4, 19, 98, 218n44; *The Female*, 53, 97, 198n16, 209n96

Torres Ríos, Leopoldo, 4, 66

Triple A, 35, 108, 204n72

Tropical Ecstasy, 11, 181, 98n18, 200n47, 210n105, 218n47; and censorship, 100, 101, 113, 121; and labor, 132, 141, 152

Tropical Lust, 11–12, 68, 90, 98, 210n105, 218n47

Tropical Sun. See Tropical Lust

Trucco, Orestes, 11

El trueno entre las hojas. See Thunder among the Leaves

El último amor en Tierra del Fuego. See Last Love in Tierra del Fuego

Vieyra, Emilio, 66
Viloni, Orlando, 7

violence, 13, 153; in Bó, 42, 112, 134, 141, 143–46, 149–51, 155, 176, 195; in film, 55, 144–46, 224n64; in society, 34, 51, 56, 83, 108

The Virgin Goddess (1975), 7, 18, 198n16

Una viuda descocada. See A Madcap Widow

voyeur, 142, 161, 174, 176, 181, 222n40; female, 176, 184, 187; in sexploitation, 136, 184; as worker, 120, 135–38, 135*fig.*, 137*fig.*, 155. *See also* spectator

Waters, John, 19, 192, 193, 202n62
Williams, Linda, 72, 129, 159–60, 184
Wolf, Sergio, 9–10
Woman and Temptation. See Naked Temptation
Wright, David, 45

. . . Y el demonio creó a los hombres. See Heat

Younis, Ricardo, 6

youth, 13, 29, 75, 100, 157, 210n102; and censorship, 89, 112–14, 217n23; onscreen, 53–55; and Peronism, 23, 30, 35–37, 40, 206nn25,31; and sexuality, 47–52

YouTube, 28, 69

Zangrandi, Marcos, 126, 138, 221nn19,21

Founded in 1893,
UNIVERSITY OF CALIFORNIA PRESS
publishes bold, progressive books and journals
on topics in the arts, humanities, social sciences,
and natural sciences—with a focus on social
justice issues—that inspire thought and action
among readers worldwide.

The UC PRESS FOUNDATION
raises funds to uphold the press's vital role
as an independent, nonprofit publisher, and
receives philanthropic support from a wide
range of individuals and institutions—and from
committed readers like you. To learn more, visit
ucpress.edu/supportus.

www.ingramcontent.com/pod-product-compliance
Lightning Source LLC
Chambersburg PA
CBHW030535230426
43665CB00010B/901